# City of Soldiers

# City of Soldiers

A Year of Life, Death, and Survival in Afghanistan

Kate Fearon

Interlink Books

An imprint of Interlink Publishing Group, Inc.
Northampton, Massachusetts

First American edition published in 2012 by
INTERLINK BOOKS
An imprint of Interlink Publishing Group, Inc.
46 Crosby Street, Northampton, MA 01060
www.interlinkbooks.com

Text copyright © Kate Fearon, 2012
Cover Image © Yola Monakhov/Panos Pictures
Illustrations: All images courtesy of Kate Fearon except pp. 160, 181, 183 and 292 taken from Wikipedia Commons; p.100 courtesy of ALCIS; p.130 Wahedullah Ulfat; pp.152, 266 Derek Griffiths; author photo taken by Eamon Kingston.
Published simultaneously in Great Britain by Signal Books, Oxford

**Library of Congress Cataloging-in-Publication Data**

Fearon, Kate.
City of soldiers : a year of life, death and survival in Afghanistan / by Kate Fearon.
    p. cm.
Includes index.
ISBN 978-1-56656-902-6 (pbk.)
1. Fearon, Kate. 2. Postwar reconstruction--Afghanistan--Helmand--Biography. 3. Women political consultants--Afghanistan--Helmand--Biography. 4. Helmand River Valley (Afghanistan)--Description and travel. 5. Afghanistan--Politics and government--21st century. 6. Lashkar Gah (Afghanistan)--Social life and customs--21st century. 7. Lashkar Gah (Afghanistan)--Description and travel. 8. Lashkar Gah (Afghanistan)--Biography. I. Title. II. Title: Year of life, death and survival in Afghanistan.
DS371.43.F43 2012
958.104'71092--dc23                                          2012007755

Printed and bound in the United States of America

# Contents

"The use of force alone is but temporary. It may subdue for a moment; but it does not remove the necessity of subduing again; and a nation is not governed which is perpetually to be conquered."

—Edmund Burke, 1775

For Derek, who has put the time in.
And to the memory of Mir Wali Khan, briefly a
President in his own land.

✳✳✳✳✳

With thanks to Piet Biesheuvel, Paul Bliss, Philippa Brown, Siobhan Fearon, Elizabeth Gowing, Derek Griffiths, Toby Harnden, Fraser Hirst, Eamon Kingston, Fionnuala Kingston, Jon Moss, Hugh Powell, Tim Radford, Abdul Rahman, Bernadette Salisbury, Lynn Sheehan, Abdul Whakiel, Robert Wilton, Wahedullah Ulfat, and my mum and dad for support, encouragement, critique, and comment.

Many of the names in this book have been changed to protect the identity of the protagonists.

# *Preface*

THIS BOOK IS ABOUT people and place, rather than politics. But the politics of the place, of its people, help explain some of what happens in many of the stories and experiences you'll find in these pages. So the following is literally a thumbnail sketch of the history and politics of where the stories in these pages come from.

In 1946 a subsidiary of an American construction company—the same company that had just built the Hoover Dam and the Golden Gate Bridge—was established in Afghanistan. Its purpose was breathtaking in scale: to bring modernity to the Helmand River Valley by constructing dams, canals, schools, hospitals, and asserting the primacy of settled agriculture over nomadic pastoralism—a Green Revolution to challenge that of the Soviets' Red one, another front of the Cold War. The effort was centered around a new town built in the image of surburban America by the same company. The new town was Lashkar Gah, which became known as "Little America."

Except that it wasn't a new town. Lashkar Gah, or Lash, as I came to call it, had existed since at least the tenth century AD when Sultan Mahmud of the Ghaznavid Empire made it his winter capital, relocating his court and his army there. Its name, in Persian, means "City of Soldiers." Genghis Khan came through, plundering, in the thirteenth century, Tamerlane finished off what was left in the fourteenth, but then it was built up again by the Emperor Barbur in the sixteenth century. The irrigation canals had been there since Mahmud's time, and there they remained in varying states of disrepair through the Great Game and the Afghan nation-building of the twentieth century when the Royal Government of Afghanistan decided to commission first the

Japanese, second the Germans, and then the Americans to build a whole new network. Despite a thirty-year engagement, millions of dollars spent, and headlines like "Ambassadors with Bulldozers" or "Taming Rivers and Moving Mountains" the effort failed.[1]

The Soviets invaded, the US funding went from development to training and resources for the Afghan opposition—the Mujahideen, out of which the Taliban emerged. The Russians withdrew in 1989, but propped up a puppet president until 1992, when the Islamic State of Afghanistan was created. The country fell into civil war, and the Taliban assumed government over their new state, the Islamic Emirate of Afghanistan, in 1996.

The Taliban in government cultivated an extreme form of Islamic nationalism, manifested in a harsh and restrictive social code, particularly for women. After the 9/11 attacks, the US laid the blame squarely at the Taliban's door for providing the training camps where the suicide bombers planned their attacks. The US was joined by the UK in invading on 7 October 2001. They quickly displaced the Taliban government (though not, as I was to discover, its hold) and the Islamic Republic of Afghanistan was established. It was the sixth incarnation of the state since the contract to bring modernity to the Helmand River Authority was signed in 1946. And the latter three all contained the prefix "Islamic."

I had lived with Islam before, in Bosnia and Herzegovina, where I had worked for seven years. I had even completed a Diploma in Islamic Studies, guided by the fine Islamic scholars of the University of Sarajevo. So while I was certainly no expert neither was I a complete ingénue. Or so I thought—Islam in Afghanistan turned out to be very different from that in Bosnia. I'd had two jobs in Bosnia. One was building political parties, training their personnel, and advising their leaders on election campaign strategy and planning. The other was bedding down the legislation required by the Bosnian peace accords, the Dayton Agreement.

Before that, I'd worked on another peace accord, my own—the Good Friday Agreement—in Northern Ireland. I'd been a founding member

1 For details on this, see N. Cullather's excellent article at http://www.nyu.edu/gsas/dept/icas/Cullather.pdf

of the Northern Ireland Women's Coalition, established to ensure that women's voices and concerns would make it into the final text of the Agreement.

None of these jobs had been particularly easy, but they'd all been done in places that bore some resemblance to each other, and all took place, more or less, after the end of physical conflict. When I opted for "something completely different" I had no idea just how different Afghanistan would be. And when I came home on leave, my family and friends would ask: "What's it really like over there?"

This book is my answer to that question.

Helicopter landing at Nawa

# 1. Getting There

THE PILOT SAYS something that I recognize. *Allahu Akbar*. At least the language of Islam doesn't change, only its interpretation. God is great. He says it three times followed by something which could be the flight safety instructions, or a prayer. It turns out it was the traveler's prayer which all pilots on SAFI (an Afghan Airline, which I am taking from Dubai to Kabul) say before takeoff. There are no spare seats on the plane, which doesn't appear to have any Afghanis on it apart from the crew, who are all male with the exception of one young woman. You can always tell something about the socioeconomic state of a country by the gender of its airline and waiting staff.

In Bosnia (where I lived for seven years) many Muslims explained how they understood religion—they saw it as a personal communication with God, there was no middleman at the mosque. I think the pilot has a direct line as the flight is really smooth, especially considering all the baggage that we (mainly white) Westerners are bringing. But we'll get back to the luggage later.

On the way in the view is literally breathtaking. The mountains are riven with chasms, valleys, peaks, and canyons, and the late evening sun shines brightly on them, throwing sharp dark shadows so that they appear dappled in bronze, beige, and black, capped with white snow. And they are high. To give some perspective, my home in Ireland is on a Ring Dyke, the remnants of a volcano that bubbled and fizzed for two million years, eighty million years ago. It rises out of a lake straight up to a height of about 1,300 feet. We call it a mountain. In Bosnia the mountains we'd hike would be around 6,500 feet, five times higher than my "mountain." These mountains the pilot now guides us over are between 20,000 and 23,000 feet high. The scale is awesome. The sky is blue, the sun is shining, and the mountains are spectacularly high. Already I want to hike in them, but know that I won't ever be able to.

We land as smoothly as a skater on a pond. And it isn't the prayer but the lack of luggage—everyone's luggage—that has been left behind in Dubai, which means the plane is (relatively speaking) as light as a feather. General chaos ensues but a sort of queue forms with people resigned to the wait. By the time we give our baggage tag information (which a guy takes down on a sheet of paper using a pencil—no electronic tracking here) the sun has fallen and we are heading into Kabul just after dusk. By this stage I've been traveling for 28 hours.

We put on our body armor in the car, an armor-plated B6, Japanese manufactured, and set off into the dusty dusk of the city. Night falls quickly so it is hard to see much, especially through our darkened windows. The traffic kicks up so much dust that I see everything as if screened behind a patchy muslin cloth.

The road we take is bounded by rickety booths of rough wood, lit now with small, single yellow bulbs. They sell roasted chestnuts, or metal tins, or firewood. One or two have strings of red and green lights framing their doors. We take a crazy roundabout where cars, donkeys, pedestrians, and cyclists (without lights) all seem to have right of way, or want to assert it anyway. I am nervous when we have to be momentarily stationary because of a broken-down car, but the driver and IBG (individual body guard)—all ex-military or police now working for private security firms—take it in their stride. And it's busy: lots of donkeys, cars, pedestrians, and cyclists moving with chaotic purpose. We pass through a few police checkpoints, the security guys showing our paper credentials so we are waved through as if we had an electronic E-ZPass. I didn't check the donkeys, but the cars, pedestrians, and cyclists are all men. Maybe just over half of them are in jeans and T-shirts, the rest in traditional *salwar kameez*—a long shirt worn over baggy trousers. Public space after dark is for boys only, I think. And then I see one woman, with her husband and child. But she's the only one.

I stay in the Embassy compound that evening and the next day wait for the luggage, due in on the next plane. The Embassy fixer is conversing with SAFI early, but our bags don't come that day, or the next. I can't move anywhere because I don't have my body armor, which weighs a ton and which Aer Lingus have charged me €160 to carry from Dublin to London. I can't get on the plane to Lashkar Gah without it.

My colleague goes on that evening. I'll take her luggage when it arrives, but my body armor is still missing, so I arrange with management in the Embassy to issue me new body armor and swap later. However, that evening the plane is canceled and I'm stuck another day. I arrange to have a drink with an old friend with whom I worked in Bosnia, and who works in ISAF, the NATO force in Afghanistan. I have a pint of Guinness in the Embassy bar, from a can, but that floating widget works wonders: it's great, and it's great to chat with Jim. On the way out we run into his associate who is "minding" Ross Kemp (for those of you outside the UK and Ireland, he's an ex-soap star in England, who has gone on to make surprisingly good documentaries on soldiers' lives in Afghanistan and is back for a follow-up). Kemp has a minder whose job it is to keep him orientated toward the positive. Jim speaks to Kemp for a bit, and what he says (Jim is pessimistic about the international intervention here, even though he's part of it) almost causes Kemp's minder to have a coronary, although she gamely grips her gin and tonic and grins throughout.

The next day the luggage arrives, but because flights had been canceled the night before, there is little chance that I'll get a seat. These are all military flights and soldiers get priority. Even if civilians get a seat, we can get bumped off at the last minute. I check twice with the ops room and it's confirmed: no seat. I arrange to have dinner with Jim on his base. The drive takes about three minutes, you could walk it in ten. It's inside the green zone (a number of streets in between embassies that have been designated as a "safe area" for walking), but the UK has additional rules and so we cannot walk anywhere outside our own compounds. We are walking around the base—it's getting very cold—when my phone rings. It's the flight coordinator from Lashkar Gah (LKG): yes there's no seat for me, but he's "heard there might be another flight going," and he can give me a number. I try the number. For all I know it's the pilot, or the Taliban. The guy who answers it says, sure, we have a flight, the check-in time is 03:40. I consult with my colleague who's gone on to LKG. I say there's a flight leaving Kabul at 03:40. "Stop, stop, stop, stop, stop, stop!" she says. I thought she was never going to stop saying "stop." I have broken the cardinal rule of never giving any timings on the telephone and fallen at the first hurdle as it were. Funny, the pilot guy was able to give it to me, but I don't say anything. I say I'll go on it. We have dinner, good pizza and fantastic tiramisu, and I call into the ops room to let them know I'll need a car to the airport for 03:40. It's nine o'clock. In the ops room Rick says I'm booked on a non-existent flight. "There are only two flights tonight, and you're not booked on either."

He sees the crestfallen look on my face and adds, "But this guy must have put you on our flight, not the ISAF flight. Tell you what I'll do, I'll get you to the airport for 23:00, check-in is at 23:30, and the flight is at 01:30."

It's the Ambassador's birthday and he is buying everyone a drink in the bar. I have a gin and tonic and then go to the airport. Of course I'm not on the 01:30 flight, but the woman says if I want to wait, I can see how many turn up for the 04:00 flight check-in (at 02:00) and maybe get on that. So I wait, unable to sleep, until we finally get on the massive C-130 Hercules, the military plane that you enter up through its guts at the back and strap yourself in.

No cabin crew, no flatbeds here. There are no armrests, so no arguments about the etiquette of whose elbow can go where. No, we are squashed in, wearing our body armor and helmets. I've been in Afghanistan four days and this is the first time I cover my head. I am next to and opposite two young Afghani military translators. The one opposite me is rolling something between his fingers and thumbs. I think "he's got lovely slender fingers," then feel slightly bad as it seems that he's rolling prayer beads, a rosary, and I have just had a quasi-lecherous thought about him. I look away, and when I look back again I see that he's been rolling the yellow foam of the ear plugs, but I determine not to have further inappropriate thoughts.

We land at Camp Bastion at 05:00. It's literally in the middle of the desert, the Helmand desert, in the middle of nowhere. Iran is about 125 miles to the west, Pakistan about 75 miles to the south, and there's pretty much nothing but desert or scrub in between. I get into the bottom bunk in a sixty-square-foot unit—half a shipping container—at 06:00. At 11:00 I'm woken by the fixer, a big burly guy with freckles and red hair and beard. I'm the only woman on this trip so I'm woken earlier than the men so I can use the showers first. It may

4

be the middle of the desert, but they have a massive power shower. I am amazed at the engineering and logistics of Bastion. Accommodation, plumbing, a water supply, catering, cleaning for over 6,000 people. And it works, daily. We check in for the helicopter at 12:00 and it's due at 13:00. I run into Clive. Clive is six-foot-three and big with it. He's going to be one of the security team at LKG. He's from Carrick, a former Royal Irish soldier. I say I'm from Newry—it's the most neutral thing to say—and we chat. Or rather Clive talks and I listen.

When there's a rare lull, I ask if we'll go on a Chinook.

"Nah, the last time I was in a Chinook was at Drumcree! That was some laugh. We sure scared the f' outta 'em! We were caught in the middle—if we were at the Prods, they didn't like it. If we were at the Ka-licks, they didn't like it either. And now look—what was it all about?"

I think that the last time I remember a Chinook was when one landed 500 yards in front of my home, in front of the ancient volcano, with soldiers swarming out of it like bees from a hive, the grass beneath billowing like green silk. But I don't say any of this. Not yet.

"Yeah, 'ems 'er 'r babies nawh! Sea Kings. Sweet. Many's the time they saved ma bacon. I tell ye, when you're low in rounds and you just wanna get outta there." He was talking about Iraq, not the front of my house.

There follows war zone reminiscence by about six of the private security firm staff. They don't need to exaggerate. I take my book to a corner table and read in the sun. Another soldier joins me in the silence. Obviously we're in the reading room. When we finally get into the helicopter (or "helo" as I discover is the jargon) I'm squashed beside Clive. I try not to stare at anyone's hands, and of course, I try to look nonchalant. Part of the panel opposite me has fallen away, exposing the wiring, the viscera of the helo, and I stare at it for a bit before I realize we have taken off. It's like being on a bus, trundling along the barren, brown ground. We fly barely fifty feet above the ground for the first few miles. There's a gunner at the front and the back. The one at the front swings the machine gun around on its post, then we rise up and he lets it buck and swing by itself, catching the eddies in the air, like a horse just freed from its reins.

Lashkar Gah, arriving by air

I look out of the window. The loose sand is the color of milky coffee, undercut with pale yellow. Small hillocks render small patches of black, recalling the dapple of the mountains and also their splendor, though the desert's flatness and softness is the absolute opposite of the mountains. After about forty minutes I see the backdrop darken; the yellow vastness becomes beige and then brown, a strong Brazil-nut brown. This is the delta of the Helmand River, with its system of irrigation canals built by the Americans in the 1960s and then abandoned when the Russians invaded. It's hardly Venice, it's barely lush, but it is home to around 250,000 people. It's my first real view of Afghanistan. The houses are made of mud. The walls around the fields are made of mud. Most of the fields are mud. The streets are made of mud. It reminds me of Connemara, where stone walls are built around fields of stone. There there's nothing but rock. Here, it's mud. Except that we land on concrete. Now I am one of the swarming bees, though there's not grass but only dust that billows beneath. And my brief glimpse of Afghanistan is over, for now. We're in the compound at Lashkar Gah, or Lash Vegas, as some of its former residents have wryly dubbed it.

6

Lashkar Gah is the capital city of Helmand province and site of the ancient city of Bost, home of the winter palace of Sultan Mahmud. My understanding is that Bost got the boot when the Americans built up the canal system. The Lonely Planet guide to Afghanistan says it used to be called "Little America." The canal system now irrigates wheat, poppies, and pomegranates.

It is two o'clock in the afternoon. The flight from Kabul to Bastion took an hour and the flight from Bastion to Lash took only forty minutes. But the journey took about sixteen hours. You could drive it in less than half that time, if there was no war. But there is a war, and so I turn up at my new office for my new job, to meet my new boss, five days late.

Downtown Lashkar Gah

# 2. The Other Side of the Wall

"THOSE FDD-ERS need to go to OCCD ASAP."

"But T-3 reports SIED intent from EF. We should use the MDP or the PMT as part of the SSR response up at the FOBs. HMDG needs to get his COP and DCOP to VCH near the PB. PSC has been OSMd already."

When I finally make it into work, those five days late, I find that an acronym can be a noun, a verb, an adjective or, in fact, a whole grammar system. I had thought I would try to learn some Pashto, but instead find I need first to navigate this sea of new clusters of letters, as if a fridge magnet set has fallen and the letters cling to each other randomly. And that's just the civilian vocabulary. There's another alphabet for the military side of things. BTW, the above sentence does actually mean something (not a lot, but in so far as it contains signifiers, it has meaning).

I take a break from this small Babel and go for a walk around the (as Jack Bauer would say) hard perimeter of the base. Each side is about 1,000 feet long, roughly square. There are two US soldiers jogging around the track that frames the helipads. It's a solid, concrete path, hard on the knees, hard on the feet. They are doing split sprints—in shorts with their body armor on. (We had weighed our own body armor the day before on the new electronic drug weighing machine we'd bought for the police. It weighs 22 lb.) I hate running. But the day is bright and the blue vault of sky above is high and gleaming. Everyone is running. I should run too. Instead, I walk around the side of the track a few times until I am bored of watching them. I venture out around the back of the camp, right next to the wall.

Our wall, which isn't made of mud, is about ten feet high. Inside is the 1,000-foot square perimeter where we live. It has helipads and vehicle maintenance areas, long rows of twelve-man tents, a concrete cap over the sewage pit, our living and working accommodation, the cookhouse, and a row of Hesco. (Hesco is a sort of huge felt bag, inserted into a square wire mesh and filled with sand and small stones.

Imagine if you put a thick felt inlay into a wire supermarket shopping basket and filled it with sand and gravel. Then imagine it was a six-foot-cubed basket, and you made a wall by stacking two of them atop each other. That's a Hesco wall. There are Hesco walls everywhere in the camp.)

It's safe to walk inside the walls of the compound, except of course when joggers come panting up behind me and I have to leap to one side if I don't want to be mown down. It takes about forty minutes to walk the circuit. I can see nothing of Lashkar Gah in that time, but on the other side of the wall I can hear children playing, hear them laughing, an infectious silver warbling, for much of the walk. So we must be very close to town. Later in the evening I hear the call to prayer clearly. We are right on top of it. The odd thing about evening prayer is that I only seem to hear it from one mosque. In Sarajevo at the turn of the twentieth century, there were 108 mosques, one for every family. Not many new mosques were built until the end of the 1992–1995 war, when (mostly) Saudi money poured in for "re-construction" of what became new-builds. But in each of the 108 original mosques the call to prayer was fractionally staggered (as in Islam itself, there's no central synchronization of watches), so each muezzin was on a slightly different time, and all these fractionally separated layers of sound gave the prayer great depth. Here, it is clear and unilateral, sounding strong in the evening air, on the other side of the wall. I wonder where the minaret is.

The next day is my first day on that other side of the wall. We are going to visit the prison and some local women. I am very nervous as I get into the car. The body armor slows my movement—"how can those guys run with this stuff?" I think—as I heave the seatbelt around me. The security team (let's call them Chris and Ian—there is a marked preponderance of Chrises and Ians on the compound) go through the drill: if anything happens we are to get as low as possible and stay down until we are told to get out of the car by them. On no account are we to leave the car until they direct us. Once we're in the car, our lives are pretty much in their hands. It's a trust thing.

If you ever wondered where white Toyota Corollas go to die, muse no longer: it is Lashkar Gah. Although only about fourteen percent of the population own cars, if there's a car, it's a white Toyota Corolla. I think about the Afghanistan Independent Human Rights Commission (AIHRC) report I read the day before about the extent of Taliban "justice." Virtually all the atrocities were carried out by men who arrived in a white Corolla. Story after shocking story spoke of the white Corolla. Now I see why. We pass a whole yard full of them. When they are moving, that's OK. I am nervous when they are stationary, but again Chris and Ian are engaged, focused, and have done this many times before. It's a trust thing. I relax a little and begin to take in the streets.

There are lots of little children, and virtually all of them wave at us as we pass. We wave back, even though our windows are darkened. It hasn't rained since I arrived and so the road is hard-caked brown. The many mud walls give the impression that everything is slightly rounded off, as if done in medieval times, with no spirit levels. There are brick buildings too, and houses that are set back, behind courtyard walls that face onto the road. There are one or two concrete palaces, huge ugly narco-mansions that have sprung up, testimony to Helmand's position as the leading cultivator of poppy in Afghanistan.

Unexpectedly, there is a good deal of commerce, the backbone of which seems to be giant cauliflowers. There is also stall after stall of red onions and potatoes, the onions' oily skins shining in layered purple and pearl, a pile of amethysts beside the dull spuds. A small child sells pairs of used Wellington boots on the grass verge. He's little higher than the tallest boot. The boots have floral patterns—yellow background with pink flowers; green raindrops on white. There are fruit stalls (green bananas, apples, oranges, lemons, though none of these is of the hypertrophic proportions of the cauliflower). Further on are little wire roadside pens containing (separately and together) chickens, goats, and sheep. All the donkeys seem to be attached to owners already for they stand patiently in their harnesses. After the livestock displays comes homeware, then hardware. In the homeware department there are stalls and stalls of bed frames and doors. These have floral prints painted in bright colors—cerise on cyan; canary yellow on bright red or deep blue; emerald green on lilac. The metal frames of beds are also painted in bold hues, in stark juxtaposition to the brown mud of the streets and the muted monochrome clothes of the men, who wear greys, blacks, and browns. In homeware there are multifarious metal objects, and great piles of firewood, gnarled driftwood from the desert collected and piled like giant dried mushrooms at the side of the road. Then there are stalls of red diesel, perched on planks in dirty once-white plastic drums and jugs. Mucus-colored uremic sludge lines each side of the road in shallow open drains.

The diesel stalls are where the tasseled tuk-tuks (tassels, as we shall see, are big in Lash) and the many motorbikes come to fill up. Like circus elephants, they have sparkly headbands of crenellated cloth. There are tuk-tuks a-go-go, and their colors, like the bed frames and the doors, are a welcome foil to the white Corollas and the brown mud. The bazaar is like a huge open air department store—as if Ikea had no roof and sold fruit and livestock.

We turn away from it to the prison, weaving snakelike around the bollards. The gate swings open and I fix my headscarf in position. I am wearing my new *salwar kameez* that I bought in a shop in Tooting Bec, South London. It is blue chiffon with embroidered pink flowers and a matching headscarf. When I went to the shop to buy it I said to the Indian woman behind the counter: "I need clothes like yours."

"Hmm, I don't know if we have any in your size, dear. Why do you need it?"

"I'm going to work in Afghanistan."

"Hmm, what size are you, in European clothes?"

"Ermm, twelve." She made no effort to hide her disbelief. "Or maybe fourteen," I offered. She looked at me with a razor sharp eye. She was about four foot three high, and nearly as broad.

"I think maybe sixteen," she'd harrumphed. I comforted myself with the thought that I and my non-Indian physique were clearly descended from broad-shouldered Amazonian princesses.

I looked around her shop. The outfits were in pretty colors, which was good, but I could only see short sleeves, which was bad.

"Do you have any with long sleeves?" I asked.

"What do you need long sleeves for?"

"It's a Muslim country. I need to cover up."

"Nonsense, my dear. You don't need long sleeves. It will be hot over there. It's hot in India, that's why we don't have long sleeves—look around!" She trotted this out in a sing-song Indian accent. I touched the blue outfit I'm now wearing. It doesn't have long sleeves.

"Try it. It's extra-large. Your size, dear."

I tried it on. I wasn't sure it fit—there was plenty of room for expansion in the drawstring trousers, but at least there was no way my bum would look big in this, because it was impossible to tell which body part was where underneath it. I had to get back to central London for briefings, so I bought it, another in pink with blue flowers (and matching headscarf), and one more for good measure. The three outfits came to £103 and after a brilliant piece of negotiating I managed to get all of £3 discount, "because there is a recession, my dear." They all had short sleeves. Which is why I'm now wearing a long-sleeve T-shirt under this particular one.

I fix my matching headscarf, Chris opens the door—I can't get out until he opens it—and I leave the car. Or rather try to. At first I think it's the body armor weighing me down, so I kick my legs for greater leverage. I only end up squirming like an upside-down beetle. Chris smirks, then grins. "You might want to try taking off the seatbelt."

I am flustered, the scarf falls off my head, and I am rearranging it hurriedly when I am introduced to the deputy director. I place my right hand on my heart as if I am swearing an oath and say "*Salaam al-lekum.*" He mirrors my gesture and returns the greeting "*Al-lekum Salaam.*" He doesn't look me in the eye, nor shake my hand, as he does my male colleague Fraser's. Fraser and I go down a few steps and through a thin nylon green-brocade curtain. It has crimson tassels. Each of the windows has the same curtain, with crimson tassels. The director comes forward to meet us. He shakes both our hands. We sit down on brown velour sofas, which line either side of the room. He sits behind his desk. There are carpets depicting Hamid Karzai, the President, and another man on the wall behind him. There's also a framed photo of Karzai. On the desk is a vase of plastic flowers—green leaves and gaudy pink petals. A young man brings tea. He is either very sour, or very shy. It is fresh green tea, with the roughly chopped leaves nestling at the bottom of the glass cup. In Bosnia the meeting drink was unutterably bad coffee, in the Turkish style, thick as tar, with sugary sludge from about halfway down the cup. But here I like the taste of the tea—it's tart and refreshing.

For the first few weeks I will sit in on all of Fraser's meetings, to get some idea of the personalities and the lay of the land. We talk business for a while. We are here to get an agreement on where to blow a hole in the prison wall. (I should explain that it is to be a temporary hole, to give access to a contractor to build a new complex within the existing walls.) The military engineer, H, has come with us. Pencils are produced to relocate our proposal. Then the director says, "Why don't we go have a look?" So we move out. We walk to the other side of the prison compound, but are escorted by the director's security and our security.

Our security is comprised of muscled guys who tote semi-automatic guns, are electronically wired up to the ops room and the cars, and have body armor with many little extras: a pistol, light sticks, knives, ammo. Most of them have an additional pistol strapped to their thighs. The director's guards are little more than kids. They are thin, in grey uniforms. Their old guns have yellow shoulder straps, but they carry them much more casually, as if they were children dragging spades at the beach. One of his kid-guards has beach sandals on, and no socks, even though it is freezing.

Having renegotiated the position of the new temporary entrance, we go up the watchtower for a look. It's like going up the spiral stairwell of a medieval castle, like the chateau at Angers, perhaps. It's dark. On one dusty floor there are two blankets folded, somebody's bed. The top floor is not yet finished, but already there is a makeshift shelter from where the guards look out over the prison yard. There are no stairs up to the very top level. There's a pile of stacked bricks, then a V-step onto the outer wall (if I fall over, it's over thirty feet down) and up to the platform. Not easy in the blue dress and the long coat and the body armor. The weight of the body armor has more of an effect than I thought: it causes my heart to race and I am more lightheaded than I will admit. I do actually sway over the thirty-foot drop, but I am quite determined to get up—I grew up playing on my dad's scaffolding, after all. I have to haul the various skirts up a bit to do so, but no one seems to mind. The director smiles as I clamber up, surprised that I've made it. It's the best view of Lashkar Gah: an expanse of flat roofs, basking in the sun. Far away to the right is a huge hill with dark eyelets that could be caves, like a red Fraggle Rock, or the mountain in *Close Encounters of the Third Kind*. I still don't notice any minarets. On top of our tiny platform—three is definitely a crowd up here—there is another negotiation which negates the decision we just made on the ground, and then we go to get down. This is even trickier than getting up, so I just jump from halfway down. I almost land on top of the shy young man who served our tea. He is showing us his doves. There are two of them kept on this level in little wooden cages, nestled in a corner. He takes them out and strokes them, smiling broadly as he does so. He has very white and even teeth. It is clear that the birds give him great joy. I'm glad he's not sour.

Fraser isn't leaving without a signed agreement and so back in the office I dictate the terms to our translator who copies them into Pashto and the director signs. Mission accomplished: Phase 1 of the new prison build can begin.

We go from there to a women's group. Here we discuss the literacy project they are running (with our funding) for women prisoners and the office furniture we will provide them. They talk of what they'd like to do for the street children, a worthy but outside-our-remit project. The women wear bright clothes: a pink and green embroidered ensemble; a day-glo orange *salwar kameez*; a turquoise top over jeans and high-heeled boots. All wear matching headscarves. I am not out of place. I have no idea what ages they are, they could be thirty, they could be fifty. I read in an Asia Foundation report that life expectancy in Afghanistan is 44 years. I was 39 during that week. If I were Afghan, I'd be looking at only another five years of life. The conversation is effervescent, like a fizzing aspirin in water. It bounces and bubbles so much it's hard for the translator to keep up. Then another woman enters the room and when she says who she is I am dismayed, for she is the person about whom we heard something only hours previously. The Taliban are targeting her because of her position, they want to kill her as a lesson to other women. She is graceful and calm and has presence. She also has a small child, dressed in red.

We finish our business and while I am putting the armor back on again the women feel the blue *salwar kameez*, admiring the pink stitchwork and ask where I got it. It really does fit, after all.

Hesco walls, Lashkar Gah Main Operating Base

# 3. In Memoriam

I AM INTRODUCED to a tall blond soldier. He has freckles, lots of them, and his blond hair is spiky, whether by accident or styling-gel design, I can't tell. He looks like a stretched out Tintin, and I almost expect Snowy to come round the corner, similarly elongated, but not having aged as well. The soldier wears second-generation horn-rimmed specs, little windscreens across his eyes that exacerbate their earnestness. That's when he also reminds me of fair-haired Father Mulcahy (who, to be honest, had selected better glasses, even though it was the time of the Korean War). He is the padre and he makes me want to giggle a little, not because I think his position is ridiculous (I don't); not because he's cute (he probably is, but I can't really move past having compared him to a cross between Tintin and Fr. Mulcahy), but because he is such an utter caricature of himself and his work. He exudes honorable intent. There is a near translucent glow of it from him. When he speaks he speaks with a soft but strong Scottish lilt (I later learn he comes from one of the very remote islands in Scotland and on that island his church doesn't use any musical instruments. It's all human harmony: pushing air from the diaphragm so it pulses through pliant vocal chords and produces sounds of incredible range and beauty). So when he speaks he reminds me now of a third person: a blond brother from The Proclaimers.

We shake hands and he tells me about his church. It's the big racing green tent on the way down to the canteen (galley, apparently, because the current brigade is the Navy, even though we aren't on a ship). The door has always been closed over when I've passed, but the entrance is around the other side. Next time I go past I take a look. Yes, it's got all the church gear all right: simple bench seating that's bound to be painful to sit on, a central aisle, and, at the top, a table altar and a small lectern. The altar is demurely dressed: white cloth and a gold chalice. It waits, mutely, for souls. Over the next few days I take a look fairly regularly and I never see anyone in there. I have no idea what denomination it is.

I ask one of the officers about the church. Charles is from Northern Ireland as well, from Coleraine. We would go through the usual rigamarole of asking which school we went to (this is how, in polite society, we are able to label each other), but we don't have to because he's in a Britmil uniform, which is a pretty clear label. Charles comes into my office one day, which I share with my boss, Piet, and Fraser. It's before we really know each other and Charles explains our little would-be ritual to Piet. Charles says my accent has confounded him because it's not so pronounced, but when he asks where I'm from I tell him and he says to Piet, "Now I don't need to ask her what school she went to." We all laugh at these fissures that still exist, ten years after our conflict has formally ended.

I say that I don't need to ask either, but I'll tell him anyway: Coleraine Inst.

"You're right!" he says, grinning. Piet presciently observes that when we speak together both of our accents thicken considerably, to become much more like each other. In the British army Charles is treated as Irish, and defines himself that way when in England. Confusing, huh?

It is because we do some work together and have laughed at the still extant divisions in our homeland that I feel able to ask him about the church.

"Pah! No one goes! I don't think any of the men are religious."

"So why have the padre?" I ask.

"Dunno," he says, chomping on a slice of melon. Our last meeting of the day is at 18:45 and we often go to dinner afterwards. "The men only need him sometimes. But at least he's there when they do."

When I go outside to downtown Lashkar Gah, I won't travel in anything other than a Toyota B6, a state of the art (though you can't really tell from the dust and mud caked on its sides) armored vehicle. We aren't allowed to travel in anything below that standard, as they are practically blast-proof. They cost about £80,000 each. Mounted on the dusty dashboard is a Motorola radio with a handset, an electronic GPS handset, a high-frequency phone handset (if all other comms are down, this is the thing that will still work), two devices (I don't know what they do) with day-glo green screens and red and green buttons below, like a double taxi meter. There's room for some black digital text but I've never seen anything other than "greater than" or "less than" signs. There's a big rear-view mirror (which the navigator uses, not the driver—he uses his side-views only), and all sorts of things that I'm probably better off not knowing about. The guns are there, ubiquitous, omnipresent. I wonder if the security guys ever sleep with them, they are never without. In the back there's us, and a small med kit. I always take my own med kit out with me as well, so that's two. Then there's a really big med kit in the last section, as well as a winch, a couple of tow ropes, and other various bits and pieces. On the outside are at least three aerials—one on the hood, a black bakelite rod as thick as my furled fist, and two on the roof, more aluminum-like, metallic, wiry.

The Americans' desert cars are fortified Hummers. The wheels are up to my chest, and almost as wide as tractor tires. There is all sorts of crazy stuff going on in those cars, which are more like mounted Hudson River-tugs on wheels. There's armor plating, aerials, guns, shooting holes (probably not the technical term). They're like the antennae of a prehistoric and huge insect or one of the short stubbly and spiky dinosaurs, the antecedant to the armadillo writ large and fueled with limitless supplies of red diesel (not purchased at the tuk-tuk stands).


One evening I am really hungry and go for dinner right at 18:00, the official start time. The canteen is the size of a tennis court and it's the same tarpaulin technology air pumped through it—the artificial lung— to keep it up. There's a bit more of a queue than normal to get in, but I am not unduly concerned. There's the wash drill first: wet, soap, rinse, dry at the three freestanding basins outside (freezing in the winter) and then round the corner: splat! squirt hand sanitizer onto your hands to really be sure. Hygiene is a really big thing here. If you get an outbreak of anything in a confined area like the camp with a thousand people on it every day, there's no stopping it. Prevention is the cure.

When I get into the galley there aren't any civilians there. Usually there's always someone, but no, this time there's nothing but a sea of beige and brown camouflage. I think, "Is there an unwritten rule that the military get to go first?" But my plate is full and so I walk right down to the first empty table, near the end. My lilac and purple fleece seems much brighter than it likely is. I sit down. I am joined by two young soldiers. We rarely sit at the same table as them—all the military I mix with professionally are officers, and in the canteen civilians usually eat together. The guys opposite me now are right on the frontline. They are the people I meet going off to spend the day in the netted and leafy Snatchers, on their way out to patrol, as I make my way to the gym in the dark of the scarcely morning. These two look quite young. They are talking about those patrols. They are saying: "We took some incoming this morning. I just laughed."

"I don't like the rockets when they come in. Small arms fire, that's OK, I don't mind that, but I don't like those RPGs."

"I dunno, mate, I was just able to—" he hesitates, "react. It was cool."

The next day we are—and by "we" I mean the whole camp, civilians and military alike who are on base at that time—called to a memorial service for those who have been killed in the past ten days or so. The following week another service is held, for one person. The drill is the same both times. We gather on the old helopad. The sand and cream uniformed cohorts line up around three sides of the dirty grey concrete. It's a ribbon four or five men and women deep, forty or fifty men and women long on each side. The civilians line up behind them, in assorted fleeces—purple, mint green, gravy brown, maroon, khaki, charcoal grey. The police officers are in navy. Then the soldiers are called to attention. It really is how you see it in the movies. A man screams, I think he's going to cause at least minor inflammation of his larynx, if not a tear: "PAARRRRAAAAADDDDEEEE STAAANNND T'AAAATTTEN-SHUN!"

There is a precision and synchronicity of group movement that I didn't really think possible outside of the parading armies of former communist countries—though this parade doesn't quite have the same sharply ironed corners. The communist regimes must have used more starch. But there it is, right in front of me. And then, just as we civilians shuffle our feet, square our shoulders, and straighten our backs, the corps is invited to be at ease. This too is hurled with considerable volume. Definitely some tissue tearing around the tonsils this time, I think.

And there, making up the fourth wall of this rectangular humanoid box, is the padre and his simple altar. The souls have come. The padre wears the same uniform as the others. There are no liturgical vestments: no alb, no cincture, no surplice. The only exception is the squat black stole that hangs around his neck to below his knees. His fingers falcate around a Bible; he reads from it. The words have ballad meter and he reads, steadily, in a baroque timbre, the consonants of words like "Lord" and "remember" ringing out clearly across the at-ease parade. The combination of content and tone lends itself well to the occasion. Then there is real remembrance. Words not from two thousand years ago but from yesterday, when friends of the deceased wrote about them.

For my previous work I had to reduce many complex policy positions to two or three bullet points, without losing the meaning. What's the message? This paper is a hundred and fifty pages long: sum it up in three points, without losing its essence. What does the audience need to know, really need to know? We have five minutes with the prime minister. What do we tell him in that time? How do we make sure he gets the message?

It's all about reducing to the core. What we're about to listen to is the salt-solution boiled dry: we're down to the white powder in the pan: absolute desiccation. There's no going back. This is what these friends of the deceased do now. They have five minutes to vocalize the virtue of lives irrevocably interrupted. Two or three well-chosen sentences on a cold makeshift parade ground on the other side of the world must encapsulate all that these young men were. And they are young. "Lee was born in 1986." Or 1988. I remember what I was doing in 1988, and how it would be if that were my last year. They were just starting out. But they wanted to experience it all: they asked to be "sent to the most dangerous place in Helmand," or were "always gubbin' off, always getting in'te shits w'sergeant—we called him 'ASBO'!" (this sets off small laughter) or "one of the bravest officers who led by example and who would do anything to defend his men." I am reminded of the better qualities of Lermontov's Pechorin. These boys are heroes of their time. The camouflage of the uniforms in front of me is a pale sand-colored base with almost-ochre splashes of dark. The dark patches fall like a scattered pack of Rorschach cards across the backs of the army uniforms. On the lower back of the man in front of me a shadow of almost-ochre looks like the silhouette of a winged angel in profile holding a rifle. I think that I shouldn't tell anyone this or else the psychologist whom I saw (whom we all are required to see) before coming out might amend her report. I look away and look back again. No, that crusading angel is still on that guy's back.

One of the readings is from Wilfred Owen—"I too saw God through mud"—which is particularly and poignantly apposite for Lashkar Gah. There is something slightly off about the reading of it, though, and it doesn't strike me until afterwards what that was. Then I realize: the officer read the title in English—"Apology for my Poetry"—as opposed to Owen's Latin—"Apologia Pro Poemate Meo." Maybe he thought the ordinary soldier wouldn't understand it otherwise (there is such a stark class differential between officer and soldier manifested mostly in accents gained at private schools and bearing gained from a sense of entitlement taken at birth). But they all understand, all live and die the words in the verses of the poem. Then the laryngeally challenged officer recites, surprisingly gently but firmly, Laurence Binyon's words:

> They shall grow not old, as we that are left grow old:
> Age shall not weary them, nor the years condemn.
> At the going down of the sun and in the morning
> We will remember them.

The padre turns and walks away. The parade is dismissed, and we go back to work.

Street scene, Lashkar Gah

# 4. The Toilet Paper

FRASER, MY COLLEAGUE, is a mellow yellow kind of fellow. His hair, normally tamed into a wiry ponytail by a purple elastic band, descends a fair way down his back in frizzy salt-and-pepper spirals. Occasionally one wisp will escape and tickle his forehead but more usually there will be a general wispiness all over, a corona of calm capping him. Even though he is the only person in the office to wear a suit every day (with a pretty spectacular line in high volume ties), he seems somehow unkempt. But this combination of calmness and unkemptness is one of the reasons I've felt so instantly comfortable in our little team. One cannot but be at ease in his company. This external demeanor of an extra who has remained behind in an Adam and the Ants video with a love of 1980s tunes (which he'll sing without even the drop of a hat) belies his manifold accomplishments. He is a qualified junior soccer referee, he is a qualified diving instructor, he has been the de facto Attorney General of the Caribbean island of Montserrat. (The AG was sick for nine months, and Fraser was head legal honcho in that time. The island of Montserrat has a parliament of eleven MPs.) He will be running the Barcelona Marathon in March and does many laps of the helo hard track every day in preparation for this. His second language is Lao because he was "kind of" married to a Lao woman for a while. We discuss this:

"Er, Fraser, 'kind of'? I 'kind of' speak Bosnian. I 'kind of' like parsnips. But marriage. I've been to a few. It's a legal act: you either are, or you're not. 'Kind of' doesn't seem to me to apply."

"Well, I wasn't there when it happened."

Obviously this was a conversation that we had to finish over drinks on a Thursday night (equivalent to Western Friday nights—we work six days a week, Fridays are our day off). Perhaps this is a good place to explain what it is I'm doing and for whom I'm working, if you will forgive the digression.

Fraser's been here for a year so far, working in the Rule of Law team of the UK-led Provincial Reconstruction Team (PRT) in Helmand Province. Fraser's the Justice Advisor. In the same team, I'm the Rule of Law Governance Advisor. That essentially means that I'm supposed to identify opportunities for the local community here in Lashkar Gah and in the surrounding districts to increase their engagement with, and potential participation in, the main rule of law institutions. In a formal sense this means the prosecutor's office, the courts, the police, the prison. But Afghanistan has a very strong cultural and historical tradition of dispensing justice outside of the formal system. Tradition has been for local Tribal Elders (all male) to deliberate on matters of dispute between persons in their community. In a sense there are elements in this of what we'd recognize as deliberative or restorative justice mechanisms today. Certainly in Northern Ireland such systems began to be developed in the latter stages of the troubles as alternatives to going through the formal court system and as a way of seeing the crime as damage to the community as a whole, not just the victim. It was not just a response to keeping bad men out of the way of the formal justice system, but also to keep them out of the hands of our own informal system, administered by paramilitary groups. The IRA, the UVF, the UDA, the INLA, it didn't matter: punishments administered by these groups were harsh, physical, effective immediately and irrevocable, and handed down without due process.

In Afghanistan it's rather similar. There's the formal system. But there are also two informal systems: informal (Elders) and informal (Taliban). The Elders tend to follow customary law, a blend, so far as I understand it, of tradition and religious law. The Taliban version is (as they see it) pure Islamic, or Shar'ia, Law. Punishments administered by the Taliban are harsh, physical, effective immediately and irrevocable, and handed down without due process. But there are certain ironies in the differences between the two informal systems. For example, under Afghan customary law a woman has no inheritance rights over a piece of land. Under Taliban, or Islamic law, a woman very clearly has rights of inheritance. In addition, in the Pashtun areas (like Helmand), the Elders and the community are guided by and adhere to the particular code of the tribe, the Pashtunwali. The primary pillars of the Pashtunwali are *badal* (revenge), *melmastia* (hospitality), and *nanawati* (sanctuary). It's all about regulated revenge. *Badal, melmastia,* and *nanawati* can all play out in one act of revenge. Thomas Barfield[2] explains this well: For example, there is a murder. The person taking revenge should be a close relative of the victim. The most honorable revenge attacks take place face to face, but killing in ambush is also acceptable as long as the revenger takes public credit for his deed. Revenge attacks cannot be carried out in a mosque or against a guest, even if a host discovers mid-lamb-roast that his guest is an enemy, he must not harm him, such is the primacy of *melmastia*.

People believe the formal system to be corrupt, expensive, and sluggish. So they invariably turn initially to the Elders. But the Elders' system—tough at times, there's no doubt, but generally focused on repairing damaged relationships within the community (it is also aimed at ensuring that absolute adherence to honor doesn't mean that small illegal acts spiral out of control into vendettas that cascade down through generations)—is coming under threat from the Taliban system. Actually, in areas that are controlled by the Taliban the Elders' system is smothered, stunted, and as dry and dead as driftwood in the desert.

The Elders' system isn't perfect—not, to my mind, by a long shot, not least because of the absence of women—but it's part of my job in the context of this war to bolster this informal system, to bolster the formal system and, if and where possible, create a workable nexus between the two that enjoys community consent and confidence. The trouble is, when you start dabbling in an informal system that's been around for hundreds of years, say, by having Elders write down their judgments, by having Elders' judgments be consistent and cognizant of all the facts, by having them take principles of universalism and human rights (as set out in the Afghani Constitution) into account when considering a case of theft in a village, what does that mean for the Elders' system? For us, the written word is sovereign: nothing exists unless it is in writing, particularly where disputes and their resolutions are involved. But here, over half population cannot read, cannot write.

2 For further reading, see Thomas Barfield's very interesting "Afghan Customary Law and its Relationship to Formal Judicial Institutions." United States Institute for Peace, Washington, DC, 2003

They can't read the calligraphic twirls and whorls of the right to left letters that grace the few billboards in downtown Lash any more than I can. So if we encourage judgments to be written, recorded, and archived, enabling the admission of precedent and consistency, does this very act of writing alter the whole process? Does it create a mutation that is unrecognizable and unworkable in the community it must serve? At base, does it mean the informal becomes formal?

It's not as if customary law itself hasn't changed over time, however. Community consent has been, and will be, key. In the process of getting at the truth of disputes, it used to be the case that the accused would be asked to swear an oath before Allah. This is taken very seriously and superstitiously. But there also used to be an additional way: the accused would be asked to undergo an ordeal, akin to medieval trials to establish witchcraft. If the accused got through the ordeal (taking seven paces with a red-hot piece of iron placed on your hand over seven pieces of paper, or picking three stones out of boiling water) without suffering any epidermal abrasions, then he was innocent. I'm thinking the laws of nature will have trumped all other laws in this instance: there cannot but have been boils and blisters and suppurating skin, post-facto. But, says the Barfield article, the popularity of the ordeal was declining in favor of the oath alone by the 1970s. The community had simply lost faith in the capacity of the ordeal to determine truth. Plus, swearing oaths had a justification in Islamic law while ordeals did not.

Fraser has found a way to fuse the two systems, though not by means of red-hot iron or boiling water. It's fragile, but it's a start. The traditional means by which the Elders take a decision is through a shura, basically a meeting. This week he helped the Head of the Legal Education Department organize a Legal Education Rights shura. It was held in the front yard of the Department, on great red and burgundy carpets fringed in cream, under a cream cotton tent. Stevie, the projects manager, had set it all up. Everything hadn't gone smoothly, it must be admitted. Stevie had had an argument with the Head over the kettles he'd bought for the occasion. They were stainless steel: too bright and shiny. They'd only turn black when heated over the wood fire that would burn in the corner. The Head didn't want to serve the Elders from dirty kettles. It would have been better to have black cast-iron kettles from the start. Honorably, Stevie apologized and said if the Head accepted the shiny stainless steel kettles, he would try to persuade Mr. Fraser to address the crowd of esteemed and honorable Elders for at least an hour.

Fraser spoke to them for five minutes and then they just got on with it, Elders learning about basic rights. Whether they will use this alien knowledge or not is completely unknown, and to be honest, at this stage, unknowable. So we will need to figure out ways to track this. Before we leave this technical intermission, a word on the formal system. There are 1.8 million people in the province of Helmand. There are plenty of judges. And there are around 3,500 prosecution lawyers in the whole country, who, even with only the most tenuous grasp of the law, attain an incredible 85 percent conviction rate. Before August of last year there were no defense lawyers in Helmand: none. Not until Fraser managed to persuade some of them to come from Kabul and set up shop in Lashkar Gah. There are no jury trials. I think momentarily of Diplock Courts. And there were no students at university studying to become lawyers for those 1.8 million Helmandis. Not one. Again, Fraser found the money for four of them to take the entrance exam (they passed) and to study at the university in Kabul. They're there now, and will be for four years. I don't know how this place will look when they are ready to come back, if they come back, to practice law in this chthonic and contaminated system.

But today, Fraser and me, we're on a top-priority mission: to get the judge to agree to one of our three proposals for new toilets in the court building. We are conscious of the great responsibility that lies on our shoulders: the fate and fortune of the formal justice system in Helmand is riding on this meeting. So, of course, we get down and dirty when discussing it in the office as we put on the Kevlar.

Fraser: Do you have the toilet paper, Kate?

Kate: Why, no, Fraser, I thought you were the keeper of the toilet paper. Did I flush it maybe? Oops!

Not a clever pun, or even a word-parry, but we giggle nonetheless.

Sometimes you just can't beat toilet humor.

We enter the court building, clutching the toilet paper. Two toilets and a shower OR a toilet and two adjacent showers OR a toilet and a separate room with one shower. These are the No. 3 judge's choices. Chubby and ebullient he is a burnt copper version of the tawny lion from *The Wizard of Oz*. He greets us in English, "Hello! Hello! Come in! Come in!", giving each word its own exclamation mark. He is as confident as the lion is cowardly. I have quickly developed the habit of waiting to see if men will shake my hand or not, though my natural inclination is to extend my hand first. I recognize that I have adopted a subtly subservient position, something I'm not so used to, but I also acknowledge that it doesn't cost me much. This particular judge is brimming over with smiles and handshakes of greeting, his brown eyes flicker, his spade-like hands engulf even my sausage-like fingers.

His companion, who remains seated throughout, is older, and doesn't speak English (though he speaks German). He has a magnificent beard, as white as snow in its first hour, in contrast to the lined nutmeg skin of his face. His eyes are palest translucent blue, bleached by too much sun, perhaps. His white turban is perched magnificently on top of his head, he wears a brown dress-blanket wrapped like a shawl around him and his cream *salwar kameez* swirls around his ankles. He has the aspect of an elderly and esoteric white cat. His feet are bare, except for his sandals. It is freezing in the room—the biggest and grandest I've been in so far. There are massive red carpets on the floor, and pale rose-petal pink velour valances—with cream tassels, of course—dress each of the low windows, confident as if they were adorning one of the minor rooms in the Palace of Versailles. There are four filing cabinets standing rather forlornly at one end (which the PRT has paid for to support court administration), and there are low brown sofas lining each of the two longer walls.

It is freezing. I am wearing Peter Storm maximum weight (mountain) hiking socks, heavy hiking boots, Berghaus base layer underwear (usually used when skiing), a sweater, a black *salwar kameez* (with a silver trim—bought from the "occasion wear" rack in an Islamic-dress shop by the old Orthodox cathedral in Sarajevo). I'm also wearing a full-length black wool coat and black headscarf. With my white face and white hands, I'm like the corner of a grubby chessboard. My feet are still cold, and he is wearing no socks. The Afghans are a pretty tough people.

It takes them two seconds to decide on the toilet arrangements: showers and toilets are to be separate entities. This effluvia-management decision is also guided by Islam and its emphasis on the principle of cleanliness. It's the right decision for the No. 3 judge to take: one does not excrete and ablute in the same place.

Like the fine dust from the desert, Islam gets everywhere.

The sad irony is that forty years ago there was running water (and electricity) in every home in Lashkar Gah, and now there are only street pumps, which always seem to attract hordes of small children, never tiring of seeing the clear as crystal water gush from the metal pipe. It may not be in every home, but you can drink the water here, not like in Kabul, where you can't. If the Taliban really cared about Islam and the cleanliness which is a core tenet, they'd be supportive of rebuilding the hydro-infrastructure.

Later that week we get a project bid in from one of our partner organizations, an Afghan NGO, to run classes in basic hygiene. The first lesson plan proposes to teach how to use soap, the second how to brush teeth. We're starting from a low baseline here.

Landing strip, southern Helmand desert

# 5. Getting Out of There

Day 1: Tuesday

It's Tuesday, the day I am meant to travel to Kabul to meet with people at the Ministry of Justice, and then depart for my first breather break on Thursday. The day does not start well. Ian is the flights coordinator at Lash. I go to his desk early in the morning to check what time I'm leaving. There's no Ian. Instead, there's a sign stuck across his screen, in upper case black lettering saying: THERE ARE NO SCHEDULED FLIGHTS TODAY. My heart sinks. All rotor aircraft today are being used in support of a military ground operation.

Then, at midday, the first in a series of miracles: Ian comes and tells me that I can get to Bastion, the massive camp in the desert, on a flight, wheels up at 17:35. Hurrah! I'm going home. I rather foolishly assume that means I'll get all the way to Kabul on Tuesday night, taking the Stampede (the huge big military transport plane), but at two o'clock, Ian breaks the news that I'll have to stay overnight at Bastion, as the Stampede has been canceled. I'll have to go the next night. My sunken heart deflates further on hearing this, crinkling like a week-old balloon. But I remain positive. That's OK, I think, I can rearrange the meeting with the MOJ (on establishing a Lay Prison Visitor's scheme in LKG Prison) for the Thursday morning, and I'll fly out on Thursday afternoon as planned. A night in Bastion won't do me much harm, surely?

I'm getting ready to go to the HLS (Helicopter Landing Site), where Fraser runs most days, when Kevin, the Deputy Head of Mission, puts his head around my door. He brings the gift of a second miracle. Hugh, the Head of Mission is no longer going to Kabul that evening, so I can have his seat on the earlier Stampede! My heart leaps like a dolphin doing tricks in a pool. Hurrah! I'm going home.

We get to the HLS at four-thirty, well ahead of time. I'm sitting chatting to Peter, discovering that he is as fluent in Amharic as in

33

English due to a childhood spent in Ethiopia, when I notice people actually checking in. It's my first time on the outward journey, so I amble up to the desk and here encounter the next problem of the day. I'm not on the flight manifest for the first flight. I'm on the manifest for the second flight, but that one won't be flying until 19:00, and that will be too late to catch the Stampede.

Then the third of the day's miracles. Major Tom is to fly on the first flight, the VIP flight, but he doesn't need to be in Bastion at any particular time and he'd only be waiting around at the other end. He offers to swap seats with me. It's very sweet and kind of him. Again my heart leaps in my chest.

But it all goes very badly wrong after that. Given the UK operation, flights are being supplied this evening by the Canadians. It's 17:45, and we are told that the Canadians want to wait until it gets darker before they fly. They won't be here until at least 19:00. We all groan. There are about twenty of us now, including the civilian Head of Mission, the brigadier, and the provincial governor, all bound to meet a party of UK MPs. Invariably, there are lots of complaints about the Canadians being big babies, don't-they-know-there's-a-war-on, and a host of other yellow-tinged terms that I couldn't possibly repeat.

We are told to go and eat, but my stomach is such a bundle of knots that I don't think I can. There is a silver lining, however. Though I just paw over the dinner, I do manage (valiantly in my view) the dessert: bread and butter pudding, with custard. This is a dual-function dessert. It both tastes fantastic in the here and now, and carries with it in every succulent mouthful the memory of every time I've had it as a kid. It's not quite as good as my mum's, but it is close.

Fed and watered, we clamber back over the rough shale pebbles to the HLS waiting area. It's now dark, really dark. And the wind is coming up. The Canadians announce that they won't be flying, even in the dark. Because it's the brigadier and the Head of Mission and the governor, Britmil get on the phone and rustle up a Chinook. Though the flight time is only about fifteen minutes, by the time it gets crewed up and over, it will be here in an hour. We are BOGSAT for the hour, Captain Rob tells us. We stare at him blankly.

"Bunch of guys, sitting around talking," he reveals, grinning, "it's from the Americans, they think up everything!" On the reception table sits a beige camouflaged helmet, with a glowing orange lightstick cocked semi-horizontally across it, like a rooster's comb, or a centurion's helmet's plumage.

I go around the corner out onto the HLS itself. This comprises two large concrete rectangles. Blue lights mark the corners of one of them, and green lights mark the corners of the other. When I go out there is only one green light and two blue lights on. I have no idea why they all come on at different times. The green light makes me think of the green light at the end of Daisy's dock, the one that Gatsby looked across at, or the dashboard that you see from being warm and safe and small in the back of the family car when you were driven home in the dark.

The helo is coming and we huddle behind the Hesco wall that separates us from the blue and green lighted concrete pads. Above us the night is clear, an infinity of stars twinkle just like the lullabies say they are supposed to, little astral asterisks all. The bright opalescent moon is a few days short of its full belly. We are signaled to come out from behind the Hesco, in a single-file line, down the running track, our little head torches in white and red bobbing as we walk. The two blades of the Chinook raise so much dust that I can't see the helo, even though it is only twenty feet away. The Chinook is a truly majestic metal insect. Its two rotor blades seem to defy the natural order of things. I've been told that when they are in full rotation, whirring furiously, they distend by four inches. The metal stretches because of the speed and the rotation. It's truly amazing. And they still don't touch each other, it is pure unadulterated parallelism: two vectors that stretch to infinity without touching.

Right now I can't see any of this. Because of the dust, I'm viewing things behind the grey-brown gauze again. All I can see are soldier silhouettes, carrying stuff out of the back of the Chinook in a line, as if they were passing buckets of water to put out a house fire in the Wild West of old. They sway slightly sideways on the shale, their helmets exaggerating the size of their heads, on several of which are perched, like plumage on a tropical bird, a number of the orange glow sticks.

Our orange-lit leader stops us. We are to turn off our head torches as soon as we turn into the pebble dash. I in turn sway from side to side as my luggage, the Kevlar, the helmet, and the hope that my heart must contain alter my center of gravity and disorientate me. It is my first time in a Chinook. Four green spots light the insides of the great man-made grasshopper. I am second in line after Andy (another marathon runner). We sit at the top, furthest away from the gaping hole which is the entrance and exit. The four green spots go off, and there is darkness. The electronics are black with green text, like the very first computers, a toxic, glaring, warning green, almost fluorescent.

The gunner is next to me, and he stands up, his head even more swollen than most: he wears a bigger helmet, to accommodate his night vision goggles. His big bug-eyes are a matte milky green, and give off a small phosphorescence, like a deep-ocean creature. The gunner looks around and smiles down (I think) at me in the darkness. I smile back, still hopeful of an early flight to Kabul. We take off. The Chinook is amazingly silent on the inside (and not just because I'm wearing earplugs). As we rise vertically up I get my first real night sight of Lashkar Gah. There is darkness and brightness, but it is patchy. Houses with generators, public buildings, they have electricity, light. The others do not. There is no light pollution because there is no street lighting. This community is too impoverished to pollute in the ways we do.

The approach to Bastion could not be more different. It looks like a city from an airplane, all orange sodium lights, white lighting around the cookhouses, the perimeter and other camp amenities, purple and red and blue spots on the HLS and runways. The darkness of the desert is all around.

We land. As I'm getting out the gunner comes towards me, his big bug-eyes still bulging. I'm a little bit afraid he's going to scold me about something. Instead, inexplicably, he shouts in my (plugged) ear: "Your perfume or deodorant smells so good I feel I should be buying you flowers!"

Let's have a look at this little tableau. I'm wearing navy Kevlar that squashes, squares, and generally de-genderizes my whole upper body. I have a bright, my-first-paintbox blue helmet on, that looks like my toddler-nephew's upside down dinner bowl sitting on my head. There are small canary yellow foam cylinders jutting out of my ears. I look like an extra from a Pixar animation, *A Bug's Life*, perhaps. This is not a good look, in anybody's book. Perhaps the helmet/bowl is set at a jaunty angle? Perhaps the gunner needs to go on his R&R break? Perhaps there is something wrong with the night vision goggles? (This last thought is all the more disconcerting given that he's the guy who is supposed to be looking out for any incoming Taliban action on the flight.)

In any event, I have missed the Stampede, so will have to go out on the one the next day, Wednesday. What if the Stampede doesn't go for some reason on Wednesday? I think, before banishing such negativity from my mind. But it pops up again; these planes can be very fickle. There's not much I can do without it, however. I am sharing a pod with a woman, Jane, from the Embassy in Kabul. The pod is half the size of my normal one in LKG. There, I have one bed, a desk, two doors that open onto a shelf and a wardrobe, a door that opens into a toilet, a sink, and a shower cubicle, and a door that opens to the world of the camp. There is a two-drawer bedside table combo, and a foot-high fridge. There's a TV that doesn't work, and an internet connection that does, so I can listen to Radio 4. It's spare and spartan, but pretty comfortable. It's about twelve by six feet. The walls are cream, the floor is slate blue with a small red carpet on it. In Bastion there are two of us in bunk beds in a regular pod split in two. Our "room" is about eight by six feet. We must dress and undress the beds ourselves, but the mattresses are better than those in LKG. The ablutions block is separate and unisex. It's a bit smelly, but at least the power showers still work.

## Day 2: Wednesday

The next day, Wednesday, we wake up and are told that there's no Stampede to Kabul that night. That deflated heart of mine turns to lead and sinks to my toes. There's no way I'll make the plane to Dubai on Thursday. I am resigned, except there's a chance, with the morning flight to Kabul, on Thursday. Ian's schedule said the plane left at 09:30. If it left on time, I'd still get into Kabul on time. It would be tight, but I would give it a go.

I decide to explore the mighty Camp Bastion, home to around 7,000 military personnel—mostly British, but with some Danish and American. I go out to the perimeter wall nearest the Foreign and

Commonwealth Office encampment (a once-white tent rising from above the pods, pinnnacled around a central pole like the big top of a circus. The FCO transit camp has garden-furniture-green Hesco, which, possibly coincidentally, matches the cushioning on the wooden bench that sits in front of the tea/coffee/*Nuts* and *FHM* magazines/left behind paperback thrillers/TV table). The roads are long and flat, cut into the desert floor on a grid system. Bastion can exist only because of a vast underground water system. There is so much that it bottles its own water, which is what we all drink while we're here. It's only nine in the morning, but already the sun is high and I want to walk before the sun gets too hot. I don't have any sunscreen with me. I know I'm such a pale face that I'll get burnt, but my desire to explore and walk far outweighs my fear of a fried epidermis and even more crow's feet.

I walk around the back, to what looks like a gap in the wall. Behind it there are mountains—not very high mountains, but something of distinction on the landscape. I come to another road that beckons between two empty sangars (which I think is the military word for watchtowers). I go up to the gap. There's no gate. On the other side of the gap the desert seems to sprawl untamed by any fence. There is a road, and I can see some shipping containers. I put my head through the place where I think there should be a gate. I'm like a prisoner who wakes up one morning and finds the cell door inexplicably left open. It is surely a trap, but the air and the space outside are beguiling, enticing. I entirely expect a gruff voice to tell me I'm breaking some rule or other and to go back. But no, there's nothing. I can go forward. But I don't. I self-censor, I curtail my own freedom of movement. I don't take the risk, like I normally would do. I backtrack and turn on toward the HLS. I'm getting toward the end of that when a soldier comes out of a little hut and tells me I can't go any further. I ask him about the road that I've just been on. Is it safe?

"Sure," he says, "people run out there all the time."

So I go back to the gap in the wall and this time venture further on.

I discover that the sense of being truly out in the desert was an optical illusion, an apposite mirage given the location. There are fences made of wire and set farther back, that's all. But it doesn't matter. I've been walking for almost an hour now and I'm only halfway around the camp. I could never be in this situation in Lash.

I take in the desert, literally. The dust is omnipresent and, I think at times, omniscient. It furs and films everything, becoming an integral part of my clothes, my eyes, my tongue, my nostrils. It coats the very water we drink, even if newly opened. It settles in the teeth of zippers making them stick and stutter when I open and close them. The desiccated powder that blows everywhere and settles as the desert's top layer is a chalky brown, the color and texture of dried yeast. Kellogg Brown & Root employees are building a new road, part of the Bastion expansion programme, and the dirt they cut into, further down, closer to the water supply, is the color of soft Sequoia flesh, redder, more fertile. I come to a sign that exclaims: "Explosive storage! No runners!" I turn back.

My phone rings. It is Ahmad from the Ministry of Justice. He wants to know if I'm coming today. I say I won't make it today, but Clive from the embassy is still intending to go to the MOJ. If I get to Kabul tonight, I will go tomorrow. He is very understanding and says they will meet Clive. It's about 9:45. Then Clive calls. What's the line on the Lay Prison Visitors Scheme? I give him the line, which he will include among other business. I walk back toward the HLS.

A car pulls up—it's our facilitators, Simon and Mark.

"We've found you a flight! The Danes are flying. We need to check-in at eleven!"

I don't need to be told twice to get in the car. The three of us, Jane, Tim, and I, head over to the airstrip. The Danish flight controller has cornflower blue eyes that glimmer next to the wheat-blond of his beard and hair. He is my own personal savior.

We are to come back at two. We decide to go for lunch. Tim has the inside scoop from the facilitators that the shortest queue is the one which is farthest away. There's only one cookhouse in Lash, and the line is never very long, feeding maybe 700–800 people a day. Bastion has at least three cookhouses and feeds 7,000–8,000 a day. The only drawback with the short line is that, because it's situated near a sewage pit, there's a bad smell.

Tim and I confer. We decide that minor nasal discomfort is a small price to pay for early eats. Did I say minor nasal discomfort? We walk around the corner and it's as if we have vaulted onto another planet, one which is governed by smell. And it's not a democracy: it's a malodorous dictatorship of smell. It is putrid and it is pungent. It is foul and it is fetid. It is lithe and it is alive. It reeks, it is rancid, and it rocks and roils my stomach so much that the proper order of digestion is interrupted and my breakfast is hurled upwards to my esophagus, where it burns my throat. I barely manage to keep it on the inside. We both gag. I cover my nose with my shirt. I try not to think that smell is really microscopic particles of the original substance airborne to my bloodstream via the nasal passage and other ducts. We never use that line again.

We go back to the Danish airfield at two, ready to fly. We are told to come back at three.

"But the plane is coming, it will fly?" I ask the blond Dane, Johannes.

"Yes, it is coming, and it will fly," he smiles, his eyes reflecting the bright sun.

We go back at three. We are told to come back at five.

"The plane…" I start to ask Johannes.

"Is coming and it will fly," he smiles.

We come back at five. At six we hear the plane land. We are going to Kabul! We get on the plane, do up the seat belts. As usual I need some assistance with this. Tim takes a photo of Jane on the plane. Jane takes a photo of Tim. I take a photo of them both. Everyone is smiling. We are going to Kabul, and then home.

Then, dismay. The guys at the back get off the plane. We have to as well. We are crushed. But Johannes doesn't let us down, not yet. There is a slight technical problem. The Danes carry four mechanics on every flight, they must be able to fix it.

We go into the airfield tents and wait. The hours stretch by. At 20:00 Johannes brings news. He hollers in Danish for about five minutes and then turns to us and says in about thirty seconds: "We are missing a little rubber ring. It costs $2. We need to see if we can find one in Bastion. We will fit it, and then we will go."

Someone has told me that the Hercules has four propellers, but can fly with only one working. And it can't go without this $2 rubber ring?

By this stage news has filtered in of incidents in Kabul. We learn that the Ministry of Justice has been attacked. Clive and Ahmad were in the building at the time of the attack. If I hadn't been stuck in Bastion, I would have been there too. Everyone has survived, but I do feel bad because the meeting wouldn't be taking place if it weren't for me. And I can't call Clive because we don't have network coverage.

At 21:00 Johannes comes back. There is no rubber ring of the right size on the camp. What they will do is to ask the British to take a ring from Kandahar Air Field (KAF) when they come in on their Stampede.

Johannes then arranges for us to have army rations. This turns out to be singularly the coolest thing I've ever seen. The outer reinforced-foil bag is dull brown. The inner bags are a muted spearmint green. I need to use Tim's serrated knife to open each one. I get a vegetarian meal. I take out the little packet of foil-wrapped tortellini, similar to what you'd get served on airplanes. I look at it trying to figure out where to put the knife to cut it. I must have been looking pretty perplexed, for a young Danish soldier leaps over and, excitedly, as if he is about to get a sign-up fee for inducting me into an arcane and ancient ritual asks me if I've done this before. I shake my head, and smile, self-deprecatingly, perhaps a little coyly.

"OK, here's what you do. You get this bag (he points to a clear plastic bag), put this inside (the spearmint green foil pack), then put in some water up to here (a line about a finger's width from the bottom of the clear plastic bag), close the bag over, sit it on the box like this for five minutes, and then you're done.'"

I thank him, and wonder what will happen. Then I notice all around me little chimneys of steam spouting from the clear plastic bags. I put cold water into the plastic bag. I put the ration pack inside. I twirl the ration pack around the corners of the plastic bag. And then the magic happens: as soon as I'm done twirling, a head of steam builds up and pillows the bag, like microwave-in-the-bag popcorn. I almost burn my hand because of the steam. I nearly drop the whole thing in surprise— it happens so fast! I set it down and wait. In less than five minutes the tortellini has heated up so much that it cooks the sauce it's sitting in, and is ready to eat, in the absence of any visible heat source: no fire, no microwave, no gas oven. A chemical reaction that gives off enough heat fast enough. And both things—the water, the chemical—start off cold. It is like no other "just add water" instant food I have ever seen. The air afterward smells a little acidic, but nothing like the smell from the cookhouse earlier in the day. And the tortellini tastes great.

Day 3: Thursday

The hours pass. Around midnight, Johannes comes again, offering Tayto Cheese and Onion chips and hope. They are working like crazy on the plane. It will be late, but it will fly. The postprandial atmosphere in the tent is getting more than a little boyish and gaseous, as people leave the seats and lie on the floor, stretched out, holding PlayStations or Wiis or iPods, or sleeping. Very few read. These guys have just finished their tour—this is the plane come to take them home after six months. Earlier they were exuberant, but now they are tired, and they just want to go home. Johannes watches a documentary on polygamy with us. We chat. At this stage I think I'm a little bit in love with him. It is of course a love predicated on his ability to get me far away from him, but love manifests itself in mysterious ways. We watch *Desperate Housewives*.

It's 02:00. No fly. It's 03:00. Still no fly. Johannes comes again. The plane is canceled. I am devastated. We go back to the Danish base and wait for our luggage to come back, on two huge pallets. I get my bag and say goodbye to Johannes. He touches my arm in parting. He's sorry too that we haven't been able to fly. I touch his arm back in a gesture of acknowledgement. If we weren't so tired and frustrated about not flying, who knows, it might even have been a beautiful moment. It's 04:00 when we get to bed. Another day of disappointment beckons.

I wake up too late for breakfast in the cookhouse so I have a grapefruit, half a packet of Sour Cream & Onion Pringles and some Minstrels. We go to Pizza Hut for lunch, and await news of Stampede movement. It's got to go today.

Then, mocking our plight even further, there is a great sandstorm. The wind whips up massive clouds of dust that rob us (and any pilots) of visibility. It sucks and spits and spews the sand in a frenzy of furious eddies, for hours. There is a rumor that the US will fly some planes, but they won't do it in this sandstorm. I sit under the canvas canopy in our transit camp. The wind howls and shrieks and eventually it tears the canopy to shreds. I sit through it watching an old (very camp) episode of *Batman and Robin*, leafing through a *Nuts* magazine for the first time ever (all seems quite boring to me, the parabolas of the human anatomy being, by definition, at least conceptually similar to all) as the tent cracks and caves inwards, and the canvas falls down literally onto my head. Great, I think grimly, just great. Then the rain starts. It's like being on holiday in Donegal. Sun-burnt one day, rained-in the next. I remember "sympathetic fallacy" from when I did my English Lit O Levels. Unsurprisingly given the degree of grimness in his books, Hardy was very big on it, the weather reflecting the emotional state of the character. Well, this sandstorm just about sums it all up for me, all the misery of *The Mayor of Casterbridge* and *Tess of the d'Urbervilles* rolled into a morning.

We try not to have hope for the evening's flight, but the storm clears and around 18:00 we see the sun for the first time that day. We feel good. Surely we'll be flying this evening. We go to the check-in before dinner, just to be sure.

Captain Billy is waiting at the desk. "The flight was canceled due to bad weather in Kabul."

"No way, Billy! You're not serious!" I can't believe it. He isn't kidding. My heart goes crashing through my feet and into the chalky dust. I'll never make it to Kabul. One option is for us to go to Kandahar Air Field if we want. KAF is much bigger, and there are more flights out of KAF to Kabul on a daily basis. We call KAF. The FCO transit camp there can only take one female. Because I am the one who is trying to get out of country, Jane generously allows me to go. Tim decides to go on the 03:00 flight, which means that he won't need any overnight accommodation, so he will join me the next day.

Day 4: Friday

KAF is vast and ugly and gray and soulless. It is like being on a huge industrial estate. It's maybe ten times the size of Bastion. I'm down at the TLS (this is the name of the airport, the so-called Taliban Last Stand because this is where the Taliban were earlier defeated) trying to get on an ISAF flight, when Tim arrives, not having slept. We sign up for the waiting list for two flights: ISAF 27 and ISAF 64. Both are on time.

By the time we go to check in, both are canceled. The young woman behind the desk gives me a tip: "Try the Americans, sometimes they have flights going."

I find the US desk. No problem, I'm in their system. They have a flight at 20:45 and a flight at 01:00. I have a good feeling about Team America. In addition, we put ourselves down on the British Stampede, to go at 17:00. While we are still there, the ISAF 27 suddenly comes on again, only to depart at 19:00 Zulu. (Zulu time, I discover, simply means GMT. I don't know why they just don't say that. 19:00 Zulu thus means 23:00 or 11 p.m. in Afghanistan.)

We go for a walk, confident that of the four remaining options we have secured for the day, at least one of them is bound to fly. KAF may be soulless but in its favor it does have more retail opportunities. I buy a new bag (rucksack, not handbag), new trousers, and a new wash bag. I am conscious I am defining myself in terms of my ability to shop, but I don't care: this is the rough edge of retail therapy. We go along the boardwalk where there's a Subway, Greenbeans coffee, and Pizza Hut. I stop in my tracks as I see the next sign: Beauty Center and Spa. Oh boy. I almost salivate. Earlier that morning, as I stood, precariously balanced on one leg beside the stinky urinals in the shower/toilet area (and thinking there's something to be said for the judges' choice of separate showers and toilets in the Court at Lash) I caught a glimpse of my lower leg. It was more recognizable, in a follicular sense, as the limb of a baby bear than that of a human female. A beauty center would soon deal with that. I try to open the door, but it's locked. There'll be no beauty today. To compensate I buy a pain au chocolat from the French bakery, which is pretty good although the accompanying coffee is not.

We learn more about each other as the day goes by. Tim has two kids with his fiancée, who's an airline pilot, all of whom he wants to see on the weekend. He was a cartographer in the army and now his field is tracking the counter-narcotics effort. Tim learns that I have a first date on the weekend, my first first date for about two years. The Date will fly in from New York. I will fly in from Lashkar Gah. There's a window over the weekend. What could be simpler, what could possibly go wrong? Right now, I'm a day behind schedule. The earliest I can make it to Dublin now is Saturday, but that's still doable if I get out of KAF today.

At 17:00 we go down to the UK flight line. We don't get on the British flight, it's full. We learn later that it didn't go, in the end. We go back to the TLS. The ISAF flight is canceled again. Team America had better come through.

At 21:00 we get called to the window. They can take us, but there is a problem. We need a form filled in to say we are authorized to fly on a US Military flight. We rush around and get the form made up, on time. We are booked to go on the flight. The plane lands and the soldiers go on. We get ready to board. There's a last minute addition of ten extra soldiers, which means we get bumped off. I call the Date.

"I think I'm going to be at best half a day, at most one day, late. We might need to think about moving it back to the following weekend. Are you around then?"

"Hmm, I'm in Sierra Leone that weekend for a few weeks."

So, if it doesn't happen this weekend, it isn't going to happen. Relationships, like wars, I realize, are won and lost on logistics. There's one more chance to make it: the 01:00 flight. We go back to the pod, where Tim takes the top bunk and I take the bottom one (thus probably breaking FCO rules on gender segregation, but it's either that or one of us sleeps outside—which isn't allowed either: our duty of care policy means that we have to sleep in hardened accommodation—i.e. not in a tent—and that probably trumps the gender segregation diktat). We get up at 00:30 and go back to the TLS for one in the morning. The flight has been canceled. My heart is sinking through the earth's igneous layer. But we take the positive from it: at least we won't be sitting around all night, waiting. We can go straight back to bed.

Day 5: Saturday

I don't sleep so well and wake early. In the dull and cold hour just after dawn I am in despair. I just feel like I'm never going to get out of here. And the earliest I'll get to Dublin now will be Monday. The Date is logistically impossible. My lower lip curls around my chin, my jaw contorts, and saline suspension seeps out onto my pillow from red eyes. I am feeling very sorry for myself and yes, have a wee weep.

I wipe my eyes, get up, and go back to the TLS. Maybe there's another

ISAF flight. But no. I go back to the Americans. They have a flight going at 16:45. We are "in the system" so we should be in line for it. In the terminal—concrete arches, peeling yellow paint, walls pockmarked by bullets, airport chairs—I see a young guy whom I thought went on the US flight the night before. He recognizes me and we say hi.

"Didn't you go on the flight last night?" I ask.

"Yes." He seems close to tears. So I'm not the only one. "We got to Kabul, the pilot took a look at the runway and decided not to land. So we came back here."

I'm sorry for him, but, selfishly, more sorry for me: it means the 16:45 flight will be chock-a-blocked. No room for civilians, yet alone non-US civilians. We are never getting out of here. The Date calls me. He can rearrange, after all, by juggling his calendar around a bit. That takes the pressure off, but it's still frustrating, not knowing when I'm going to get out.

I trudge back to the transit camp. Tim gets up. And then the miracle, the real miracle happens. A plane is coming to rescue us.

It will be arriving in KAF around 12:00. We go down to the TLS, for the umpteenth time in two days. So far we've missed, been bumped off, told to come back in an hour, not gotten on, or been canceled on around sixteen flights in the past four days. Sixteen times there is hope and then there simply is not. It takes its toll, that amount of rejection, on any heart. It's taken us five days to get around sixty miles. We could have walked in half that time.

At the TLS two fighter jets whizz past, their sonic boom following in their wake. A drone comes in, the first one I've seen up close. It floats past like a big white paper plane. There are no windows or doors, just cameras, taking shot after shot of the chalky dirt and the dapple-gray rock. We drive up through a double row of stationary helos. One pilot lovingly polishes his aircraft with a sponge, like he's grooming a horse. There are Chinooks, Apaches, Lynxes, and Sea Kings. I wonder how I suddenly know so many makes of helicopter. The Apaches are particularly vicious beasts, shimmering black metal with blacked out windows and machine guns mounted up front, for attack, not defense like on the Sea King or the Chinook.

We throw our stuff in the back of the plane. It takes off and forty minutes later lands in Bastion, where Jane gets on board. We're also joined by other passengers from Lashkar Gah. Dave and Ali have recently landed by helo. The trip to Kabul from Bastion lasts for about an hour and a half. The journey that has taken us five days takes Dave and Ali five hours. The day is clear and bright. We move from the white dust of the desert, to the dusty white of the snowy mountains at the base of the Hindu Kush. Kabul blanketed in snow. I stay there for one night and the next morning get the flight to Dubai. At last, I really am on my way.

If Lashkar Gah is the graveyard of the white Toyota Corolla, then Dubai is the kindergarten of the white Lexus. It's only two hours flying time from Kabul, but it might as well be on a different planet, though it is a Muslim country too. As I go through security I notice the woman in front of me has a particularly sparkly hijab, lined with either Swarovski crystals, or real diamonds, and I am curiously covetous of it. I wonder (a) where I can buy one and (b) why I'd want to buy one. There seems to have been some form of subtle shift in what I find fashionable. This is not a values shift, but it is a perceptual shift and though not to be overstated, it takes me by surprise.

Thankfully, there are no more cultural, political, or social surprises en route and after sixteen hours waiting at Dubai then seven hours on the plane to Amsterdam, I get onto the plane to Dublin, on the plane home.

Posing for photos, near Nawa

# 6. Gender (I)

IT WAS THE FINAL question that completely floored him. He started to say something, but it got strangled, mangled in the now constricted cords of his throat. An inarticulate "urrhgh" was all that squeaked out. He stared at me blankly with his dark eyes, soft and luminous, confused, like a doe caught in car light.

We'd just spoken for over an hour, one on one (well, with the translator in tow) on pretty much everything: the police, the courts, the Elders, the Taliban, Afghan society. I had been surprised. It was the first time we'd met and he'd been far more open than I would have been had a stranger from another land, speaking another language, come along and asked me questions (which, in Northern Ireland had happened a lot around the peace process). He'd been articulate and enthused, intimate even, in his responses. He answered everything without hesitation, yet with consideration and care.

So when I asked "What do you do for fun in Lashkar Gah?" I was semaphoring the end of the serious stuff, a wind-down question, a rapport-building question, but was stunned by the non-answer.

Though he knew how to speak English, he'd done the interview in Pashto. I was even more surprised that he now turned to me directly, excluding the translator, and spoke to me in English.

"Nothing!" he hissed. "We have nothing here!"

I held his gaze, but my mind was blank and impotent: I could think of nothing to say. He continued: "I was in London, they had discotheques, nightclubs there. There were men and women dancing together, talking together. That never happens here."

Anguish and despair contorted his voice and his face as he continued, his eyes no longer soft and luminous but hard and incandescent, nailing me to the chair: "My mother will decide who I am to marry! Can you believe that? A girl will be picked and I will be expected to marry her. I won't know her, won't have anything in common with her!

What's that going to do for our future relationship? What good is that for our children? There is a darkness here. There is a darkness," he finished, barely audible.

And I could offer no hope, nothing. That is the way things are in Afghanistan. I'm not going to change that. I know that. I am impoverished, incapacitated, impotent in this context: completely devoid of agency. But the difference is, as always: I can leave.

This was a young, thinking, man, who'd traveled, who'd seen what was possible, who'd grown, yet in his own country was expected to allow others—who hadn't seen, felt, heard all the things he had—to make those major life decisions we take for granted. We may make good choices, we may make bad choices, but the point is that we make them, we live with them. I used to think of arranged marriages entirely in terms of the impact on women. I never contemplated the possible impact on men, or if I did, it was only cursory, fleeting. But the penny drops and squashes my own prejudice. Here is a young man who craves the *company* of the woman who would be his wife, every bit as much as, if not more than, anything physical. The apotheosis of his ambition is autonomy. But he is bound, against his own volition, by those invisible bonds, those ties, that darkness.

As I leave I ask him if there's anything he wants to ask me. It's only fair. He doesn't hesitate before he asks me what used to be the Balkan taxi driver's favorite questions: "What age are you?" and "Are you married?"

I answer: they are statements of fact. The ensuing baby-bird rictus of his mouth means I can tell he is amazed that at my age I'm not married. I think though that that gape also holds some envy about the series of choices that led to that fact. The Balkan taxi drivers—to a man (there was only one woman driver in Sarajevo, and she never asked this question)—also had the same fly-catching gape, except their jaws would almost immediately slacken and then stretch to an opportunistic grin: "Ah! Then you must meet my son!"

Fraser and I meet with another, older man, a provincial official. His office is a pale mint green with large windows and rust-colored curtains, edged by the omnipresent tassels—cream ones. It is cold and the room is heated by two small gas heaters. The white blocks glow orange and an azure and purple flame gasps at the gas feed, making a disconcerting rasping sound, as if the heater has a respiratory disease, TB perhaps, and we are overworking it by our very presence. The official has a full beard, dark, kind eyes, and a bulbous, fleshy nose, the kind with large pores. He wears a plain white turban. He shifts the conversation suddenly, to women.

"These men, they treat women like animals; no, they treat their goats and camels better than they treat their women! It is very sad. It is a blight on our society. That needs to change."

Two sincere young men come to pick up money from the PRT for a literacy project we are paying for (increasingly it seems to me that literacy and education should be the cornerstone of the international effort). They are both rotund little boy-men, with smooth, light brown skin and virtually identical facial hair—wispy beards around chipmunk cheeks, like two little Afghan Hobbits. But they have set up and work for one of our most trusted NGO partners. They can't be any more than 22 or 23, and easily administer around $100,000 a year, accounting for every cent, and delivering detailed written reports on activities, which is amazing in a culture that doesn't exactly value the written word. They have taken a taxi from Kandahar to Lash. It takes about two hours. Remember how long it took me. But at 30,000-feet-plus you don't run into the Taliban. There's another man, in his late twenties, who turns up to meet Fraser and me a few days late. He has an impressive CV: he's a lawyer (a rarity in itself) who has specialized in human rights and women's rights in Shar'ia Law. He is calm and centered, wears a plain wool cap. He tells us the reason he is three days late is that he was kidnapped by the Taliban. He was traveling on a bus to Kandahar when the Taliban stopped the vehicle. He threw his ID and mobile phone out of the window when he saw what was happening. If they spotted any Western names in his call records, he'd be dead. Also, he is tall, which doesn't help him melt into the rest of the detainees, mostly farmers. They took him away, with all the others on the bus. He was asked why he was going to the airport. He replied he was in a hurry

51

because he was going to pick up a relative who was just coming back from doing the Hajj at Mecca. This bit of bluster worked. He was let go. But turning up at the helo pad with no ID was almost as problematic—except without the same threat to life. But he persevered and here he was, sitting in our Pink Lounge, telling us about his plans for providing legal aid to the citizens of Lash.


With Andre, a police mentor from South Africa, I meet a big ursine man, fierce looking. His face is annealed by the sun: a hardened rust backdrop and softer red patches over his cheekbones. But he's a big softy, even though he's in Russian-influenced uniform. He doesn't wear a turban. One of our translators has told me that before the Taliban regime hardly anyone wore turbans, but then it became a matter of assimilate or become isolated. Lots of men who aren't Taliban continue to wear turbans, in a very Afghan tradition of hedging your bets.

This man looks anywhere between fifty and seventy. As usual, it's hard to tell the age of Afghans. A small boy—about eight or nine—dressed in navy comes in, weighed down by a red "Power Rangers" backpack. It contains his schoolbooks. He bursts right in, to what we realize is his father's office. This office is up two flights of banister-less, uncarpeted, concrete stairs. There's a desk and a sofa encased by pale yellow walls. No computer, no filing cabinets. Not even any plastic flowers, garish or otherwise. There is the framed photo of Karzai. There are two windows with no glass. Though it's set back from the road a little, we can see out into the street. The boy whips into the room and brakes when he realizes his dad has company. His dad waves him out, but relents at the boy's crestfallen face, and beckons. The boy scurries around us to his dad, who cocoons him in a giant bear hug, breathing in his scent and his love. Then he is released and he flies off to play with his friends.

There is a real paradox where children are concerned. There is a real threat of kidnap here for kids, and yet at the same time there is real freedom for kids in Lash—they all play on the streets all the time in a way you'd never see in the UK, Ireland, or the US these days. You never see parents go to pick up kids from school—they all walk home themselves.

The official smiles after his son. It is my first meeting, and Andre introduces me and what I'll be doing. The man is genuinely pleased.

"You will have all the help I can give you. You are my sister!" He repeats this several times during our conversation. He has shaken my hand directly and looked me in the eye. He's not just saying this. I am welcomed, completely. He even asks for my help in resolving a case that's been ongoing for a while, even though it is a delicate matter. To Andre, he says, "she can come any time, she is my sister."


I speak about justice issues with a man who will be district governor of an area we will clear. He has a trimmed beard, and a black turban with a gold and white tartan stripe through it, twisted so that a long tail comes down decoratively over one shoulder. He understands English but only speaks a little, so we use an interpreter. He also understands and speaks German as he has lived in Germany and still has family in Frankfurt. He offers himself as someone who understands both Western and Afghan legal practice.

When I ask him about informal justic mechanisms in his district-to-be he says: "Pashtunwali as a way of life is very good, but there are some very bad aspects to it that we should not accept. For example, if I kill someone's brother, I will have to give my sister to be married into his family. That's not good. But, if I have a neighbor who has just arrived into the area, say from Musa Qala, it is my duty under Pashtunwali to protect him, because he's in my area. That's a good thing. If you have a problem you can talk with the Elders—there are lots of examples of this. But because of the thirty years of war we have lost everything. Right now we are obeying no law—not European law, not Afghan law, not Pashtun law, not the Elders, not Islamic law. It is all very confused, mixed up. Some follow a very strict Pashtunwali, some do not. We need to remove the bad stuff from Pashtunwali.

"In respect of women, though, our Pashtunwali respects women more than other laws. In the past we did not search women ever; if there was a fight between two men they would automatically stop whenever a woman came by."

He pauses to answer his mobile phone—this happens a lot during our conversation, but the topic seems to strike a chord with him and he unearths a memory from long before: "I remember one time, during the Russian occupation, when there was lots of fighting going on. It was up near Musa Qala and I had taken my motorbike to a high position, so that I could look for my friends and my brother. The Russian helicopters were to the right and the Mujahideen were to the left.

"I saw a black speck come towards the high ground and go back. I couldn't see very well—I'm color blind—so I wasn't sure what it was. It did this a number of times and I then wondered if the person was scared of me. But the fighting had started and the figure was still going backwards and forwards. I decided I would go down on my motorbike and take them out of danger. When I got close I saw it was a woman with a kid and a big bag.

"I wanted to help her, but there is the Pashtunwali rule that says women shall not talk to men who are not their relative. But the fighting was on, so I asked her anyway. She didn't reply. So I told her that she was like my sister and I brought her and the child to her village. I felt that if I brought her to her house they would kill her and maybe me as well. So when I went to the village I said to a boy I saw working in a poppy field, 'How much do you get per day for that?' 'A hundred afghanis,' he said. I said I would give him 200 afghanis if he would take the woman to her home."

He stares momentarily into the wall, absorbing the recollection. He turns to look at me and removes his glasses.

"I never told anyone that up to now. But this is part of our law—and things like this should be removed from Pashtunwali. I'm sorry if the story is boring, but this was a big experience in my life. You can imagine how much darkness is in their mind—we were all in trouble just because I wanted to help her."

He laments the fact that it is because his countrymen—and women—are uneducated, that they know nothing of the world, that these types of rules are still in place and in force. Then he says something immeasurably sad: "You know, there are three things in the world that I love: God, the Prophet (Peace Be Upon Him), and my wife. But my wife, she is uneducated. When I try to tell her that I love her, what love means, she just doesn't understand. Still, I try to tell her, but this is difficult for me."

I meet a group of farmers and ask them if they've grown the enormous cauliflowers that I've seen on the street stalls of Lashkar Gah. Or do they come from Pakistan?

"From our farm!" they shout, "not Pakistan!"

There are twelve of them, and they immediately beam. We are meeting in a room at the Bost Hotel, now used as the governor's offices and residences. The table is surrounded by forty black chairs and there is a plastic cover featuring peach, tangerine, and apricot flowers on large green and white gingham. A few black ants labor fruitlessly among the plastic flowers. Out of the large bay window is the Helmand River. On the other side of the river a lightning storm fires vertical swords of white phosphorescence into the wheat fields around Bolan, where these guys have the farm that grows the preternaturally large vegetables. Several of them wear elaborate turbans of silvered or sequined material that seems incongruous to their labor on the irrigated earth. Their faces are either as furrowed as their fields (the older ones) or as smooth as the surface of the river, still now the storm has moved behind it (the younger ones). They wear their shoes with the backs flattened down so they approximate sandals, even in winter. They don't know me, yet they are open and frank in our discussion. For all that, they don't see any issues with the (exclusively male) Elders making decisions on cases for women. They laugh at my suggestion that women might not be satisfied with that situation, but it is not a cruel laugh. It is a "she can't help it if she's from another planet" sympathy laugh.

So I am confounded somewhat by the men I meet. These men, whether in officialdom or ordinary farmers, are courteous and chatty. The strong silent type is largely absent among them. They want to talk. I have had no trouble at all in getting men to talk to me in groups or as individuals, even though there is some risk associated for them in doing so. I have no idea how they treat the women in their own families, but their interaction with me (pasty-faced novelty though I am) suggests they are *capable* of having a mature relationship with women.

I guess the point is that these men are all different to what I expected, and different from each other. There's diversity. They all may look similar, in whisker and waistcoat and squashed shoe, but they are not. They are all subject to the same social bonds, but they all respond to the restraint in different ways. Some seethe, some are stoic.

I ask another group of young men the question about fun in Lashkar Gah. Again, we have conversed for over an hour on Rule of Law issues. They have been exuberant and enthused, yet earnest too. They are dressed in a mixture of Western (black leather jackets, blue jeans, thick-buckled belts, bare-headed) and Eastern (plain blue or grey *salwar kameez*, and wearing small skullcaps) dress. Their responses to my questions have been quick-fire, stumbling and jumping over each other like puppies in a basket. Though they all answer as one, they don't answer the question. Instead they say what they'd *like* to do for fun in Lashkar Gah, not what they actually do now.

"Go to nightclubs!" they shout. There is a collective grin and giggles. It's as if they have accepted that it's out of reach and the husk of the dream is good enough for them: thinking about what it would be like.

I wonder if there's a special kind of Afghan anhedonia—a collective psychological inability to experience happiness. I see from these men—boys, really, some of them, in their late teens—I see from the very young children playing and laughing on the street, that there is a capacity for happiness. It does exist, but that it is always on an ever-higher top shelf, so that the potential for realizing this capacity for happiness reduces with age. It's hard to explain, and I'm not sure I'm yet in a position to. Something seems to happen in the journey to adulthood that knocks the stuffing out of them. Life is just so hard, it's as if there isn't time for uninhibited joy. I think it's about lack of choice. I may be wrong. And I hope I'm proved wrong on this point the more I get to know Afghanistan.

As before, they get to ask me questions too. As before, it is about my age and marital status (some things are universal, it seems). But there is another question: "What do you think of Islam in Afghanistan?"

This is a hard question to answer. I want to be honest, but I also want to remain respectful. Even though these guys might be clamoring for a nightclub, I'm pretty sure they wouldn't be clamoring for a detailed critique of Islam. So I tell them that in Bosnia where I lived for seven years, Islam was interpreted in a very different way. Dress, mosque attendance, the way in which men and women interacted in Bosnia: all were very different. I tell them how things have changed over time, how a lot of how Islam is experienced there today comes from recent and far-off history, history driven by individuals. In modernity, it rests pretty much in the work of one man, Džemaludin Čaušević, the Reis ul-Ulema of Bosnia in 1914. Čaušević studied in Turkey, and traveled in Egypt and Syria. He took back stories—and pictures—of women working in the fields, without hijab, to a Bosnia where women were veiled. He commented that in Egypt "Muslim women who work in the fields or in factories have their faces and hands uncovered... In Syria Muslim girls who are studying have special dresses and their faces are uncovered. All the teachers at girls' schools are Muslim women and all go about with their faces uncovered." He further insisted that veiling was a mere custom (*adat*) rather than a religious duty (*ibaddat*): "I had rather see a Muslim girl unveiled and honorably earning her living, than a girl who walks around the streets veiled in the daytime and spends the evening in a café." There is also the fact that Bosnian Islam belongs to the Hanafi school of Islamic jurisprudence. (The Hanafi school interprets Islam in liberal, relativist terms, taking account of the social environment in which it is implemented.) So it seems to me, I conclude with them, that there is room for developing how Islam is interpreted in Afghanistan. It seems to me that there is room for both Islam and a nightclub in the same town.

There is an awed silence for a moment. And then they go home, back to houses they need to get to by nightfall, when there will be no electricity, and no nightclubs. Into the darkness, indeed.

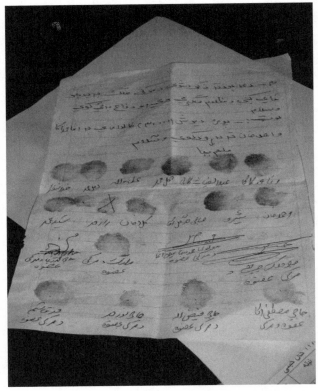

Land dispute agreement, brokered and signed by Garmsir
Community Council

# 7. Language

I AM FRUSTRATED by my attempts to find a language teacher. In part this takes so long because, naively as it turns out, I have asked for a woman teacher. No woman can or will work as an interpreter—all our "terps" are male, generally young (in their early twenties), and usually from Lashkar Gah. They earn more in two months than a police officer earns in a year. They earn more in six months than a judge earns in a year. But no Lash woman will ever earn this. There has to be some form of correlation between such skewed and asymmetric salary systems and post-conflict reconstruction, sustainability, and state-building. But that's too big a question for me right now. Right now, I just want a language teacher.

I ask Ahmad, the military terp, if he can help me find a teacher. He's a little older than the others, and is from Kabul. This is to have its advantages and disadvantages.

"You want a female teacher?"

"Yes, if I can. Women can't do any other work for us. It's not a lot of money, but it is something. It would be three times a week. She'd have to come here, to the PRT."

"OK, I will ask Razia on the Provincial Council. She's an English teacher, so I'm sure she'll know someone."

I step away, elated. It will be easy, after all. But no. Ahmad can't get her on the phone. Then he goes on leave for two weeks. I pace around the HLS with my Eurotalk "Learn Pashto!" on my iPod. Anyone who's heard me annihilate Serbo-Croatian-Bosnian will know that I am not a linguist. But I am fascinated by language. It's not the translation and what words match and mean that is the main thing. The main thing is that, in broad terms, language is *translatable*. We use language to describe our experience as human beings and to interact in the world and yet the range of emotions and observations that we articulate are, at base, the same, no matter where we are in the world, no matter how developed or impoverished our countries are. The other thing about language is that it encapsulates something of the character, the culture, the soul of any society. If you want to understand these things, then knowledge of the language will help.

It is interesting what words the linguists at Eurotalk choose as important as "First Words in Pashto." "Sa-Hil," I repeat: beach. I've seen nothing but desert. It's a land-locked country. Why would I want or need to know about "beach"? Then "Kush-tee": ship. I haven't seen any ships either. On the "Shopping" section, inexplicably I am given the word for teddy bear ("de-tu-krai-lo-hetz"). I walk around the camp repeating an approximation of these words, and become exasperated at myself for not remembering. I am wading in a thick soup of linguistic chowder. I think that I'm going to need an extra tongue in my mouth to scrape and squash and squeeze out some of the sounds that the words demand from the darkest crevices of my throat. There's no way my Anglo-Saxon-trained mouth is going to be uttering any kind of soft gutterality, which is what I'm, technically, hearing, but which is just not recognized by my brain. It's right outside the pale, this stuff. There are glottal stops galore and an abundance of affricates: a soft stopping and starting of the breath as it loops over and under consonants and vowels like thread being teased into elaborate embroidery. There seem to be words without vowels, only consonants vying for space and sound. I think that Georges Perec and the lipogrammatic Oulipos would feel right at home with Pashto. It's just impenetrable. No need for self-imposed constraints.

But then some words that I vaguely recognize, like a figure still blurred around the edges, emerge from fog. "Jar-ra-pee": socks. In Bosnian socks are "charapee," from the Turkish. So here's one link with the known and a tiny chink of light for me. I didn't think the Ottoman Empire ever came this far, but the word could have carried up through Persia and across.

Then there are a group of words that have come from further West, and much more recently: "postcart," "da postie ticket," "nek-tie-ye," "pant-a-lon," "T-shirt," "pen-cil," "twole," "sho-wer." No prizes for guessing the meanings of these, borrowed from all over. And not just the word, but also the concept. When did "shower" arrive? Was it with the English explorers-cum-colonists of the nineteenth century? Or before? Or after? When did its "wash" meaning arrive in English? A shower of rain has been with us since Old English and Old High German, but I don't know when we started to use shower to describe the process of washing in artificially produced hot rain.

So, not just because the runners look at me askew when I try to pronounce Pashto polysyllables on the walk around camp, I quickly come to the limits of my learning by iPod.

Ahmad has passed the task of finding me a female language teacher to one of his colleagues. But the guy isn't forthcoming. I've now been looking for a month, and it's coming to the end of my first rotation. I decide to ask Muamer, one of our own translators, from here in Lash.

"Muamer, I'm looking for a language teacher, preferably a woman."

"A woman? To come here? To the PRT?"

"Yes. Three times a week. Ten dollars an hour."

"But that's impossible. No woman can come here."

He isn't being awkward or unhelpful. He is being honest and realistic. So he gets me his friend, Aziz. Aziz is, like Muamer, from the Hazara tribe—much more Asiatic than Middle Eastern or Mediterranean in appearance. Though he has brown eyes his skin is much paler than others. When we meet for the first time he wears a cream cotton *salwar kameez* and a black waistcoat. He carries a cream shawl. As I get closer, I see that the shawl has purple and blue stripes with a line of silver woven in a tartan pattern on it. It's beautiful. An Afghan man wearing so much color. I like him already.

Which is just as well, because he pushes me hard. We start with the alphabet. There are 44 (yes, 44) letters. alif, aalif, bay, pay, teay, tteh, seh, jeem, che, hay, khay, tsee, zeh, dol, ddaal, zaal, ray, rrhea, dzeh, zheh, zhay, seen, sheen, shen, swaad, zwaad, twoi, zwoi, ein, gheine, fey, qaaf, kaaf, gaaf, laam, meem, noon, roon, wow, hyderdakay, hydercheshma (yes, a letter with five syllables), yeh, yeah, yeeah.

Of course, they are all written in a much more florid font than this. Adobe Garamond just can't contain the shapes of letters which are somehow lithe and fluid on the page, wriggling and squiggling like tadpoles in a tank, waiting for me to understand them. These hyperactive hieroglyphs are very beautiful, but I cannot make out one from the other. So not only the sounds, but the look is also impregnable. And there's more: when they elide, they evolve, in shape and sound. When they are joined up together in words, they change shape. And when they change shape, they change sound. But the calligraphy of the letters extends to their cadence—they are all soft, even the ones that require a broadening and flattening of the tongue on the ceiling of the mouth.

Aziz has great patience. We start with "alif." One of the first words I learn is "Allah" (alif + laam + hyderdakay, if you're interested). The one thing I can do is write the letters, which slide easily across the page from right to left. It's much more simple than I would have thought, like switching driving from on the left to on the right. It just fits. We have two lessons and then it is time for me to go on leave. Repetition and listening are the keys to learning any language. I forget to take my letters home. So, for two weeks I hear nothing and cannot remember anything beyond the first four letters, then a gap, then another sequence of three or four. There are massive lacunae loitering with intent in the middle of my memory, keeping back any remote chance of recall.

On the way back in I have to wait in Terminal 2 of Dubai International Airport. They have a new Costa Coffee. Alongside the familiar burgundy and white logo in Latin font is the Arabic equivalent. I go through the letters, making out "kaf + wow + seen + teay + alif: k-aw-ss-t-a." Costa. The first word I can read by myself. Never mind that it's taken about five minutes to put together five letters, I can read it! I am, disproportionately perhaps, elated.

Aziz and I work through the alphabet. Right now we're on "tteh." It's going to be a long haul, but I am beginning to recognize combinations of letters and sounds. It is no longer an unassailable fortress, just a very high one.

A few days ago I was facilitating a group of Elders trying to put together a community safety plan. This is hard enough to do in developed societies, let alone one that is so impoverished and in the middle of a war, so this was never going to be easy. First off, we had to identify the main threats to security in their district. Robbery, intimidation, and kidnapping were pointed out. One member of the group, an old man with a full white beard and mint green *salwar kameez*, told us about being kidnapped. He had green eyes and a leathery brown face. Thankfully his kidnappers were pretty inept—or their vehicle was. When the door accidentally opened, this old man made a break for it. He showed us the holes still in his long shirt where he'd fallen in the dirt. The would-be kidnappers didn't notice or just didn't give chase. He left the room at one stage when I was talking about kidnapping, so I referred to him as "the gentleman who was kidnapped." All the other men immediately started laughing. Several of them grabbed their ears and pulled them out, like characters from the newer Star Trek series.

"You mean Hairy Ears!" they guffawed, almost rolling around in the aisles.

I had been feeling rather good as I'd used two letters of the Pashto alphabet to illustrate a point about the importance of collecting good statistics. I was able to put, instead of (a) and (b) on the whiteboard, alif and bey. (OK, I realize that's close to (a) and (b), but I did write them in Pashto.)

Needless to say, it's pretty unprofessional to laugh at someone in a group you're facilitating. But they were right. He had the hairiest ears I'd ever seen. They were virtually separate stick-on attachments, like the talaria of Hermés or an angel's wings, if an angel's wings were black and hairy. And who can really say for sure they're not? I had to laugh.

So Pashto, like English, has words to describe ears that are hairy, confirming once again that language is translatable, and therefore learnable—in theory.

The office, Garmsir

# 8. Garmsir

LAST NIGHT there was a mighty, but brief, thunderstorm. Raindrops fell like fists out of the old-bruise yellow sky and the wind whipped up a thrashing sandstorm that raged all night. This morning my windowsill is covered in small piles of dust, about three times as much as usual. Until I wipe down my computer, it's like typing on emery boards. We are due to fly today, to Garmsir, to run a four-day workshop for members of the recently elected Garmsir Community Council, part of the Afghanistan Social Outreach Program (ASOP). Derek and Jon, the Governance Team, are organizing, and Fraser and I are going to facilitate the drafting of the local security and justice plans.

We go in two helicopters—Cougars (another name added to my repertoire)—eight of us in each one. The Dutch are moving us this morning, and the trip is fantastic. The Cougars rip through the air, but the flying Dutchmen steer us at a low altitude. We're almost tipping the tops of the dunes at times, we're so low to the ground. And the ground is marvelous. Just outside Lash is the Helmand River-fueled horticulture: some wheat, some poppy, all, at the moment, green cutting into the ground, the color of crushed coriander seeds. We quickly whizz past this landscape. The doors on the Cougar don't close, they only have little half-stable doors, over which the gunners cock their weapons, one looking out of either door, over the desert floor. There's lots of space to see. Perhaps because of the rain the night before, or perhaps because the Helmand River has underground tributaries that feed the sand, there is a great deal of green. It's not a strong green, only a pale, timid pigment, yet it is tenacious. It only comes in clumps—bushes, plants, grasses, even occasional trees—but it's there, softening the reach of the sulphur-colored sand.

As we travel out into the desert the green loses its fragile hold and the sand dominates. Down here the sand is more a dull yellow than the ochre and coffee to the north. It forms into frozen waves of gold silicon, lipped with fine dark shadow in the sun, which highlights the waves' beauty, like eyeliner. Incredibly, huddled around the few spots of three or so trees, are tents. I see one camel.

After twenty minutes we arrive in Garmsir, about sixty miles south of Lashkar Gah, a district that is bound by the Afghan–Pakistan border. The Helmand River, the main water source in the whole province, runs north to south down through Garmsir, opening out in a kind of enclosed estuary near the village of Darvashan. This is where Britmil have a Forward Operating Base (FOB), and this is my first trip to a FOB. Immediately I can tell that Lashkar Gah is the Helmand Hilton in comparison. There's no HLS, only an area with stones. The rest of the camp defines "basic." The only place where there's running water is the kitchen. Everything else is what you load and carry yourself.

As soon as you get off the helicopter, the first thing you smell is the burning. The burning happens once or twice a day. Five or six oil drums are cut down to about a third their size and are slotted in under wooden thunderboxes. Five or six times a day the drums are removed, new ones (well, more or less empty ones) slotted in, and the shit is burned. The smell is not actually as bad as you might think, because the burning kerosene, the accelerant, produces so much thick black smoke by itself that it dominates. There is also the fact that I don't get too close. It's waste management at its most rudimentary. Solids and liquids are deposited in separate receptacles. The women have just received a urinal, which is the cause of much celebration. Previously there was none. I hear that the reason it was built was because the environmental health inspector person said it had to be. The notion of an environmental health inspector on this camp is, at first thought, incongruous. But it makes so much sense. D&V (diarrhea and vomiting) can fell a camp more quickly than the Taliban can. I can add another thing to my list of things that are necessary to win a war: first logistics, second cleanliness. During the week we are here the procedure changes to "Wagbags," the human equivalent of poop-a-scoop. Everyone gets a biodegradable bag… you get the picture. By the time we leave that slightly acidic burning smell is no more.

There's a makeshift step (an empty metal ammo box) up to both the thunderbox and the urinal. In the dark, on two separate occasions,

I manage to miss the step and fall out onto the pebbles, my head torch making insane parabolas in the process. Not awfully graceful exits, but at least it was dark. Hopefully no one will have noticed.

I am sharing a room with four other women, all in the military. Home for the next four days will be a twenty-inch-wide camp bed (no mattress) under a fixed mosquito net, a small cupola of green mesh cupping the cot zipped horizontally along the edges of the bed and vertically to its apex, about three feet above the bed-frame. It's in the corner, and it's dark. No natural light gets into this room—the one window is blocked out with sandbags—and entering it is like entering a cave. The walls are made of mud, badly plastered on the inside, the remnants of a School of Agriculture built here by the Americans in the 1950s. The whole FOB utilizes bits and pieces of the long abandoned college. There's no Hesco on the outer wall, so we might as well be in a tent. There's no door on the room either, just a sheet of racing car green nylon then a sheet of white waxed canvas, weighed down by a small plank of wood.

The one advantage of our room is that the communal wash area is right outside. There's a huge water container, and a pipe leading from it that feeds three old-style bins (the kind that Top Cat had in his alley) and a tap. The tap water is always cold, but the water in the barrels is generally warm. This is because the cold water goes into the bins which act as a kind of kettle. Sunk into the water is a pipe which cuts through the bottom of the bin. Just like in a kettle, this is the heating element—a hot pipe heating the water. Only it's not heated by electricity, this element. There's another pipe that feeds it, from which kerosene drips silently, small drops of amber dropping down and fizzing when they hit the fire below. Thick black smoke comes out of it, and if you can stand the sting in your eye and you look down it, you can see the naked orange flame sputtering at the bottom, under the water in the bin. It's an odd juxtaposition of fire and water. You reach down into the barrel to draw some warm water and you can see the flame that's heating it under the water. It's basic, but it works.

To shower, there are two choices. Take a relatively warm Solar Bag shower, or go for a cold electric power shower. I decide the cold shower will wake me up a bit more after my gym session, so I go for that. There's some research to do before I realize that these showers aren't working, or don't work in the mornings. The Solar Bag shower it is, then. This is a black plastic bag with a red seal at one end and a small clear plastic tube with a tiny shower head at the other. You're supposed to fill them and leave them out in the sun, which warms them, but we fill them with the kerosene-drip-fired water. It's the second day before I work out that there's a small clamp that stops the water running straight back out (for the first day I just held the plastic tube up while I was waiting in the line). Once in the shower (a roughly hewn wooden cubicle, with a corrugated zinc roof and door—the door is closed by the weight of sand in a plastic bottle—and black plastic decking underfoot) you soap up, and rinse before the water runs out. It makes you think about how much water you really need to wash, and what a luxury a long hot shower is. This shower is perfectly serviceable. There are three solar shower cubicles and three power shower cubicles for 300 people, give or take, on a daily basis. Around the back of the showers are the wash basin stands—roughly cut wood, with car mirrors mounted at face level for shavers. You have to fill an aluminum basin from the hot water bins and wash. There's usually a line here in the mornings, a lot of taut and tanned torsos and bleary eyes. The basins are emptied into a surprisingly nice Japanese garden-like feature: a large pebble pit, smooth stones in all the greys, light through dark: dove, mercury, lead, and slate. Then you have to wash the basin out and replace it. To the side are the black plastic basins where all the hand washing is done. All clothes are hand washed. There are washboards underneath, made from the same corrugated zinc as the shower doors, wrapped around plywood. I recall both my grandmothers' washboards: emerald green rippled glass boards bound in wood. The zinc and plywood boards are a crude pastiche of these and I'm sure that they must do more damage to clothes than clean them.

We go out of the FOB to the District Center to check out the facilities we'll be using for the next four days. Again the topography of the town is mud buildings the color of ground white pepper, slowly melting under the heat and wind as if they were made of wax. But there are some differences to Lash. As we turn out of the FOB there is an abandoned building, long and low, fronted by a cloister of perhaps forty arches. This was the teaching center of the agricultural college. Beside it is a small, square building, painted white, and with crisp edges: a traveler's mosque, with a well, that we have rebuilt.

We turn into the first street and see that it is a long row of bazaar shops, scooped out of the mud. But there is no produce, no people: it is completely empty and a bit eerie, like a ghost town. Then we turn a corner and there they are—the vegetables, the bikes, the glittery tat, the plastic drums of purple diesel. There are also cobblers working, and tailors in front of garish rolls of sparkling cloth from Pakistan and India. There are no women. For the four days I am there, there are no women on the streets, not even one, not even in a burqa—only men and boys.

Downtown Garmsir

The District Center is also a new building, behind a pale pink concrete wall. It should only take us twenty minutes to check it out. I have not donned Afghan dress for this as we haven't planned to meet any locals apart from those we've traveled down with, and I meet them in Western dress all the time when we're inside the PRT. But news of our presence quickly travels and we meet the governor and most of the community council. Only we meet them in tranches of twos and threes, so that Jon has to do the introductions about eight times, and I am mortified because I'm not wearing hijab, and worry now about being able to be a facilitator and give direction to these men. We eventually escape the jungle of pleasantries ("it's an honor to be your guest," "no, it's our honor to have you as a guest" and vice versa, etc) and inspect the main room and the smaller breakout rooms. In one of the smaller rooms are the carpets that we've brought, the cushions, and a couple of green mortar shells (that we haven't brought).

"I think I want a room without mortars," I say to Derek. The next day they have been moved and I am pretty sure this has been done without the assistance of any ordnance disposal expert.

We look at the kitchen, where our lunch will be prepared. There's only one word to describe the worktop nearest us, a word that doesn't appear in Merriam-Webster, but which is often heard in Belfast: mingin'. There's no way we aren't going to get D&V by the end of the week. We sigh, but commensality is part of the trust and relationship building process, even if the price is an upset stomach for a few days. George Mitchell used this to great effect in the Northern Ireland peace process, I think, remembering a particular dinner I was at, many years ago. We go back to the camp, through the ghost bazaar, which takes about five minutes.

The first night we are there, we take some indirect fire (IDF). Well, one rocket. It lands outside the FOB walls, but the boom of its crash to earth is loud and frightening. It's followed by a few rounds of small arms fire (SAF). Then things are quiet. We have to stay inside. Then we start firing mortars. I don't realize until the next day that they are "lumes"—shells designed to light up the sky to see where the Taliban is. Launching them makes as much noise (to my uninitiated mind) as real rockets. The episode lasts for about an hour and a half, and then we sleep. I had been thinking that living in Lash was much more like growing up in Northern Ireland than living in Bosnia. The scale is different, of course, and the society much less developed—and there's a lot more heat and dust, but some things are the same: bombs at police stations, attacks on police officers and other state personnel, bombs under key infrastructure targets like bridges (if I had a pound for every time my school bus was rerouted), bombs left in cars, in trashcans, army patrols supporting police checkpoints, temporary police checkpoints. All these things happen here, though what we used to call "bombs" are called IEDs. They still make the same sound, cause the same death, injury, and general destruction, though. What I am not used to, what is different, is this back and forth of fire. In my recollection at least, at home it was generally one-way traffic. Outside of riots, only on rare occasions was there any exchange of small arms fire, let alone rocket fire. Yet none of the night rockets, lumes or not, is louder than the loudest explosion I have heard—the 2000-lb Forensics Lab bomb in Belfast in 1992, and I draw a freakish and perverse comfort in this, conscious as I do so that it is freakish and perverse.

IEDs are not, however, the only hazard here. Heat and its sidekick, dehydration, is another. There's a special chart outside the gym that warns when no working out is allowed, scaled from Green (20°C and below) to Green Alpha (20–25°C), Yellow (27–29°C), Amber (30–32°C) to Red (32°C and over). At Red there's to be no non-essential physical activity. While I'm there it's mostly Green Alpha, though there is one Red Day, at 39°C.

There's also wildlife. A notice describes the various snakes to be wary of. The snake *Echis sochureki* (I'm sure it must have a shorter, more pronounceable name) is "extremely toxic," its venom a potent hemotoxin. The anti-venom is "debatable." Its colleague the good snake *Eristicophis macmahoni* is "very aggressive." Its anti-venom is "unavailable." Of more comfort is the fact that, although the Iranian scorpion works hemolytically, leading to swelling and necrosis, "no deaths in Afghanistan have been reported." Plus they only come out to hunt at night, the day being too hot for them. So that's all right then.

The first day of the workshop goes well. The men are keen to learn. I notice more things about them, ornamentation and decoration. There are tattooed hands and wrists, nail varnish, hennaed feet. No one wears shoes in the meeting room and as the day goes by the smell of feet begins to overpower.

The district governor is present for most of the day, as is his youngest son. He looks about seventy, the son about six. The boy is very cute, is doted on and indulged by all: the police officers at the gate, the community council members, his father.

For lunch a long green plastic cloth is rolled down the center of the room: the table. Slabs of naan bread are thrown down at intervals: edible plates. A small stainless steel bowl of salad (fresh mint, parsley, a green chili, red onion, peeled cucumber, sliced red tomato—all organic) and a small glass bowl of goat stew accompany. I won't bore you with my long and complicated history with the goat and its associated products, but I am persuaded, for the first time in my life, to taste of its flesh. Surprisingly, I like it. For dessert there is fruit: oranges and small bananas. Lunch will be exactly the same for the next four days. There's more fresh fruit and vegetables than at the FOB. They've even run out of UHT milk, and so are down to milk powder. There's no fruit until mid-week.

There are no rockets the next night. Next day we continue the workshop. The governor's son, Simonon, has spoken to me the day before, so I learn some Pashto slang from a six-year-old. I bring my "100 First Words in Pashto" book with me the following day and we read it together. But I see quickly that he can't read: he is following the pictures only. When it comes to the exercises of picking out words from a letter-grid I realize that he only knows the first three letters of the alphabet: alif, beh, and peh, so I end up telling him what the other letters are. I learn that he's been to school, but only for two days. He didn't like it (perhaps he didn't get the deference there he finds all around in his dad's office) so he wasn't made to go back. This particular parental indulgence is sad and is going to be very costly.

The next night at base there is a trivia night in which we humiliate ourselves in astounding fashion, though Fraser is a wizard at the math round, and Derek pushes us up on the general knowledge round. But on "Music and Movies" and "Movie Quotes" we are abysmal. Of course this is because the questions are set by a twenty-year-old quiz mistress from Wales and cater to 18–25-year-olds, a demographic that is a mystery to us (as our result confirms). It also brings home the fact that this is the demographic that is out doing the fighting, the demographic that we get told about when we attend memorial services on the HLS at Lashkar Gah. I think I've been to around five services in the short time that I've been here now.

Later that night there is another rocket attack, this one landing close to the District Center. More lumes are fired from the FOB. There is a suggestion from the governor that there is a connection with our presence. Yes, four unarmed civilians with a load of flipcharts, some pens, and a few ideas. There have been no attacks in the area for seven months and there have been two in the time we are there. It is unproven, but plausible. It might seem unlikely, but the stuff we are doing—bolstering the capacity of the nascent community council to represent its own community—is, on one level, much more of a threat to the Taliban than any military attack. The battle for hearts and minds can be more important than that for territory. Land can be taken and retaken, but, as my mother wisely always did say, no matter what else you lose, no one can ever take an education away from you.

After we finish on the last day, a real adventure: we are allowed to walk partway back. It's my first time "outside," on the street, in Afghanistan. Everybody stops and stares. Mind you, I don't really blame them. Here we are, in our body armor, walking behind one armored vehicle and in front of another. We walk up the main drag, then up to a small police station by a bridge over the main canal. An old Russian tank has recently been pulled out of the canal and sulks, muddy and disgruntled, by the side of the road. We go up to the other end of town to see the hospital. The doctor there is from another province. It's the only place I've seen any women all week. There's a big maternity ward, which is necessary. The men in my group—the Security Sub-Committee—had asked me the usual two questions about marriage and age one day, and insisted I ask them questions also. I found out that one of them had three wives (the others giggled like teenagers at this. In Derek's group, they all mocked the one with three wives, saying he always falls asleep), one had two wives, and the rest one. But they had a combined total of over sixty children between the five of them. The maternity ward is a busy place.

Our last stop is a small checkpoint by the Helmand River. It's the first time I have been this close to the river which is literally the life-blood of the province, feeding as it does the myriad and intricate network of canals and irrigation channels, some of which work, some of which are in disrepair, and some of which are destroyed. The flow is much faster than I had imagined, the water a chalky gray-green, swollen by the melting snows of the Hindu Kush far upland to the north. There's something here I've also never seen: crushed scrap metal in an old yet still colorful truck, one of the "jingly-trucks" painted bright blue with faded yellow flowers with bells across the windscreen, like a headband. We ask the commander where it has come from and where it's going. He's a small man, in a yellow-bronze *salwar kameez* and cream turban. He has one leg much shorter than the other and walks with a pronounced limp, even with wearing an improvised built-up shoe. He is well informed, telling us the truck has come from Nimroz and is headed to Kandahar, a journey that takes around nine days. At the end of our conversation he asks Ian, the local stabilization advisor, for a well. Ian says there's one 100 yards away. He gives some reason why they can't use it. Ian says "we'll see."

It is the final lunch that proves to be the killer. It is exactly the same (perhaps it is the exact same) as the previous three days. I don't know that at the time, however, and eat the goat with the same gusto as before. Then something noxious brews in my innards and during the night my stomach feels as if someone's in there scraping it out with a metal claw. I think of the Iranian scorpions out hunting for food as I go to grapple with the wagbag during the night. I have to report to the medic center the next morning and am fearful that they'll put me in isolation and not let me get on the helicopter home to Lash. But I have to go—anyone with diarrhea must report it. If it's a bug it can infect the whole camp. The med center is quiet at 07:00 and the young nurse immediately says "admission" and "isolation." Oh no!

"But it was the goat," I protest, "and I didn't vomit. I need to leave today."

"OK, let me ask the doctor," he says, and toddles off. I look around the room. This is where field casualties are dealt with. Like everything else in the camp, it's basic. There are two cot trolleys and shelves of medicines on roughly hewn shelves. When I get back to Lash and report in there they have computers for taking my pulse, computers for entering my details, two very plush trolleys, and a lot more equipment.

"OK," he says, "the doc says you can go, but you must report to Lash Medics when you arrive there."

On the flight back (which comes exactly on time), I see nothing of the desert, in all its loveliness and loneliness. I concentrate on keeping everything on the inside that needs to be on the inside, against the constant vibration of the Chinook. It all stays put, and I'm back in Lash, back to running water (hot and cold), a toilet en suite, and decent food. This is five-star compared to Garmsir.

The Peace Globe, Lashkar Gah

# 9. *The Drive*

KAREN AND I ARE GOING downtown to give some gifts to the women prisoners in Lashkar Gah prison. By gifts I mean basic necessities: soap, shampoo, sanitary napkins, plus some unwanted clothes that we have collected around the PRT in the previous few days. There is some very nice soap in the packages, like lavender. It may not be by L'Occitane, but by the smell of it you can tell there's real lavender essence in it, and it makes me think of the matte green lavender fields and the sweet astringent scent of their crushed leaf and petal, on the island of Hvar, fusing with the dense smell of pine-sap in the summer, baking in the heat and creating an intoxicating Adriatic aroma, an aroma which is a million miles away from Lashkar Gah prison. Karen is from CIMIC, the Civil Military Co-operation component of the army, and it is they who want to deliver the excess welfare packages. Because we'll be talking to the women prisoners, it is me, and not Fraser, who will accompany her.

It had seemed impossible to me at first that I should ever be able to recognize our route, never mind anticipate it. But here it is: we set out and I know which way we'll be going. We head off past the graveyard, the road surface underneath the B6 scabrous and pitted, seriously stressing the chassis. The graveyard, like most of the rest of town, is dug out of and made of mud. Graves are slightly raised mounds, except for one or two that have small walls or even iron railings around them—family plots echoing, but a far cry from, the great marble crypts found in the graveyards of New Orleans. It is the same principle nonetheless: a demonstration of wealth and power, even in death.

One of these more elaborate graves has long been untended: the mud headstone eroded by the breeze that perpetually runs, sprite-like, across the graveyard so that the squares of small alcoves where (I'm assuming) plastic flowers were once laid have softened and rounded.

It makes the headstone look as if it is slowly melting. There are always people here; it's like a social gathering place, a café without the coffee, a teahouse without the tea. Groups of men squat on their haunches for hours (strong and elongated calf muscles abound), sometimes interspersed (but sitting separately) by a sprinkling of women, usually with children, who run alongside our cars, often with their thumbs up. On virtually each corner of every grave are flagpoles, two or four tall and thin bamboo sticks on the hundreds of desiccated mud mounds. And from each pole flies a fluttering flag in a thin cloth, nylon perhaps, so that the barest whisper of a breeze lifts it. These are mainly green—the Islamic color of peace—but also crimson or black. These are like little sails, so the graveyard seems to me sometimes like a shimmering regatta of small sailing boats, run aground in solidified sand, their tiny canvasses full and tugging, darting like tied birds. But they are not going anywhere, destined only to become thinner and more shredded, so that they hang eventually in ribbons over the graves they mark.

We go round the near side of the graveyard, which means going past a couple of trees. They are willow-like in that their leaves droop down and their branches are soft and supple, but their leaves are broader and their green is perpetually frosted by dust, so the color is muted, cowed, like the overall aspect of the trees. I don't know the tree's taxonomy, type, or name. I have never seen trees like it before, not in any European arboretum that I've been in, not even in the garden at Tršteno, on the edge of the Adriatic, which holds at its core two massive and mighty planes from the Orient. I can never get out and look at the bark, or touch the leaf to find out if these might be relatives of the Tršteno trees. I'm a girl in a bubble, sometimes on wheels, sometimes on wings. It's a heavy bubble: there's always sheet metal or glass between me and Afghans, like I'm in a deep sea diving bell, when I travel.

So I can't look at the tree, and we go round the corner, past the beige crumbling house with the big green double gate that has a huge pink flower painted on each side, through the concrete anti-bomb blast blocks at the small police checkpoint, past the baby-carriage-wheel-mounted wire cage of fat white-feathered chickens, past the bright yellow cloth sign advertising the "New Ideal Engush Centre" (I trust they get the Pashto spelling right—we are going too fast for me to read the letters), and into the town proper. As usual, it's buzzing, though I've never seen anyone actually buy anything.

The urban fabric takes on a distinctly industrial feel, metal and concrete prevailing. There are yards of cubby-holes of shops and stalls. They hawk horticultural and agricultural implements (the poppy season will be coming up soon) of twisted metal, some shiny, some rusty. There's a yard of white Toyota Corollas and a yard of red tractors (some will be used for poppy eradication, some will be used for poppy cultivation, they are all bought at the same place). There are rows and rows of bikes—old styles that we would no longer recognize. There are no aluminum or carbon frames, no shock absorbers, no spring-loaded wheels, no gears. On some of them you simply pedal backwards to brake. The frames are heavy and painted in matte colors, black and grey, dark green and maroon. There are rows of bamboo in varying height and circumference—thin short canes (I don't know what they're used for) and long and thick sticks that I've seen used as precarious-looking scaffolding, tied with little more than ribbon. There are pygmy pyramids of bricks piled up by the side of the road, codified by color: ochre and sulphur. Beside these are cement blocks, made by hand by the roadside using a square mold. The cement is gray-green and shiny, the color of a cold sea, as it waits to set. I have not seen anything made out of brick yet, but have seen some walls of cement blocks. But they weren't plastered together, just stacked to make a wall. Donkeys stand patiently as their carts are loaded up with the blocks and bricks. Surely they'll keel over, but they don't. They just look straight ahead, swishing their tails against the flies. A man sells popcorn in paper cones to the traders from a wheelbarrow kiosk.

We are heading down the main drag, towards the giant and kitsch "Peace Globe" that marks the biggest, the only true, roundabout in Lashkar Gah. The enormous plaster earth is painted a dark, yet almost fluorescent blue, as if it were made of blue Plasticine. It sits over quite a deep tiled moat that must have at some stage held water, the kind you throw coins into for good luck. There are no coins here, only dust. Around the moat there's a faux wooden fence, with buoyant little branches linked and waltzing with each other, skipping lightly around the world. It's all the more incongruous since there are piles of real driftwood all over the place. The continents and countries are slapped across the sphere in appropriately located rainbow colors: France is purple, for instance, China yellow. The names across them are in black, in English. The body of water between Galway and Boston is labeled "Pacific Ocean." From the nether regions of Brazil and Bali respectively rise two white(ish) alabaster doves, wings akimbo, breasts jutting out, with flat black eyes; impassive sentinels fated to forever look down at the long two-lane (and tarmac) roads that are the arterial routes of the Lashkar Gah Bazaar. It's the only road on which there's anything resembling a central median—a small curb that rises to mark the halfway point in the road, with gaps every hundred yards or so for donkeys and popcorn producers to cross the road.

Gasoline for sale

It's packed with people, animals, and produce. We move to the left-hand side of the road, and increase our speed. The switch over in lanes is unusual, but not unprecedented. The acceleration is. A young boy, his head down as he races his bike up the right-hand (and correct, for him) side of the road gets a honk of our horn. He looks up and sees our massive B6 bearing down on him. His mouth drops into an "O." A four-and-a-half-ton armor-plated exoskeleton versus a soft and fleshy wisp of an endoskeleton weighing barely eighty pounds. There's just no competition. He swerves off to the right, we veer slightly to the left, and he is left unscathed. All that extra weight means that response time and ability with the B6 can be much slower than with a normal car. It's a much less accurate car, but that doesn't matter, because it's built to withstand bomb blasts. The boy is even luckier than he thinks.

We switch back rapidly to the other right-hand side, but we are overtaking and undertaking, darting in and out as quickly as the mechanics allow.

"Why are we driving like this?" I ask, "we're going to kill someone."

"There's a silver Corolla following us, we have to lose it."

Karen and I fall silent. We roar off switchback to our right-hand lane, and begin to turn left around the roundabout. We go past the misplaced Pacific Ocean and the sullen white sentinels until we're at the third exit, about 270 degrees of the way round, as if we are going back on ourselves, heading back up after the little lad on the bike. The navigator barks directions at the driver: "Stop. Stop. Now. U." We brake stop, and (relatively smoothly) do a U-Turn, at small velocity.

Karen and I look behind us. All we can see is the other B6, our escort car, the one that holds our interpreter. It's just reached the globe. We do the turn and take off in the same direction we've just come.

But there's a problem: a herd of about fifteen or twenty camels are milling around at the exit we want to go down.

"Fantastic," I think, "the first camels I've seen in Afghanistan have to be a full herd and happen to be in the way of escape from a potential suicide bomber."

I am sure they are going to end up as hairy auburn skittles, splattered across the road. We beep the horn and the driver and navigator gesticulate wildly, (not that the camels can read human semaphore), but humans can, and they run. They are frightened, for they have no idea what is happening, just that the foreigners need to get out, fast. They run across the little moat, under the off-white doves of peace, in their sandals and bare feet, stalls abandoned, popcorn left popping. Later, the bodyguards in the escort car tell us why: the driver of the silver Corolla suddenly abandoned whatever quest he was on. He stopped his car at the roundabout, got out, leaving the door open and started to run. Either entity—him or his car—could have been a suicide improvised explosive device (SIED). No one is taking any chances, least of all us.

We have to go slower through the camels. There's no point in speeding, scaring, and scattering. We'd lose control of the situation for the sake of a few seconds. These could be vital seconds, granted, and I don't doubt the security guys would rip through them if we had to, but for now short-term caution means longer-term safety. We steer around them, veering mildly. They move as a bunch, oddly organized, their hairy hides henna and tawny, these ancient beasts calm even in the face of SIEDs, B6s, wildly gesticulating humans and now, as news of the activity spreads, flashing blue and white lights on the dark green Afghan National Police trucks as they race past us, to the silver Corolla.

We go to the nearest safe house—the compound of the security police, the NDS. We have to wait until the all-clear is given. It's there that we are exposed to the greatest direct danger, and it doesn't come from any SIED. No, it comes instead from the inspired actions of the guards at the gate. Somehow they have managed to get a red pressurized gas container—the kind you used to get to heat your three-bar heater when you lived in student accommodation—on fire. Yes, there are flames shooting out of the top of it, about a foot long, and it is spinning round, like a firework that has failed to fly, spewing yellow fire across the dehydrated mud. And the NDS guards' response? Oh, poke it with a stick. Jump over it for a laugh. It's the most nervous I feel all morning. The security guys get us back into the cars and drive to the far end of the compound, as far away as we can get from the incipient rotating rocket. We will have to cancel our trip and make our way back to the camp. The women will have to wait for the lavender soap.

Just as we reach the walls of camp there are a further three camels being driven. They hold their heads high and still, and have large, curious eyes, with long lashes. I know from a desert safari in Dubai a year or so ago that they stink, but inside the B6 you only get the visual angle, and they are beautiful beasts. They thrust their legs out from the knee joint, heads held high and looking forward, parallel to the ground. Their upper bodies remain smooth and straight, no matter how rough the ground, like a debutante descending a stairwell, heel down against the upright of the stair.

You wait a couple of months to see a camel, and like buses, several come along at once. They pass in front of us, and we go back inside our gate. The drive, for today, is over.

A walk through Nawa

# 10. Gereshk (I):
# Speaking Up, Speaking Out

THE AFGHANS ARE LATE, very late. They are always late, but this time they have skidded past infuriatingly late to angry late. They are cutting things just too fine. We are taking the same team to Gereshk, about forty miles north of Lashkar Gah, a well-connected urban hub with a bustling bazaar. Gereshk sits on the main trade road to Kandahar and Kabul. The commerce—it's the only place I've seen real traffic jams of jingly truck after jingly truck—brings relative wealth. Gereshk is also relatively liberal, and though I suspect that's something to do with wealth and the commerce, I can't say for sure. It is a place that is known for giving women a voice, a place in its public space, and we are confident the election of five women on its community council two weeks previously is testimony to that. But first we need to get there.

I'm not feeling particularly liberal toward our Afghan colleagues right now. The helicopter is due at 08:00. We are supposed to be there forty minutes in advance, in case they come early (yes, this is known to happen, even though you may not believe it, given my experience with late and canceled choppers). Derek asks me to go with him to the gate to take in the Afghans.

"No," I say, "they are always late and I always get too stressed."

Derek looks at me mournfully, with his big brown Labrador-puppy eyes.

"OK, OK," I relent, "but only until a quarter to eight. Then you're on your own. I'll be going to the HLS."

It's 07:35. Derek and I go down to the front gate of camp. They aren't there. Even Derek gets angry. He phones Wahedullah, the young, brilliantly energetic and bright governor's advisor.

"Wahedullah, where are you, are you at the gate?"

"No, I'm at the governor's office!"

"What are you doing there? You're meant to be here!"

"Don't worry, I am coming!" He cuts off the call. Derek hates it when he says "don't worry." Especially when it's followed by: "I am coming!" He generally does it with an endearingly discombobulating and exceedingly exasperating smile which you can see even if he's on the phone. Wahedullah is approximately 21 (no one knows their real age here; most people only know what month their birthday is in, if even that). He has green eyes, skin color halfway between olive and corn drawn over finely sculpted cheekbones, delicate as porcelain. He has short dark hair, and a shy soft beard that creeps up his neck but doesn't advance any further than his jawbone.

The governor's office is a fifteen-minute drive away. They'll never make it. The other travelers are Shah Wali, of the NGO WADAN, who is our administrator—he accounts for every cent that Derek gives him on immaculate spreadsheets. He knows how many squares of toilet paper the project has used. He doesn't look especially Afghan, actually more generically Balkan in color and bone structure: dark and strong, respectively. Except that he is at the small and round end of the Balkan continuum, with a large flat forehead, large dark eyes, and short black hair. He is clean-shaven. He is getting rounder. His growing girth is a subject of much mirth for Wahedullah, who continually ribs him: "Mr. Shah Wali—he is getting too much food, Derek, yes?"

"I think he's eating all the program money! Are you having lunch today, Mr. Shah Wali?" Derek usually responds.

Mr. Shah Wali (we always call him by his full name and title) laughs with them and pats his expanding tummy. Perhaps he is eating all the project money. It's been quite a prodigious spurt, his spherical stomach that you can see, even with the forgiving folds of the ivory *salwar kameez* that he usually wears.

But right now, neither of them is within view. Derek shouts down at the soldiers on guard to see if there's anyone outside the gate. Yes, there are four people in an Afghan National Police (ANP) car and three others. They are here. It's 07.50. The three (Mr. Shah Wali included) need to be searched. More time. They are in.

Now they all speed off ahead of us to the HLS, as the ANP driver speeds to get them there. Derek and I walk briskly, we refuse to run, although we would have done so had we heard an approaching chopper. We get to the departure point and the buzzard announces that the Sea

Kings will be here in three minutes. It's the tightest it's been yet. I am cross and when Wahedullah shakes my hand and smiles that smile, saying "see, you shouldn't worry," I want to strangle him, but only say tersely, "Wahedullah, it is disrespectful to be this late." His face crumples, and I immediately admonish myself. I smile at him when he takes photos on the helo and he smiles back.

The flight to Gereshk takes only fifteen minutes or so. It would have taken less than an hour to drive, but road travel is not safe—for us. For ordinary citizens road travel is possible. It is not without risk, but it is possible. From the air, you can really see that it's spring, but also that already it's harvest time, for poppies. The fields are full of verdant stalks, vibrant and green against the brown earth. By this stage most of the poppy heads have been lopped off, the bulb ready for scraping, but there are blotches and patches of speckled mauve and lilac and violet and white across the green, a whisper of suffragette-colored confectioner's sugar sieved over the fields.

FOB Price, where we'll be staying, is out in the middle of the desert, next to one of the main highways. It has much better conditions than those in Garmsir. There are fewer people than in Lash, but the camp covers more ground—a walk around the perimeter is almost two miles. Charlotte (known as Charlie), who's come out from London to observe our work for a few days, has come with us to Gereshk, and she and I check out the toilets—very important. We find ourselves in sanitary heaven: all shiny stainless steel and polished rubber matting. The ship showers (a twenty-second push button) are spotless. And you can set the temperature. There is slight confusion as we wonder at first where to wash our hands, holding them under a long steel trough looking for buttons to push before we figure out that it's an unused urinal and we should go around the corner to the sinks. We giggle at our collective stupidity and wash.

FOB Price is run by the Danes, who are very cool. Take their Commander's evening brief for example. We have a similar brief every evening, where all the staff officers (SOs) chip in with what they've done of relevance during the day. It's pretty standard stuff, and generally takes place in a room where there's no air conditioning, so everyone is hot and sweaty at the end of it. The Danes take some time out from the routine. One of their SOs shows a slide with photos of knights in medieval garb. He gets everyone's attention instantly.

"I want to this evening tell you about my medieval theory of warfare."

When you talk to people who've been in Iraq in various guises and ask them what are the differences between the two societies (there and here), they'll say immediately that Iraq is a very sophisticated, highly organized society, but Afghanistan is just medieval—in architecture, in social organization, in culture. The current Afghan year is 1388, and for many that is apposite in the context of the Gregorian calendar too.

So I wonder where the young Danish SO is going with this.

"You see, this war is kind of like the wars fought in medieval times. We have castles we build to defend, and then people attack them. Slide please."

The next slide is a close-up shot of a medieval archer's opening, the kind you see on a castle. It is a sliver of a slit cut into the stone, with enough room for a soldier to observe outwards without being seen, or an archer to aim and fire in safety. No one will ever be defenestrated through this window. Only the most anorexic archer might even slip a wrist through. The next slide shows another castle window. Same principle: narrow aperture, wide firing zone—on the inside.

"See, this is an example of medieval engineering. Those medieval engineers, they were quite clever, yes?"

The room murmurs with puzzled agreement.

"Slide please."

The next slide shows one of the sangars outside the door, here on the camp, which is halfway through being constructed. It's big and square, made of silver-gray concrete. At the top are four great big window spaces, maybe three feet square.

"And this shows our contemporary engineering."

The room laughs. He's made his point, and made it well. At the end the Deputy Commander cites Frank Zappa as his thought for the day. Another evening he quotes Sir Francis Bacon: "When a man starts out full of certainties, he ends up full of doubt. When he starts out full of doubt he may end up with some certainty." The next night we go to the meeting it is W. H. Auden's turn: "Those to whom evil is done, do evil in return." How cool are the Danes?

They even grow flowers out of their Hesco baskets, little sacks of green stem and red petals peeking across the gray gravel. There's no beer on camp, but they do have one Carlsberg sun umbrella. They say that if Carlsberg did FOBs, FOB Price would probably be the best FOB in the world.

We are here in Gereshk to deliver the same workshop on community planning that we had done previously in Garmsir. Derek has already laid the groundwork, organizing an election commission that decided who would be community council members.

This story starts two weeks before, with a conversation that Derek has had with the district governor, who is a young, energetic, liberal man. When Derek was discussing the election, it was the district governor who said "I want to get some women onto the council."

The district governor then proceeded to put out the word, and so it was that seventy women turned up at the hustings, voted in the election, and five were elected. It was a bonus that we didn't ask for, a circumstance that we didn't think possible, but, challenging our perspective, Gereshk has elected a mixed gender 45-member council. The day after the election Derek, with the Afghan team, facilitates an initial training. The team sits the five women of the forty-five up at the front. During the training one of the women, Tutija, feisty at the best of times, gets vocally angry on a small point, and there are some disgruntled looks from some of the older men, and the man who has been elected Chair. He has only one good eye, the other is turned perpetually outward, a bulging planet in its own orbit. He has a big bulbous nose that nestles under his mismatched eyes. His default look is a stern stare and he holds himself stiffly. It's an intimidating look. Derek can tell that he's not happy with Tutija being a bit too vocal, but perhaps because Derek is there he says nothing. The rest of the day passes off well, and it is agreed to hold the workshop in a few weeks' time.

So two weeks after that election, we return. We are on a high going in to deliver the workshop; it's before anyone gets killed and we have energy and a buzz. We'd learned some lessons from Garmsir and were confident that we could do a good job here.

But the problems begin before we even get into the main conference room. On arrival, we are shunted into a big side room, the size of a tennis court. It has dirty cream walls and the floor is covered in carpets of burgundy, cabernet, and crimson. There are huge windows at one end, and our security guys ask us not to stand by them, as we would be too exposed, even with the outer wall of the compound giving some cover.

"There is a problem, a big problem," says Wahedullah gravely. The district governor nods his head in agreement.

"What do you mean, a problem?" asks Derek.

We soon learn what the problem is. The Afghans are nothing if not direct: the women cannot stay on the council.

"Why not?" asks Derek. I sit beside him on the brown velour sofa. The Afghans are sitting across the room from us, a huge chasm between us, literally and culturally.

"It is too dangerous for them to be on the council," says the Chair, gruffly.

"But they are here now, waiting to go in. Clearly they don't think it's too dangerous," says Derek.

"Well, the men won't work with them," comes the stern reply.

"The men seemed to want to work with them when they were elected," retorts Derek, gently but firmly.

There is a taut, tense silence.

Have you asked the women what they think of this?" says Derek.

"Yes. The men won't work with them."

"Well, could we ask the women?"

The district governor interjects: "Perhaps we could increase the number on the council to fifty?"

"No," says Derek, firmly, "there are forty-five on the council. Forty-five were elected, and forty-five is what we will work with. Women are people, not something that just sits on top."

"We will ask the provincial governor about that."

"You can ask whoever you like, but that number is staying at forty-five. If you want five extra people, you have to lose five men."

"It is too dangerous for the women to be on the council."

"This is what democracy is. You can't change it just because you don't like it."

"We will not go forward to the workshop if you insist on keeping the women on the council."

"Well, it looks to me like those people who were elected are already here. They are all very brave to be here, both women and men. Let's ask the women, shall we?"

"We should have the women be part of a separate shura. They can have their own shura."

"But they were elected onto this shura, by both women and men. We cannot ignore that."

The negotiation is as delicate as milk skin. And only Derek, as the man, can do it. I must sit by his side, and shut up, not letting any of the emotions I'm feeling (anger, sadness, frustration, despair that we won't be able to do this, belief that we can do this, hope, optimism) show through. The district governor, too, is similarly sidelined. What has happened in the intervening two weeks, when he was the one who pushed for women to get onto the council?

What has happened is that, unbeknownst to us, the profile got too high. The election was covered on national TV and that was a step too far, too much, too fast, too soon. Conservative social networks began to get activated and pressure came down from Kabul: this is too far, too much, too fast, too soon. The Helmand MPs, resident in Kabul, put pressure on the provincial governor's office, and on the district governor.

I also suspect that there's something to do with all the women being literate and educated, and the possibility that they simply show up the men who aren't.

After an hour and a half of the same circular argument we reach a mutually hurting stalemate. We are going to lose at least a day, if not the whole event. They have not succeeded in getting us to back down. Derek remains gently persistent. "Why don't we just go in and see what happens?" he asks for the umpteenth time.

And suddenly, for we are on the same turgid track, something breaks, and there is a general shuffling and preparedness to go into the (even bigger) shura hall. We go in and the women have wisely positioned themselves behind the men, their burqas cast off, a splatter of pastels on the floor.

I don't really know what has happened. It could be that in the tension between being a host (paramount in Afghan society) and having a guest, being a host trumped conservative mores. It could be that the Chair just got physically tired of the discussion. Whatever, we have a result, and I am very proud of Derek. He didn't have to stick his neck out and argue for the women, especially when our usual allies—the district governor and the provincial governor's office—abandoned us. Normally we wouldn't push for anything that doesn't have the backing of the district or provincial governor. But they had been got at. This is the first time we have unilaterally pressed for our agenda. The easier thing to do would have been to acquiesce, but the right thing to do was to fight for the inclusion of these women who had already accepted great risk in putting themselves forward for election.

After the workshop is over I ask Derek if he ever thought at any time during the negotiation that he would have to let it go.

"No," he says, "it was so important because the people of the district had made the decision that they wanted to do this. All the external pressure had nothing to do with the women themselves. All that bullshit about the women being in greater danger—they didn't really care about the women. Those were just fatuous excuses, they wouldn't have dreamt of letting the women on the council under any circumstances. No one else was speaking for them, so someone had to speak for them. And look how it's worked out: now they can speak for themselves."

Mapping exercise, Gereshk

# 11. Gereshk (II): Where, Now, How?

SO WITH THAT opener we begin, and the Afghanistan Social Outreach Program (ASOP) workshop is really hard going this time. The council members have only been elected twelve days previously and don't really have a sense of themselves as a body as yet. When we break into smaller groups they declare that they are uneducated. This doesn't mean they are stupid, by any stretch of the imagination, but they do want, in my group, Dr. Jawid to do the writing for them. And this they present as a statement of fact: "We can't write ourselves, we need someone to do that for us!" (Even though I can see two or three of them taking notes. This is less than in previous groups where only two were illiterate, but it doesn't mean that this group couldn't do it if they really wanted to.) Nonetheless, Dr. Jawid is going to be doing the writing. Dr. Jawid is the oldest member of our team. He is a tiny sliver of a man, thin as a whippet, professorial in aspect, with his ever twinkling black eyes buried deep in his crinkly face like currants pressed into dough. He has a fluffy gray beard that stretches almost to his collarbone, and is never without his white skull cap, so I have no idea if he has hair on his head or not. He is the academic on the team. No matter what the temperature is he wears a beige V-neck sweater over his *salwar kameez*. He understands and speaks some English, but we are never sure exactly what and how much of any conversation. He nods a lot. Perhaps he's just being polite.

We are doing basic community planning: a basic plan for community security, one for justice and one for economic and social development, all feeding into an overall community plan. We introduce the planning process by using the words "NOW," "WHERE," and "HOW." What is the current situation (NOW); what is our goal, where do we want to get to (WHERE), and what things do we have to do to reach that goal (HOW).

The Taliban fight on four fronts: military, political, judicial, and social. NATO, in the form of ISAF (International Security Assistance Force), is about fighting the Taliban on the military front. On the civilian side we've got three other fronts to fight. There are no clear-cut targets, and there are no quick wins, as there can be on the military side. We can expect the Taliban to push back against us if we are making any kind of impact. These Elders on the council are taking big risks to be with us this week, and we are made acutely aware of that when news comes that one of the councillors who lives in an area controlled by the Taliban has been kidnapped by them for a few hours, beaten up, and warned off from attending. He is in the hospital, as we start the introductory speeches. ISAF has big tanks and guns. The Taliban have guns, mobile "courts," enough people to intimidate, and a parallel public administration. We have flipcharts and markers. It's going to be a long haul.

Thanks to Charlie, I learned a new word in the past week: homosocial. She tells me it's an anthropological term used to describe a society that is segregated by gender, particularly one in which men are dominant. It is the social organizing principle of life in Afghanistan, and it is in this workshop that I experience it really for the first time, because this is the first time that we are working with a group that includes both men and women. I start to see what homosociality means in reality. The women arrive in their burqas, but discard them once they are inside. They sit quietly on soft sofas behind the gap of the two row semicircle of hard chairs (that we have arranged—thoughtfully in our mind—the day before, to include all and offend none). They find their own level. In fact, in one way they get the better deal: soft seats instead of hard. They bring two children with them, a boy and a girl. The little girl has swarthy Afghan skin and dark hair, but bright blue eyes. She wears a different outfit every day, but the fabric—pink flowers on white; bright red—is cut the same way, as a short swirling skirt, almost a tutu. The most amazing thing about the children is that they are completely quiet. They sit and behave without any toys or books, all day, with their mothers.

They take a separate room for lunch, and Charlie and I dine with them—rice with plump and juicy raisins, hiding some lamb; mint, tomato, red onion, meatballs and charcoaled chicken breast, with yogurt that would strip paint. The women are better company than the men. They are funny and witty and laugh with each other. Over the course of the four days we talk about driving, marriage, children, the Taliban, wanting to go to the UK, eating too much, poppy, the family dog, the seating arrangements in the hall, the workshop, the fact that they are all literate and many of the men are not.

Tutija has become the second wife of a man who is uneducated. She married him for his looks. She shows me his picture on her digital camera. He is indeed ruggedly handsome. There's one picture of him and four pictures of her dog, a Labrador of some description. She tells me it started out life speaking English (it belonged to an American couple who had it in Kabul for a while) and now it is fluent in Pashto. The next frame is me, her, and Charlie, in a shot she took earlier at lunch. I am wearing my latest Afghan outfit, a gift from one of the men on the Nad Ali Community Council, where we were a few weeks previously. It's red, very red, and gold, very gold. There are lots of sequins snaking across the red satin, and there's a matching headscarf, replete with its own gold sequins. Charlie is wearing a shiny sky-blue nylon number, borrowed from my ever expanding Afghan wardrobe. It was a gift from the Garmsir Community Council. I consider whether or not I should start formally declaring these gifts. Or at least ask Management for a bigger wardrobe.

The next photo is of a friend of Tutija's. She is dressed in an emerald and serpentine green speckled outfit, sitting in a porch, wearing a cream veil. She smiles at the camera. The next frame shows her corpse, laid out on a concrete slab. She wears the same green speckled fabric, across which is laid what looks like a goat-skin of shaggy black hair. The next shot is a close-up. She no longer wears the cream veil. Her long dark hair falls back from her face, away from her forehead which has a short jagged crimson line of blood in the middle, like a slot in a moneybox. There's another carmine crust cut into her cheek. Her dark skin is now sallow and yellow over her cheekbones and under her eyes is tinged with green, from where the blood has drained, never to return. The Taliban shot her. She was pregnant when she died.

The Taliban have tried to kill Tutija as well. She says that there was a shooting attempt on her about a year previously. We both know why that was: not only did she establish a school, but it was a co-ed school to boot.

"Why did they try to kill you?" I ask anyway.

"Well, I didn't stop to ask them!" she laughs, as the camera shakes with her giggles, the millions of pixels still arranged in the image of her dead friend. The silver arrow is pressed and the electronic reel moves on to the next picture which shows her in her husband's poppy field, all smiles and green stalks and pink and white petals. He's not just a pretty face, he'll have some money as well.

The next day we are late because of a technical problem with our ops room. Wahedullah doesn't waste the opportunity to make a point: "Ah, so this is English time, yes?" he says, smiling that smile. We are suitably sheepish.

That day Tutija shows me a video-clip on her mobile phone. It's very disturbing, more so than the still shot of her friend from the day before. It is the body of a man, still, stiff, and still hung from a tree, hands tied behind his back. He actually looks very peaceful, as if he was sleeping upright with his head up to the sun. The rope makes an odd protrusion at his neck, so that it looks, on the low grade mobile phone footage, like he has a yellow cravat tied at his neck, a nineteenth-century dandy. His turban is still on his head, which makes me wonder if there was any struggle at all, or just acceptance of his fate. But it is the scene around him that is more difficult to watch (it's about a five-minute clip). The Taliban executioner is still there—the man was a spy, they say—with his turban not twisted around his little skull cap, but over his face, like the balaclavas of the paramilitaries who used to come out at funerals at home and fire a volley of shots. But more, there is a (all-male) crowd. The homosocial public has been invited to view the hanging, both spectacle and semaphore. There are children too, who sit on a fence and look around them, at the dead man, at the living men. The jagged high-pitched music accompanying the tape gives the whole tableau a weird, fairground feel. The hung man could be an effigy, a perverse pastiche of a piñata for all the attention paid him now. He's become part of the backdrop, to these people, to this life.

Maybe it's because of these images, pegged together like clothes on a line, maybe it's because of the direct telephone threats from the

Taliban that come into a member of our local team during the workshop, maybe it's the discussions around the women's participation that make this particular workshop much more difficult than the previous two. It seems, somehow, much more real, or much closer to reality, than before and maybe that is because we ourselves have experienced a little of what a minefield it is to navigate and negotiate daily life in Afghanistan. Somehow I feel I have a little more understanding, and yet know that I am only starting to appreciate the baseline we're starting from. The scale of the task is enormous.

We finish our last briefing with the Danish battle group, but, because of an earlier IED strike, the helicopter is delayed, and later canceled. While we are waiting I flick through a surprisingly not-so-old copy of *Now* magazine. It shows celebrities in their Oscars finest, and magnifies the finest fissures in their relationships. I lap it up. Few words and glossy pictures are all my brain can cope with right now. When I'm finished "reading," Abdul Nazir takes it from me. He has a ruddy purple face the color of a young grape and hennaed hair. He speaks a little English, and is starting to use it more and more with us, as we get to know each other better.

"Ah," he says, enunciating the magazine's title, "NOW." He pauses as he takes in the photos on the front.

"Is this like NOW, WHERE, HOW?" he giggles, looking mischievously at me, clearly mocking the foreigner's fancy theory.

"Not exactly," I grin.

Wahedullah chirps up, grinning too, "NOW, WHERE, HOW! Now I get it!"

We all laugh. Further evidence that the Afghans are not so anhedonic after all. We are late, very late. Our helicopter is 24 hours late, in fact. But they keep on smiling as they board in the mid-afternoon heat.

Poppy field (Courtesy of ALCIS)

# 12. Poppies: Petals, and Other Derivatives

I ASK THE POLICE officer what's in the glass jar on his desk. It looks like sultry and sour beet juice, a dark purple-brown liquid in a giant jam jar, like the ones you'd get in chemistry class at school. But this jar comes from a much more clandestine chemistry course. The officer tells me that it's a precursor for the production of heroin. It doesn't look like it could do anything, and I'm a bit skeptical. The main molecular milestones from poppy to heroin are: poppy pod resin to opium, then opium to morphine, then morphine to heroin. Limewater, in which raw opium is boiled on the first leg of the journey, is colorless. Ammonium chloride, which is added to that solution, is white. Granted, the resultant morphine is a viscid brown gunge, like dark honey, but acetic anhydride, which is added to morphine to transform it into heroin, is colorless. So I remain skeptical. It probably is beet juice.

Then he says, "do you want to see some?"

I have no idea what the "some" could refer to, but, given that I'm in a police station and therefore bound to be among those on the side of what is right and just, I say "yes." What can possibly go wrong?

He reaches into his bottom drawer and pulls out an opaque gray, dusty, crumpled plastic bag.

"I'll show you, look."

I think he's going to mix up some powders there and then, and half expect him to whip out a conical flask and a Bunsen burner, but instead he simply unfurls the top, and from inside it takes a once-transparent plastic bag, the kind you'd pack sandwiches into. In it is a coarse green-yellow powder, the color and consistency of crushed cumin. It smells rather like cumin too, only with a bitter edge. It's raw heroin, at the penultimate stage of refinement. I look, I smell, but I don't touch: it's hard enough to get home without explaining this to airport security. He laughs and plunges his paw inside, picking up a small ball of reddish mud, wrapped in cellophane. It is wet opium, waiting for the application of colorless liquids to make the compound so coveted, now not just in the West but also in the neighboring countries of Iran, Pakistan, and China—and, increasingly, Afghanistan itself.

He drops it back in the bag, seals it—that is, wraps the plastic up again—and puts it back in his highly secure wooden drawer. There's no key. He smiles up at us in a cavalier way that says, I know this is unorthodox, but I get results, like he's an Afghan Columbo or something. That's probably a bit too optimistic of him, not that he knows who Columbo is, but nonetheless I am reminded of a story that Dave, one of the EUPOL police mentors working on counter-narcotics, has told me. It concerned a possible attempt at public poisoning, by the addition of a deadly dose to the water supply. The stuff was so potent that a small vial of it was said to be enough to knock out hundreds. The clever police officers found and confiscated the potion. If this happened at home there'd be forensics, labs, rubber gloves, dropping pipettes, white coats. There'd be scientists, lots of them, media, testing, tabloid headlines. In Lashkar Gah what happened went something like this:

Dave: "So this is potentially a very serious situation, Colonel." (I suspect that's a line that UK police officers use a lot, with the exception of "Colonel.") "Did you send the alleged poison up to Kabul for tests?"

The Colonel: "Nah, we have it here! Would you like to see?"

Without further ado, he reaches down into his desk drawer and whips out a small bottle, with a screw-top. From Dave's description I imagine it to be the size of one of those airline single servings of wine. He throws it onto the desk, where it rotates, just like it is supposed to in a game of spin the bottle. Dave's mouth drops open. The Colonel picks it up with his bare hand.

"Here," he says, proffering it, "what do you think it looks like?"

Dave has already reached into his pocket and put on his rubber gloves, even though he has no intention of touching the noxious flask. They are for just in case the glass breaks. I ponder that the same thing—ammonium chloride—is used in the production of both heroin and glass.

"Er, how do you know it's poison?" he asks, "Did you test it here?"

The Colonel chuckles.

"Yes, we know it's poison."

"How? What kind of test?" Dave asks, petrified of the answer, regretting it almost as soon as he asked.

"We gave it to a dog."

"A dog."

"Yes, a dog. In five minutes he was like this." The Colonel pushes back his swivel chair and raises his legs and arms in the air, rocking on his coccyx. He rolls his eyes and lolls his tongue. Just like the dead dog. They still have no idea of what the poison is, where it came from. All they know is that a small amount of it can kill a dog.

Back to the poppies: inflorescence comes in April, and usually we can only see it from the air—a delicate breath of candy-floss pink sprayed over emerald stems, naturally colored by chromium and chlorophyll. No other chemicals—yet. When in the helicopter you can see the distant shapes of the harvesters, earning around $20 a day to scrape the bulb back and get the resin to run. It's called lancing, and this is a high-skill, labor-intensive task. There are usually at least three pods in each bulb, and not all of them may be ready for leeching at the same time. If the pod is cut too deeply, the opium sap will run into its interior, and be lost. If the cut is too shallow, the sap won't flow. So there needs to be precision in the incision. It's a long way from picking blackberries. Lancing takes place in the afternoon, and the gum oozes out through the night, to be scraped off the next morning. And it's weather dependent: hot days and cold nights being the best combination.

But one day one of the Britmil guys who's been out fighting among the pink and emerald fields brings back some poppy flower heads. They couldn't be more different from the coarse cumin-like powder and the tarry gum slab that are derived from them. I think that a lot of thinking has gone into this alchemic adventure. Who would have thought that calyx and corolla conceal such a valuable cargo? Who thought to first scrape and *double, double toil and trouble; Fire burn, and caldron bubble?*

The petals are delicate, of gossamer fabric, like they've been woven by fairies. They are heavier than those of pansies but lighter than tulips'.

They are lilac and dog-rose pink; purple and damson; white and lemon yellow; ivory and coral; violet and vermilion. The little shawls of color that envelop the opium heart are edged with crazed crenellations, floppy fringes that casually belie the value of their core. There's none of Nature's usual symmetry here—they are all differently shaped, all uniquely inked. Like snowflakes, no two are the same. But none of this matters to the harvesters, casual laborers who flow into town for the six weeks or so of harvest, nor to the farmers, the brokers, the narco-barons, the Taliban, or the users. The petals are first to be discarded.

Even though the production and usage of heroin is *haram* (forbidden) under Islam, the Taliban get in on the act. They tax the farmers ten percent at source, collected in a single payment after the harvest. Fighting dies down during the harvest, but will pick up again afterward, around late May. I wonder what will happen this year, when all evidence points to much more wheat being cultivated than poppy. This year wheat, even though it is much more labor-intensive to produce, is simply more valuable than poppy. Also, the weather is favoring a strong yield. I wonder what the Taliban will do when they figure that out.

Earlier this year Britmil confiscated a huge haul—seventeen tons—of heroin and wet opium. It would have been worth a fortune on the UK high street (or back alley), tens of millions. And we were to burn it. A huge pyre of the sacks (think half-ton bags of potatoes, or of emergency aid rice) is made, about twenty feet by ten, and five feet high. The Afghan National Police take them off the back of a convoy of jingle trucks by hand and lay them down on the ground. In the West, this kind of thing would take place in a closed incinerator, by qualified men in white jumpsuits wearing masks and gloves. But here it is done outdoors, in the desert, brought on open-backed jingle trucks by farm laborers in their old clothes. The jingle trucks are like tuk-tuks writ large: they are brightly and abundantly painted—cobalt blue and orpiment yellow seems to be a favorite combination—and headbands of bells hang inside the cabin and outside from the chassis, like a beard of chimes. Barrels of gasoline are rolled in and around the sacks like firelighters between rolled paper to light a living room fire. The pyre is set on fire and blazes: flames of orange, red, and yellow thrust up, yielding to a thick and suffocating black smoke. The international media films the event. The EUPOL police mentors take lots of photos (which is how I know what it looks like). I ask one of them what it smells like.

"Fish paste," he says without hesitation.

It is late May now, and there is no doubt but that the fighting season has started. The next time I pass overhead, I can see the senescent stalks of poppy with the opium siphoned off, and the burgeoning sheaves of wheat—one on the way in, one on the way out. Everything is cyclical, it seems, and despite the big burn, the other seizures and the governor-led eradication program, millions of tons of heroin will still flood the market all over the world this year, a deadly derivative from such beautiful flowers.

Coming to vote, Lashkar Gah

# 13. Gender (II)

A MAGAZINE ARTICLE, from one of the serious Sundays, the *Times* or the *Observer* most likely, is stuck up on our notice board. It's a considered piece on the life story of a now elderly British woman who moved to Kabul in the 1970s, caused some kind of minor sexual scandal (came with one husband, and stayed with another; possibly there was an Ambassador involved) but got over that to be an advocate for all things Afghan. There are some photos of Kabul then and now. One is an old black and white. It's nothing fancy—a quick snap of a town square, a bit grainy. There's a heavy-set building in the background, a university or bank building, perhaps; in front of it a few people walk on their way to work, or school, or are just wandering across the great and comforting public space of the square. What's marvelously sad, but real, is that it is stark evidence of great difference between that time and now. For in the foreground there is a young Afghan woman. She wears a short-sleeved white shirt, tucked into a black A-line skirt that ends well above her knee. Her hair is cut in a bob, and sits out from her head, a dark bouncy corona. In the crook of one arm she carries books, and her other hand grips a small handbag. She is very beautiful. And you can see that she is.

Nowadays, in Kabul, in Lashkar Gah, in Afghanistan, beauty is much more difficult to see. It tends to be wrapped up, draped, swaddled, smothered in fabric, like furniture in storage.

I've come to the prison, finally able to deliver gifts to the female prisoners—you may remember we got interrupted on our first attempt. There are seven of them, sitting against the wall of the small reception room in which we meet them. There is one low window in the corner, the walls are bare plaster, crumbling in patches. A thin dirty carpet lines the floor in places. But all I see are six blue blobs and one black blob, amorphous approximations of the human form. Humans are not shaped like shuttlecocks, but these figures in front of me are, seated, docile

107

Daleks. Five sit still, two have come with wriggling adjuncts: there are children under there. But I don't *see* any of them.

I don't know what to do, how to act. I have seen the burqa-clad women all over Lashkar Gah. It is shocking at first, perverse: blobby caryatids swathed in mostly washed out blue, but also pink and mint green. For the first couple of trips I do rough counts. What's the ratio of burqas to hijabs? Some days it is 50:50, some days there are many more burqas than hijabs (and these are not just headscarves, they are full body coverings, but not shuttlecock-shaped, and not—necessarily—covering the face. Some days there are many more hijabs than burqas. It all depends which way the political wind is blowing. One day I saw a woman in a burqa carry a small child, covered in a baby-burqa, a living parody of a set of Russian dolls. A stiff conservative wind was blowing in that house. It saddened me almost more than the others.

It's hard to communicate, at first, with these women prisoners. They remain covered because we have a male translator (and we can't get female ones—their families don't allow it). A little boy of about four unfurls himself from his mother, his curiosity getting the better of him. He has no shoes. He was born in the prison and has never been outside, never been to school. One of the other children starts to cry, thin and colicky. Her pacifier is her mother's breast, even though she looks only a little younger than the young boy. I guess it's the only natural resource that she has.

We explain why we are here, trying to set expectations, trying to make some semblance of eye contact through the frieze frame covering the upper part of the face. They tell their stories. One is in for murdering her husband. She doesn't deny it but complains that she didn't have a fair trial. She wants to retain ownership of her land while she's in prison. Another is there because she fell in love with someone her parents didn't want her to marry. She and her fiancé fled to Pakistan (though given how much gender apartheid there is, I don't know how she even met someone outside the family circle in the first place). There, they got married. Then their families enticed them back with talk of forgiveness. They came, like iron filings to a magnet—the family bond here is amazingly strong. It was a mistake. It was a trap. She was thrown in jail, at fourteen or fifteen, for dishonoring her family. She'd been sentenced to five years and had been there for three years already. Another, the one in black, rocks a baby, also born in the prison. She was accused, and convicted, of adultery. I feel, again, utterly impotent.

When we go to give the gifts out we ask the translator to leave. We don't need interpretation for handing out soap. As soon as he goes out of the door, they whip off their blues, and I see them. The one who was tricked into coming back has long dark hair, bright shiny eyes and slightly pudgy cheeks, with dimples when she smiles, shyly, at me. I meet her gaze, but am afraid that my eyes only reflect sorrow, and impotence. The woman who has murdered her husband is much older than I thought, her skin wrinkled and colored like the husk of an almond. They wear jewelry, mostly costume—stones of red and green paste on gold chains and rings, though the older women have what looks like real gold bangles on their wrists. They examine our meager gifts eagerly, chatting, enthused. The only really wretched things are the babies, they barely move, soporific, sluggish, as if, like Roma street children in Eastern Europe, they've been drugged. And maybe they have, but it seems to me rather that they just don't know anything else.

We call the translator back in, to say our goodbyes. And the curtain comes crashing down, instantly. I no longer see anything but the blobs again. The worst thing is, I realize, that even though I've just seen them, communicated with them with crude signing, I can't visualize any of their features individually. They are to me now incipient women, inchoate—like grotesque full-size fetuses. It takes a second trip before I can remember their faces—something I'm usually very good at. I rarely forget a face, but I have to really work hard to recall the unsheathed images of these women. Their humanity, never mind femininity, is utterly negated. It simply doesn't exist when they are covered. I wonder who thought of the first burqa?

I recall being appalled that my Lonely Planet guidebook to Afghanistan took a positive view of the burqa; it "was once a symbol of urbanized Afghan women. Its impracticality was a sign that the wearer was free from the toil of the fields." Then how come every Afghan woman I know takes it off as soon as she is safely indoors, and wants not to have to wear it outdoors?

Granted, I don't know many Afghan women, but I recall a tough woman CID officer saying, when I asked about their uniforms worn on duty: "A trouser suit! I would love to wear a trouser suit to work!"

Her profile is corvine, she has a hooked nose and bright, beady eyes, ever alert. She once wrestled a female suicide bomber to the ground. The woman bit chunks out of her arm, and she proudly shows off the scars. She had a few run-ins with the Russians as well. She has a bird's eye for detail, especially for that one little thing that looks not quite right. For example, she and male colleagues were searching a house. When they go to search a home a female officer always accompanies, to search the women. They don't wear a burqa, but a special short hijab, and black gloves. It was suspected that this particular house contained weapons. Nothing was found inside. She watched the children play around the well in the compound while the men finished inside. On a hunch she got the children to move. The women said, "no, no, there's nothing there. Please don't disturb the children." But when you've dealt with suicide bombers and the Russians, children are small beer. She swept them out of the way and found a few AK-47s and some explosives in the well. When I meet her she's on a literacy course. It's the first time in her life that anyone has taught her how to read and write. She loves the course, she wants to do another one already. But when she goes outside the police station, she, like all the other women officers (and there are only about ten of them out of 2,000 in the province), dons the burqa.

There is some nuance in the wearing of it. It does lend some protection. Precisely because it is so shapeless there is no way of knowing who is inside it. The only time I hear women say anything positive about the Taliban regime is the security it granted, even as it exacted a great price for it. One woman told me, "at least when they were in charge I didn't have to worry. I could travel from here to Pakistan with nothing but my burqa to keep me safe."

Or consider Karima's experience. I ask her about her veil. I am wearing clothes made in her center—a purple and amber embroidered ensemble. She is wearing, as always, black, but her hijab today has a bold and broad silver stripe. It always stays put on her head, almost like it is an organic part of her whereas mine always slips. I say I like it, but did she always wear it?

"Oh no, when I was a student at Kabul University, I wore clothes like you. Not these," she says pointing at my *salwar kameez*, "but European clothes. I had skirts up to here," she smiles mischievously, marking a line halfway down her thigh with her finger.

We talk about her time at university in Kabul where she studied biology, math, chemistry, and physics. Even then, though, which must have been around the same time as the photograph of the young woman with the dark shiny bob in the square, she had to have her uncle with her as *mahran*—her male escort. Now she must always have an escort if she goes to Kabul. As she's a widow, her *mahran* is her husband's brother, whom, it turns out, I know professionally. It's a small town, I know, but it gives me a sense of how interconnected they all are. In any event, if one has to have an escort, her husband's brother is a nice man.

It's better for women to go as a group, she explains. If one or two of them go, then an escort is required. If there are five or six of them, then it's fine for them to travel unescorted. But even then, they shouldn't go out on the street.

"And when you were a student, did you wear hijab?" I ask.

"No, no!" she looks as me incredulously, as if to say: with a miniskirt, are you crazy?

"So when did you start to wear it again?"

"When the Taliban came."

"And what do you prefer, to wear it or not to have to wear it?"

"Oh, not to wear it. Of course."

I'm still appalled at the Lonely Planet's editorial stance, even though I have to admit it could be true. But the publisher didn't have to illustrate the cover of the guidebook with a smiling man and boy child in a shop selling rows of blue burqas.


Soraya Tarzi was born in 1899. She was to become the Queen of Afghanistan, wife of King Amanullah Khan. Encouraged and advised by Soraya and her father, King Amanullah worked to advance women's rights. He declared: "Religion does not require women to veil their hands, feet, and faces or enjoin any special type of veil. Tribal custom must not impose itself on the free will of the individual."

The previous king (Rahman Khan) had also advanced the status of women somewhat, allowing them to inherit property (and thus put the woman currently prisoner in Lashkar Gah prison in a position to worry about her land).Though he had many wives himself, Amanullah discouraged polygamy, and my (scant) reading suggested that Soraya was the key influencer on him. She also founded the first magazine for Afghan women, called *Ershad-E-Niswan* [Guidance for Women]. However, in the late 1920s tribal leaders organized and fought against the freedoms King Amanullah promoted for women in Kabul. They pushed against women's education and personal freedoms, and the next king (Nadir Shah) acquiesced to their behest. The lot of women was all dependent on who was on the throne, and the nexus of religious and tribal and cultural mores. Next was King Zahir Shah. That was a better time, with the first secondary school for girls opening in 1941. In 1959 women were allowed to unveil, and the wives of the ruling family, and senior government officials, appeared unveiled at public functions. Others followed. There was no social unrest in the capital, but there was a riot in Kandahar in protest, and around sixty people were killed as a result.[3] In 1964 the Constitution granted women the right to vote, and to enter politics. In the constitutional loya jirga of 2003 there were 103 women delegates, out of 500.

In Gereshk five of us are having lunch: two women in their late twenties, two of us in our late thirties, and one in her early sixties, Guliana. They are asking me what things I miss from home when I am here. For some reason, I say "milk" and "driving." (I really would love to take one of the B6 4x4s out for a good run over the rumps and bumps in the desert.) Razia, a young teacher, is mildly scandalized by the fact that I can drive. Her eyes widen and she gasps with surprise.

"You can drive?" she says, incredulously, but liking it nonetheless.

Guliana looks up with resigned eyes. "I remember driving, but I haven't done it for twenty years."

Razia looks around at Guliana. They know each other relatively well,

---

3    This information from http://www.afghan-web.com/woman/afghanwomenhistory.html, a thumbnail sketch, but interesting nonetheless.

but Razia looks now at Guliana the way she just looked at me, only more so.

"You *drove*, Guli?"

"Yes," says Guliana, smiling now, remembering without rancor. "Yes, and I liked it. But I have no need for it now. My sons drive me."

When I ask them how they feel about sitting behind the men in the meeting we are at they say only that it is their place. They don't even think that it might be different. They don't address the big group, yet in the smaller groups (sitting in a circle) they speak freely. It is not a revolution, it is them finding their level—and also their ability to influence within a stifling system, which they do. They dress, as do the majority of Afghan women, with color and panache. Fatima wears yellow-green silk embroidered with cerise thread, Razia an orange and black ensemble.

Guliana, a widow, is the most subdued in terms of dress, in soft beige and earth brown tones. The next day they won't come to the workshop because they are all to go to a wedding. It is their choice, and they invite me. I'd love to go, but know that our security would never allow it, so I don't even ask. Before we leave, one of the men gives me a gift of cobalt cloth, patterned with azure, pink, and silver sequins. I realize I'm starting to like the fashions.

One day when we are coming back from a trip into town—I have stopped doing the ratio count by this stage—I see a woman stepping across the rough mud, all whorls, holes, and hillocks. She is wearing silver T-bar strapped sandals, with three-inch heels. Bright blue trousers fall in shimmery shoals above the sandals. The pale green burqa blocks any further view, but I can imagine how the outfit was carefully put together, and, just like us, checked out in front of a mirror at home before heading out. She's a brave woman. There's no way I'd wear those heels on the topography of Lash. I marvel that she doesn't totter, that she navigates and negotiates the uneven surface smoothly, almost gliding.

As we pass her on the right, we come to the girls' school on our left. It's a fantastically uplifting place. The school uniform is a white hijab and black *salwar kameez*. They cluck like checkered chicks, their heads bobbing up and down as they chat and play. Like school kids everywhere, they are sporting heavy (bound to be back-buckling) colored backpacks, stuffed full of books. They can read and write.

Beyond that we pass the Women's Department, where I go to speak to Karima, who works there. It's the first time I've been there while all the classes have been going on. And it's fantastic. Inside, there are women of all ages, shapes, and sizes learning: how to read, how to write, how to weave carpets, how to make clothes. Outside, the garden is tended—hoed, seeded, and harvested—by women, the horticulturists of tomorrow.

We speak about the facilities and the classes. Karima is soft spoken, yet full of ideas. And she gets things done. She is largely responsible for the whole center, and for all the learning that goes on within its walls. She is especially proud of the horticulture.

"This is the first time in Afghanistan that women learn this, how to grow things!" she says, her eyes shining. "I would also like to have sports facilities for women."

"What kind of sports do Afghan women play?" I ask. I just never associated any of the women I've met with any kind of non-functional physical activity.

"Ping-pong, they like that," says Karima, "and basketball."

"Basketball!" I exclaim, "how come they like that? Where do they play it?"

"Oh, we don't play it anymore. But I used to play it, when I was a girl," says Karima.

"Where did you learn? In school?"

"Yes! I had an American teacher. Mrs., Mrs.… Hit-itch…" she struggles momentarily with the English pronunciation and her memory. "Mrs. Hitchcock. She was my teacher at school. Oh, she was old when she taught me, but she did. She taught all of us to play. We loved it."

Karima's eyes light up and she smiles. I think of the young woman pictured in the newspaper article in that square in Kabul, I try to picture Karima wearing a similar mini-skirt, or basketball shorts.

"I'd love to start it here for the younger women," she continues when we go out. "There's some space over there." Next to the center is the chief prosecutor's office, a three-story building that overlooks Karima's yard.

She points up at the building, a sign of progress, and one of our infrastructure builds.

"But they would be able to see in," she says wistfully, "so we can't."

She sighs, but then turns and regains her positive outlook, her eyes twinkling in her lined face are still the eyes of the girl who loved basketball. "But we'll think of something," she smiles, flatly but knowingly, just like the Mona Lisa.

I have no doubt but that she will.

Preparing food, Gereshk

# 14. Food

I DISCOVER THAT the name of the place where we eat, three times a day, changes with the brigade that we share the camp with. For the Royal Marines (who left in March) it was the galley. With the Army (who are here now) it's the cookhouse. I heard that a few civilians tried to call it the canteen. But it didn't go down so well. Not with the Army, not with the Navy. But what annoys them more than this nuance in nomenclature is the fact that you might confuse one for the other. "We're the Marines, Kate! The clue is in the title. The Navy. The sea. Ships." I try, but all those guys in camouflage, they all look the same to me. Toward the end of the Marines' tour, however, I do better. There are all sorts of shapes and sizes, especially given that Op Massive (lots of weight lifting in the gym) and Op Bronze (lots of vertical sunbathing—boys running topless around the HLS in the midday sun) are ongoing. No wonder I have taken up running. But we were talking about food, were we not?

The food on camp is both magnificent and munificent. There's so much of it. And it's all just right there. First, breakfast—pale porridge that greets you as you enter the tent, served from a stainless steel cauldron, then the variety of fried products that cry out to be lifted and loaded onto your paper plate. Fried yellow bread, pink and crimson bacon, sausage, hash browns, hardboiled eggs lurking in low water, and at the end creamy croissants, just like you'd get in Paris (this is actually true). I only have them on Fridays when breakfast is over late—09:00 (usual time 08:00). I take a Sunday paper (usually about two weeks old), go outside to eat, before the sun reaches full strength. I make my own coffee, and with those croissants, if I close my eyes and just let the buttery pastry flake and dissolve in my mouth, I really do imagine I am sitting breakfasting on the pavement outside my friend Owen's old Paris apartment. Then the croissant melts away, I open my eyes and here I am sitting at a long wooden bench at a rough wooden table, with a blue checked plastic tablecloth nailed down to it.

That's breakfast. Lunch is mainly salad—kidney beans and corn, prawns and tuna, beet, celery; the pizza bar, the omelet bar (made with powdered egg, spread like a pancake on the griddle, and surprisingly tasty). For dessert there's yogurt, bars of chocolate, a Danish pastry perhaps (not that I ever partake), and fruit. Before I came here I had packed stacks of multivitamins, fearful that I wouldn't get my "five a day" of fruit. How wrong I was. In six months there has only ever been one day where there was no fruit in Lash. The fruit tray is full of quartered oranges, ruby grapefruits, and green, black, and white kiwis, purple grapes, yellow-skinned and white-fleshed melons. If anything, I eat more fruit here than I do at home.

Dinners are pretty spectacular—there's at least a choice of two or three meats every night, and generally something hot and spicy. Potatoes come rolled in breadcrumbs (croquette), or sliced and smothered in creamy cheese (dauphinoise), or shot through with milk and butter (creamed), or a perennial favorite with troops and civilians alike: home-cut fries. Desserts are a range of cheesecakes or chocolate torte defrosted, but also freshly made brownies, fruit if you go early enough, Bakewell tart, apple crumble (sometimes with blackberries), Victoria sponge and, at the top of the heap for me, bread and butter pudding—all with custard.

The Lash cookhouse has the reputation of being the best in Helmand (though some say FOB Price has the edge, I don't think so). I marvel at the logistics that produce high quality food for almost a thousand people three times daily, seven days a week. The chefs and kitchen staff come from farther east: India, Sri Lanka, the Philippines, Malaysia, their remittances being sent home to prop up their families and their national economies. I'm not sure that they get any days off while they are on base (they get two weeks off to go home every six months) and yet they are always smiling as they serve us. From time to time they will do a theme evening. I've been here for "Sri Lankan night," "Italian night," "Philippines night." The staff go all out. On Italian night they made a fantastic six-foot pastry replica of the Leaning Tower of Pisa, and pasta houses from which we scooped the hors d'oeuvres. The paper plates we used were colored red and green, glued together and suspended chandelier-like from the ceiling, plastic forks dangling from their ends giving us as much pleasure as if they were crystal beads. The logistics of getting the supplies to all the big metal ISO containers that surround the cookhouse are impressive enough—in convoys of ramshackle trucks, jingling and jangling over the Khyber Pass, driving south through the desert where they line up outside the camp, next to the graveyard with its regatta of bamboo masts and flimsy green sails for days before they are called, one by one, into the camp to be unloaded. Then to be cooked to such a high standard, and with such care, is at times breathtaking, though we take it all for granted. And we take too much, simply because it's there to be taken.

We are not supposed to eat local food. It is bad for us, stored and prepared unhygienically, we greatly increase our chances of D&V if we eat it. As the summer heat stirs and I see carcasses of chicken and beef hung from street stalls without refrigeration, I am not easily dissuaded from this view. But I do learn that things are different in practice. The first meal I am due outside the wire is in the Police Headquarters, about a month after I arrive. My mind is full of the dire warnings. We go into the police canteen, and immediately those sirens are confirmed. No water runs from the taps, and there's no soap. We have to soap up and then rub down with alcohol gel before we can enter the cookhouse on camp. We only ever eat with disposable cutlery, and must wipe down our places with ethanol wipes when we are finished. Facing a meal with no cleansing products is a travesty of our hygiene regime. But we are guests and must go in. It also helps that someone has a pocket-sized hand cleaner and we squeeze out drops of the clear liquid, our only defense in our war against local germs.

I have no idea what the kitchen conditions are like—I think it's best not to think about it—but the food is great. There is fish, lamb, and goat. I am cautious about the fish—it comes from the Helmand River, and I have seen it used as a dumping ground for all sorts of effluence, but since Brian and Dave tuck in, I follow suit. It is covered in a red paste, which turns out to be quite spicy, like a hot tomato chutney. The goat I still stay clear of, but the lamb is fabulous—tender pink flesh that deliquesces in the mouth.

There's a plate of some form of tomato and onion stew cooked with whole peppercorns and garlic. It's my favorite that day. We have small stainless steel side plates with sliced onion, scallion, tomatoes, and a slice of lemon. Plates of boiled rice and slabs of pita bread are dotted around the table. Dessert looks disgusting—a wobbly milky blancmange-like substance, set in a shallow dish. I have an aversion to any dairy products that aren't fresh—my gag reflex is activated like a lightning rod if I'm within twenty paces of day-old milk. So I'm not too optimistic about this little moon on my plate. However, it's well within range, and the contents of my stomach are still firmly settled on the inside. Brian is wolfing his down (but he wolfed down the fish, the goat, and the lamb as well, so I'm not too sure if this is a good thing or not). Heartened by the fact that he is still looking around for more things to eat, I put the teeniest bit of the opaque jelly on my spoon—the first washable piece of cutlery I've used in a month—and taste. It tastes quite sweet, like condensed milk. And there are whole peppercorns secreted within, which give it a savory kick and temper the sweetness. I like it. I can't eat it all—it is far too sweet for that—but it was good. I have not only survived my first Afghan meal, I have enjoyed it.

I did get food poisoning from eating local food, but only the fifth time I ate it. In the Police Headquarters we eat at tables and chairs, but everywhere else we eat on the floor. The usual drill is that a tablecloth is laid and then the big stainless steel platters are brought out by wiry wraiths of waiters with constantly downcast eyes. The platters are huge—about two and a half feet in diameter—and there's more food there than one person can possibly eat. Everything—starter, main course, dessert—comes out at once, on that plate. The side plate of fresh salad, maybe some unpasteurized yogurt (too bitter for me, though I did taste it), a bowl of meat stew (either goat or lamb), and if we are lucky, as we are today, eating in the offices of WADAN, an NGO we are working with on the Afghan Social Outreach Program, really good spicy rice. The rice is savory with a sweet undertow of cinnamon and nutmeg interspersed with the gravy from the mutton and chickpeas for extra crunch. There's pita bread that is almost the size of the plate, rolled long and roughly rectangular. You can see this bread every day stacked at the roadside shacks, lifted straight from stone ovens, fresh for sale. There's also stuffed okra—a piquant tomato sauce bleeding from that delicate green lady's finger. As it's the season, there are also chunks of watermelon—its sliced sucrose spilt and freshly glistening in crystal beads along its crimson flesh—and whole mangoes. They don't look like much from the outside—the color a weak milky gold, skin that wrinkles when touched, shaped like an elongated pear. But I watch as Wahedullah opens his: sliced around the middle, then a sharp counter twist of both halves, and the rich orange flesh is revealed around the stone in the center. You eat around the stone, then scoop out the rest, the syrupy insides dissolving on your tongue, exciting every tastebud you have.

In town you can tell that the season has changed (even if you couldn't feel the heat). Green watermelons are stacked high on stalls, surrounded by pale gold mango mountains, all precariously perched atop each other, somehow stable. But along with these exotic fruits are the ubiquitous and universal basics, the foundations of cooked and un-cooked food everywhere in the world: tomatoes and onions. No matter how sophisticated a society, you can bet its best dishes start off with or are supported in some way by tomatoes and/or onions.

Along the side of the street huge orange sacks packed with straw are piled high. They will be used for bedding, brooms (also on display), roofing, and animal fodder. They are stacked many feet high, testimony to the bumper wheat harvest this year. The only problem with this superabundance is its management. Too much wheat flooding the market lowers the price and makes growing poppy over wheat more attractive next year. This year wheat is more valuable than poppy. Next year it might be the reverse. The Afghans are nothing if not pragmatic.

Among the mangoes and watermelons are what look like huge piles of long-stalked flat-leaved parsley. One man is weighing a stack on ancient scales, plates three feet in diameter nestled in chains over a trestle taller than most of the small men who operate them. On one side are three melons, looking lost and forlorn on the mighty plate. On the other side is a miniature haystack of the parsley about eighteen inches high and as wide as the plate. I ask Arif, who's traveling with me to the governor's office, what it is: animal fodder?

"No," he says, laughing, "it's for making juice. Either by itself, or mix it with mango juice."

"What does it taste like?" I ask, thinking of wheatgrass or another sour, yet worthy, green.

"Bananas," he says simply.

I've seen bananas grow in Australia. The leaves of the banana plant look absolutely nothing like these delicate leaves. But bananas he says, so bananas it must be. It's then that I notice the stalls selling mango juice—the Lash equivalent of juice bars. Simple wheeled stalls, tucked in between the money changers' glass safe with their thin and dirty notes of Pakistani rupees and Afghan afghanis, and the bike shops. Most have some form of self-squeeze device, but one even has four glass juicer/blenders. The juicers distribute pale gold and green elixirs from glasses, which the customer returns, to be washed and re-used. We'll never be able to stop and get one on the street, but Arif says he has some freshly squeezed mango juice in the freezer in his office that he'll let me taste when we get back.

There are local grapes on the stalls—small and round and golden green. In the winter these will be slow-dried into green and yellow raisins, and form the bedrock of the snack tray that we get at every meeting. The second staple is dried yellow corn cubes, which suck any moisture from my mouth every bit as much as the raisins flood it. The third is almonds in their shell, which when bitten seep strongly tasting sap—it's the strongest tasting, the most direct, almond essence I've ever had. The final table treat is either cashew or pistachio nuts. The nuts, I am told, come from Pakistan but the fruit that we see at market is Helmandi.

Helmand was apparently known in Pashto as *da ghaloo danou aow mehou godam*—the "grain and fruit store," the bread basket of Afghanistan. Tomatoes and onions are all very well but I can't wait for pomegranate season.

Compound wall, Lashkar Gah

# 15. Bricks and Stones

AS TIME GOES BY, Lashkar Gah moves from mud to brick and concrete. The older houses behind their compound walls are sculpted from white-brown mud, their edges smudged and approximate, scooped out of the earth and simply molded as if by a giant child making a settlement out of old Plasticine. The new build in the town looks like the child has tired of Plasticine and moved on to grey and salmon pink Legos.

There are three brick factories in town, I am told, and I see their product piled up in little pyramids of rust, bracken, and sulphur along the edge of the road, their colors given by the river and desert sand from which they are crafted. Sometimes I see them being unloaded from a jingle truck, thrown carelessly onto the dirt, chipping as they go, releasing little puffs of dust. Concrete blocks are made by hand by the side of the road. There is a whole stretch of road (and it is asphalted, not just a track) that with a little imagination could be called a boulevard of bricks and blocks, one aisle on a massive outdoors builder's yard. Here the old men stand and produce, or peddle. They all seem to be wrinkled and wizened, with long, parched black and white streaked beards. Their skin is of oxblood leather and they have white hands, dusty from the metallic grayish concrete residue.

The concrete is mixed in old cement mixers, and then poured or spaded into a mold-contraption made of wood and pulleys, almost like a medieval weights machine, with a big handle at head height that is pulled down only with some effort, and the blocks are born with every repetition. Behind those wizened exteriors must seethe sinews of steel—day-long, summer-long gym sessions, in the forty degree (C) plus heat. There are ten or twelve of these little one-man factories along the road, and they barricade themselves in behind their blocks, creating little fortresses a few feet high around them. Behind them is one of the tallest constructions in Lash: one of the three old Ferris Wheels dotted

125

around town. Silhouetted against the taut translucent sky, their mechanics are stripped and exposed and rusty, simultaneously and mutely speaking of past fun and present bleakness. There are eight cars, none of which moves, except sometimes when the older kids clamber up and sway stiffly in small back and forth movements. It makes me wonder about the time, and the conditions when it spun around, making boys and girls and grown-ups giggle. Maybe it was the time when Mrs. Hitchcock taught the girls to play basketball.

Ferris Wheel Landscape

But it is the bricks that remind me most of home. I grew up in a red-brick house and Belfast is a city of red-brick. The older ones, Georgian, were almost all handmade, from the end of the eighteenth century to the middle of the nineteenth. Each brick, like each concrete block squeezed out of the mold in Lash in the twenty-first century, was completely unique. Later, in the Victorian era, the then wire-cut bricks were more varied in hue, but still were overwhelmingly red. Perhaps this is because of the red laminated clay deposits laid down in the alluvium of the late or post-glacial lakes, or even further back, because of the red sandstone rubble of the rocks of the Triassic period (which is pretty far back—250 million odd years ago) laid down in the Castlereagh Hills and the Lagan Valley floor.

The Triassic period in Afghanistan saw different kinds of rocks deposited, rocks that have yielded much prettier things than red bricks. These pegmatite fields of granite, with lots of minerals, were hardened from the molten magma. It is commonly acknowledged among experts that the geology of Afghanistan has a "long and complicated" tectonic history. I think that this could also be applied to its politics, its tribes, and its social relations—as if the subterranean structures ordained and constrained the society from even before the time when it was settled by humans.

The basics of the formation of the Afghan Block go something like this: when the supercontinent broke up, Gondwanaland drifted north and its northern edge collided with the Tajik Block, causing in turn two other collisions, one of which created the Helmand Block, which is where I currently live. These mighty Blocks formed crustal sutures at their boundaries. *Geotimes* says that this means that "geologic maps of Afghanistan illustrate this composition with many slivers of very different lithologies and ages bounded by faults."

The big collisions kept on coming, with later crashes creating the Himalayas with the Afghan end, the mighty Hindu Kush, north and east of Helmand as well. Deposited with the granite in the making of these mountains were many, many, colored stones, gemstones, and jewels.

Stones like deep intensely blue lapis lazuli, which went to adorn the headdresses and necklaces of the Egyptian Pharaohs, are still mined today in Badakshan, a province in the northeast, up by the Wakhan Corridor, Afghanistan's only border with China. Lapis has been mined there for seven thousand years. From seven mines operational in living memory, today there is only one, at Sar-e-Sang, the Blue Mountain. It is in the middle of the Hindu Kush, at an elevation of 11,500 feet, so it can only be worked from June to September. In the Panjshir Valley the saturated green hexagonal crystals of the most precious beryl, emeralds, are found. In Jegdalek there are rubies (from almost transparent to carmine and purple-red in hue), and pink and blue sapphires. In Nuristan there is pale green tourmaline, pink-lilac kunzite, more beryl (not just emerald, but light blue-green beryl, morganite, the rose-pink variety), and multi-colored prismatic crystals of spodumene in white, yellow, purple, green, and shades in between.

Of course, though these coveted stones are there to be found, mostly they are not. Which is why the Ministry of Mining seeks many new investors.

In Helmand, though, we have nothing like this. But we do have one thing: marble. Or rather, not the rock, but the mineral: onyx. "Helmand Marble" is really Helmand Brown Onyx or Helmand Green Onyx. Commercially, there are around twenty factories in the whole country excavating and exporting rough blocks of onyx to Pakistan, where the Pakistanis process it and the Afghans buy it back—at inflated prices.

But not all of the Helmand marble goes to Pakistan. Much of it is made into plaques, heavy plaques that are then inscribed (usually in gold letters, in Pashto and English) with words of gratitude, fidelity, and friendship. Many a baggage limit has been blasted to oblivion by the taking home of these plaques at the end of a tour. Artisanship is also expressed in the form of vases, which are dotted around various offices. There is even a hawk-sized bird. It sits on Iain the flight coordinator's desk, a heavy chunk of sage-jade green shot through with vanilla and celadon bands. It may have started out being fashioned solidly in the shape of an eagle, but it ends up looking like a pale green penguin with lipstick red lips (it's meant to be a beak, but it looks more like lips). I like the green onyx better than the brown, if only because there is so much brown and beige around in the desert sand and the city mud.

This reflection of what lies beneath the surface says something about the country above ground. There is beauty and there is color in the minerals crushed to light-refracting crystals in the mines that no longer exist. But above them there is a band of calcified brown dust that both exists and is a metaphor for the drabness, paucity, and poverty, the entropy, which is the public face of the society.

But at least the jewels are there, waiting, one day, to be discovered. I'm not so sure, though, that the wizened face of the concrete block maker, toiling day in, day out, will ever light up with the joy of seeing them.

Bost Airport

# 16. The Dog, the Boat, and the Crowbar

THE PREVIOUS EVENING, Alex had asked me to send the details to the Crowbar. I had no idea what she was talking about. Alex works in Aviation for Task Force Helmand (TFH). TLAs—Three Letter Acronyms—are big in the military, and we civilians are powerless to resist. After being here for six months I find myself speaking in sentences that would have completely baffled me when I arrived. I, too, have succumbed, and use (appalling) syntax in the spoken word; sentences composed entirely of prepositions, the personal pronoun, and TLAs are no longer uncommon in my utterances. I say I have no idea what she's talking about, imagining a length of heavy steel with a hammer claw curving at one end.

"Oh, Crowbar," she says haughtily in her exquisitely expensive accent, "she sits over there. I'll take you." She can't help speaking haughtily, since she's had positive reinforcement since the day and hour she was born, and then some more as a military officer. We walk deftly through the phalanx of phones and monitors (well, she walks deftly, I stumble over various cables and crash into desks). Alex deigns to look over her shoulder with a snort as she introduces me to the Crowbar, a petite woman called Kelly, the very antithesis of what I'd imagined.

"This is Crowbar, she's the person you should talk to. Crowbar, this is Katie," she says, getting my name wrong. She actually called the other woman "Crowbar." But Kelly Crowbar turns out to be very nice.

I call Kelly the next morning with the details (the pilot's cell phone number, the aircraft call sign, the type of aircraft), which I've got from the governor's office. This morning the first commercial plane is to land at the airfield at Bost, on the southern edge of Lashkar Gah. The ancient city of Bost is the original settlement, built long before contemporary Lashkar Gah. There are reports of its existence as early as 661 when in a template-setting event it was conquered by Arabs in the anabasis of the Army of the Prophet. When the Turkish Ghaznavi took over in the tenth century Bost became the winter capital of the Ghaznavid nobility under Sultan Mahmud, who had his court here six months of the year. Today, from the top of the watchtowers at the prison, you can still see the ruins of his ancient city sited in the sand at the confluence of the Helmand and Arghandab rivers. In fact, Lashkar Gah takes its name from the riverside barracks town built to provide accommodation for Mahmud's soldiers. You can still see traces of what was once their housing—low umber and ochre walls tapering to fish-fin thin now, the wind and sun having shaved them for more than a thousand years. Mahmud's kingdom was fabulously wealthy (some seventeen plundering expeditions to India, Kurdistan, and the Caspian Sea saw to that), and some of this great wealth was put to building the Qala-e-Bost, the mighty arch[4] that still stands, but no longer functions as the entrance to the city of Bost. It was built in the eleventh century, and although today it is dilapidated and crumbling, it appears, in age-defying airbrushed glory, on the 100-afghani note (worth about $3.50). Though I'd love to go, we have no good business case for going, so I've never been to Qala-e-Bost, and have only seen it in the distance. In the picture that is most frequently reproduced two camels plod past it, their scrawny shadows stretched up its walls, their driver dwarfed by the massive structure. It is over sixty feet high, topped by a flattish arch angled obtusely in the style of Islamic architecture. It has—or once had—intricate mud filigreed tiles on the front. It's not exactly the Buddhas of Bamyan, but it's impressive, and, importantly, it's still here, unlike the Buddhas, blown up by the Taliban. Somewhere in the citadel (according to some reports, under the actual arch) is a well twenty feet across and 200 feet deep. A stone spiral staircase goes all the way to the bottom, with small anterooms dotted throughout the descent.

Mahmud's progeny couldn't keep the kingdom together and safe from outsiders, and so it came to pass that the Ghorids came and displaced the Ghaznavids, burning Bost in the process in 1151. Things didn't get much better as time went on—Genghis Khan razed Bost to the ground in 1220 and Tamerlane destroyed the irrigation system when he passed through in 1383. A French archaeological expedition

4 See http://photography.nationalgeographic.com/photography/enlarge/qala-e-bost-arch_pod_image. html

uncovered what was left of the city in 1949, but old Bost remained abandoned as the new city of Lashkar Gah was built a little to its north. Given the Russian invasion, the civil war, and the Taliban regime, you'll understand that the opening of the airport bearing the name of Bost was a red-letter day for Helmand, and for Afghanistan.

The provincial administration speaks optimistically of tourism. I can't see it. Not yet. But what the airport has the potential to do is to transport perishable food products—pomegranates, melons, eggs—to both domestic and, eventually, international markets. To make it easier still, USAID is funding the creation of an Agricultural Park right on the perimeter of the airport. The distance from plant to plane is a mere 500 yards.

For now, though, it's hot, very hot. I worry that the tar on the runway, newly laid and steamrollered, will bubble and melt. There are many distinguished guests at the opening, and many media representatives. All they see, as a swan swimming smoothly on a lake, is the plane coming into land and taking off again. They don't see the mangy dog that meanders across the runway on the plane's approach, they don't see the higgledy-piggledy nature of the behind-the-scenes organization. There has to be coordination between the governor's office, the airport, the airline, the Ministry in Kabul, the private company providing ground to air comms, ISAF, the Afghan National Police, and the Crowbar. For some reason a lot of this coordination falls to me, which is why for the first time in my life I have the personal phone number of an airline pilot.

But the whole enterprise is a success: the plane comes in, it leaves. Ambassadors address the gathered travelers and diplomats. The governor addresses the audience; this has been one of his big promises to the public—to open the airport, to put Bost on the map, to get Helmand connected to the rest of the country. Seven pilots have come down on the Ariana (the state airline) flight. All of them are presented with pale green marmoreal gifts, replete with gold lettering. There is much smiling and shaking of hands. They aren't worried about the marble plates and platter exceeding the weight limit. Everybody's happy. I know, though, that I will need to raise the question of the dog on the runway with the airport director and the governor. But I won't do that today, on this red-letter day.

However, my airport drills are over before 09:00. Then my thrice-weekly struggle with Pashto begins. I started this four months ago. I am now only halfway through the alphabet. I may never reach the end.

My next meeting is with the governor's security advisor. Taliban prisoners in Lashkar Gah jail are too dangerous to be placed with the other prisoners. At best they are disruptive, at worst they could cause serious violence. The prison director is caught between a rock and a hard place. We are building a new prison adjacent to the old one. It is almost, but not quite, ready. Though there are lockable cells, it is effectively still a building site. But the prison director has put the Taliban prisoners there. So the contractor, rightly, has stopped working. This means the new build will not be finished. We need to find a solution to remove the prisoners to a more secure location until the new build is ready. I suggest an interim solution. He agrees, but I know we will have to keep an eye on it. Then we drive back to the office. In the heat the little kids are playing in the wider culverts that they've obviously dammed up somewhere to make a pool. In winter the culverts are lined with the sludge that is the color and consistency of mucus. In the summer the palette doesn't change that much, it's merely diluted so that the kids splash in what looks like mephitic lemon barley water. But it's all they have for pleasure, for leisure.

Back in the office: admin. Two forms to fill out because I need to return $27 (due to exchange rate fluctuation) from the funds we paid for a Legal Education Shura last week. Three forms to fill out for single source justification for air conditioning in the room where we established the "Crimestoppers" police hotline, and a project proposal to prepare for the new Helmand Police Training Center. I hate admin.

Then Terry, a big Liverpudlian from our SSR cell, knocks on the door.

"Kate, do we have any money to pay for a boat for the ANP in Nawa?"

"What?"

"A boat. They've just spent $5,000 on a boat. If they use it to move supplies, they don't have to move by road, so it cuts down the IED (improvised explosive device) risk. Everyone's a winner!" Terry grins.

"Sorry, Terry. No can do. We don't have a budget line for 'Boats'." We both laugh. It is a good idea, but it should be something paid by the ANP themselves. Three days later Terry will bring a photo of the boat.

"Terry, how did they spend five grand on that? It's little more than a scooped out tree trunk with an outboard motor!" I say.

"I know, I know!" he says, grinning.

The next thing he tells me is that the officer standing by the captain, smiling with his gun in hand and standing on the sandy river shore, is already dead, shot by the Taliban.

It's high risk being a police officer in Helmand. It's high risk being any public official here. And the mighty arch at Bost bears witness to the fact that it was ever thus.

Election campaign posters

# 17. Election Heat

USUALLY MY SKIN gets a full ten minutes grace before it starts to burn. But not here. Here it's as hot as the first hell you believed in as a child. Biblical hell, except it's not a theological metaphor, it's physically real. Every cell and capillary in my epidermis tells me I'm under attack. If I walk outside it is like walking into a giant furnace—even the wind is hot and brings no relief. The sun assaults any uncovered skin, sabers of raw light stab my neck, scratching small scarlet stars into the white as if a feral cat has clung to me by its claws alone and leaving a prickly heat mark that colors me lobster.

In contrast, the normal pallor of Lashkar Gah pales to a whole new level. This, of course, makes my redness more conspicuous. The overriding hue has been, and is, beige. Before, it always hinted at something else beneath, an undertow of taupe, of mustard, of custard, of sage—browns, yellows, even greens that whispered of water, an aquifer deep beneath, that could confer color. But now at the apex of summer that promise of something more than the beige is gone. Everything is devoid of color, either inherently or because it is covered in dust. Everything is muted and homogenous, the color of moths' wings and bone-ash. The mud walls of the compounds sport great cracks. It's not just that everything is parched as a natural seasonal state, but that it's been a torturous process, that the moisture has somehow been beaten out of everything—every plant, every wall, every road, every animal—against its will.

There is a period of about thirty minutes, around 05:30, which is when the sun is currently rising, that it is tolerable. From my window I watch it peek up behind a satellite dish, the giant fireball momentarily eclipsed by the small metal disc. It hangs as perfectly spherical as a Christmas tree decoration, similarly suspended by an invisible cord, an orange ball bathing in its own reflection of carmine and coral smeared across the silver-blue sky. This carnival of color doesn't last long. As it ascends it loses all pigment so it appears from early morning onwards as a merciless white, flinging down sunbeams strong as planks of wood for the rest of the day.

Sunset is a rather more muted affair. It happens quickly. The husky hues of old women's clothes—mauve, lavender, dove gray—present themselves briefly and then the darkness envelops them all around seven in the evening. But that's not the end. The sun may be gone but its heat persists, not even the night can kill it. The choices you are left with then are: sleep with the AC on solidly through the whole night (noisy, and you're sure to catch a cold); get in and out of bed to turn the AC on and off when it gets too cold/hot (noisy, you're sure to catch a cold, and you don't get to sleep for the required eight hours); or sleep with the window open and no AC (the crickets can be as noisy as the AC, you can wake up completely drenched in sweat).

As usual, the weather is everyone's—whether Afghan or European—favorite topic.

"What's the temperature today?" is the most frequently asked starter-for-ten question, no matter who you are—a VIP visitor or the gardener.

The answer is usually something like: "Well, I saw 44°C on the Post Office door [they are supposed to post morning and afternoon temperatures and issue advisories accordingly on whether we should work out or not], but it feels more like, hmm, 46°C or so." We are all experts, of course, little barometers with fleshy feelers probing the atmosphere.

"Jeez, I was in Bastion last week and it was 59°C! Would you believe it?" says one of our team, a big burly former RUC officer from Belfast. Actually, no I don't, it seems too incredible but, like most urban myths, it's the possibility that it *could* be true that can make it so. Still, 59°C is a lot. That's over halfway to boiling water. If you take a bottle of water out of the fridge and take it with you running, it will be hot—not just baby bottle lukewarm, but toddler bathwater warm—25°C or 30°C—after fifteen minutes. So we keep on watching the mercury rising, that meniscus being pushed up a fraction each day, like the bar in the high jump at the Olympics. The only thing that seems to thrive—animal, mineral, or vegetable—is the king of heliophiles, the sunflower. In our garden there are many, heads cowed towards Hades in the morning, but in the afternoon they stretch their necks, long and graceful as giraffes', heavenward, their fuzzy brown discs with feathery coronas of canary yellow never failing to delight. Previously, the hollyhocks were the tallest flowering garden plant I'd seen here (or anywhere, for that matter). But we have a sunflower that has grown so much it must be breaking across the species barrier. It has become a tree, a sunflower tree. It is about nineteen feet tall, with a long thick green trunk about as wide as a sycamore sapling. And, from about a five feet up there are branches. At the end of each branch (and sub-branch) are the brown discs with yellow fringes.

Most of the civilians wear quick-drying, hi-tech fabrics, or natural ones like cotton or linen. None of my by now impressive *salwar kameez* collection even knows what a natural fiber is. Nylon and plastic are the king and queen of the SK kingdom. Of course, ladies don't perspire, but I cling to the scientific rationale that sweating is a sign of good health, a function of getting rid of toxins through the skin. Or maybe I just imbibe a lot more toxins than most. Anywhere there's a hint of a junction in your body—the crook of the elbow, the back of the knee, the canthus of the eye—it weeps, copiously, while you're meeting in town. Sequins and sweat. Not a winning combination.

It is at outside meetings that the electricity is much more likely to go off, or there is not to be any to begin with. On camp we do get power outages, but only because our big generator cannot cope with our AC demands. It has been belching out dirty black smoke into the shimmering sky for weeks now, its diesel fumes compounding the effects of the suffocating sun. It can't last, and then we will be in exactly the same position as the Afghans.

The Afghans, though, are preoccupied right now with something other than the heat: elections. In fact, maybe it's us who are more pre-occupied. They may well remain passive, stoic. But something is most definitely afoot. Not (as yet) something wicked, but, by the pricking of my thumbs, something sure this way comes.

The posters clinging—I don't quite know how, with the aggressive dust getting everywhere—to concrete blast walls in chicanes, on the blistering mud compound walls, on the baked wood of electricity poles, signal the event. There are no posters of Karzai, or, that I at least can make out, of any of his opponents. The posters are of candidates seeking office in the Provincial Council. It has sixteen members for the whole of Helmand, and at least two of those must be women.

Oddly, it is the poster of the woman that is the biggest of the five or six candidates who have put them up around town. She wears a black veil, but her face is clear, distinct. She has a round face, her skin is cream, almost white, with chocolate eyes. The color of her skin is so starkly white—has the picture been airbrushed? I wonder— that it reminds me of the women I met at a recent shura. Without compunction they valued my white skin (even when patchy red) over their own. They had no hesitation in saying it: "white skin is so much better than ours." They didn't mean politically, which would render the statement true, in the sense that one has so much more advantage in being white, even with a black man in the White House. They meant it aesthetically. This woman's poster is framed in green. There are no slogans on it; it is just her. I wonder which Afghan men put these up for her, and am reminded of the men who put up posters for our own Women's Coalition when we stood for office in Northern Ireland. Family members didn't have much choice, but the other guys did it out of their own free will because they believed in what we were doing. They'd just get teased for not being with a "real" party, or being "under the thumb" or "hiding behind the skirts" of women. Here, it's an entirely different situation. The Taliban are currently engaged in an intimidation campaign. They screwed up their approach to the voter registration process (half of them wanted to ignore the elections completely, half of them wanted to prevent them happening, so they ended up having little effect on the early part of the process), but are much more focused now. They send night letters warning people off from voting; they say if they find a voter ID card they will kill people. The election process itself may be a good thing, but it brings something wicked in its wake which might scupper the effect. In this context, anyone putting up posters is at risk. Anyone putting up posters for women candidates, I'd say, is a safe bet to be even more at risk.

The posters for the other men are all similar: white background, turquoise or green writing under a photo of a bearded man wearing a turban. The "Get Out and Vote" poster from the Independent Election

Commission is a simple pictogram. It's split in half. One side depicts what happens when you vote—a bucolic tableau of neatly combed green fields, houses, schools, and hospitals. The other half illustrates what happens if you don't vote—men with guns, houses on fire, buildings destroyed. But when they are up against the level of Taliban intimidation that exists right now, it will take more than a poster to get people out to vote on election day, 20 August.

Nonetheless, there is campaigning going on. On Fridays in the mosque closest to us, things are definitely more active. Prayers seem to be delivered with more of an edge. And afterwards there are long speeches, the Mullah barely coming up for breath in an hour. His voice is sonorous and has velvet depth. I don't know how he does it in the heat, and at the hottest point in the day too. But he does, and it strikes me as odd that in this country with no cohesive history in terms of a strong central state—only a motley collection of kingdoms, tribes, invaders and invaded—and no real history of democracy, that in the course of eight years the fundamental principle of democracy—the right to vote—should be embraced, even in a very rudimentary fashion, like this.

Helmand River beach at Garmsir

# 18. Here Come the Marines!

IT IS MY FIRST TRIP to Camp Leatherneck, the starter-home of the US Marine Expeditionary Brigade (the MEB) recently arrived in Helmand. So this is what an Obama pronouncement looks like in practice. Leatherneck is being built adjacent to and flush with Camp Bastion. One day it will be bigger than Bastion. I wonder where they're going to get the water from. I assume they'll probably dig deep for it, like Bastion does, so I actually wonder what the impact will be of all that water being drawn away from where it would normally be going. That's not a rhetorical question. I really don't know the answer. I suspect that not many people do.

Whatever these questions, the above-ground picture is stunning. They haven't tamed the desert yet: there isn't enough gravel, so the roads are not even semi-hardened. The raw sand of the desert still survives, spewing up into engines and shoes without discrimination. As we move from Bastion to Leatherneck the jeep starts sliding all over the place, as if we are on soft snow. There's no other way to drive but slowly, especially when there are huge gasoline tankers coming the other way, and no road markings. Several hand-painted signs exhort us to remember that "Safety is everyone's responsibilities." The sand will eventually be forced to retreat, first under gravel and then under tarmac or concrete, but not quite yet. I have a strong sense of being on an enormous building site, of being there at the start of something as yet unformed.

As we get toward our destination we pass 28 (still) white ISO containers, each fitted snugly against the next. They are 28 massive generators, creating electricity to feed the camp. Then we reach what is known as the "Ark," the command center of US operations. It is a huge one-story building with a low slanting roof, made entirely of wood—mostly thin plywood at that. Inside, it is like a half-built house that they've only half-moved into. There are no doors, so you can see into all the empty rooms and those few that have desks and chairs.

Then you'll turn a corner and the juxtaposition of high tech and Wild West hits you: there will be a large flat-screen TV monitor mounted on the wall with a black, glass-fronted box sitting on the floor beside it, both connected by a myriad of wires that run around the wall and into the General's office, out of his office and up to Kabul and Washington via some satellite or other, miles above us, far-flung in the sky. There's a large table in the room. This is the Video Telephone Conference (VTC) room. I go into a tent next door. There are at least a hundred Marines in there, all of them with at least two computers on their desks. It is like a NASA outstation. I've never seen so many computers and so many people crammed into such a limited space before. Soon they will move over into the Ark.

The Commanding Officer (CO) is, I find despite myself, inspirational, motivational. He is square of jaw and broad of shoulder, bull-like, but more intelligent than a bull. He is tight, coiled, wiry, muscled—and very focused. His sandy hair and pale eyes betray some North European ancestry. He exemplifies the "can do" attitude of the US. Even when he uses lines that are the wrong side of corny, in this context they seem absolutely apt: "we're sending you to the edge of empire, that's a very brave thing for you to be doing"; "that's like an elephant wearing a tutu; it's just wrong"; "God, this is our Excalibur moment"; "as Sun Tzu told us, the greatest field general wins a war without fighting"; "we are what we are, we're Marines. Let's embrace that—we are direct." He's a walking movie script. I'm sure people in Hollywood would kill for his ability to speak in hyperbolic, but believable, soundbites. His troops pick up on the quotes and quote Shakespeare back to him in their presentations. He makes them be absolutely sure about targets and goals when they talk about their campaign goals. "OK, so I'm the First Lieutenant down in Khaneshin—what *exactly* are you asking me to do? Talk me through it." Leatherneck he may be, redneck he isn't.

I had no idea why they called the camp "Leatherneck." I envisaged something scrawny and awful, like the neck of an old chicken. But I find out it is the term for the Marines, and the name of their in-house magazine. It comes from the use (and here there is some dispute as to whether it was by British or US Marines) beginning in the late eighteenth century of leather stocks or neck collars. Officers wore collars of black silk or velvet. Soldiers wore collars of stiff black leather, which inhibited their ability to move their necks and thus aim properly. Some say it may have been more about etiquette—improving military bearing, making a civilized man out of the savage soldier. Whatever the case, I like General George Elliot's view shortly after the Civil War that the leather collars made the wearers look "like geese looking for rain." The collar was dropped from Marine uniform in 1872, but the name has stuck fast.

At Leatherneck command and control center the MEB is discussing Operation Khanjari, the US equivalent of the UK's Operation Panchai Palaang. (The translation of "Panchai Palaang" is pretty straightforward: Operation Panther's Claw. Khanjari is Pashto for—approximately—"Big Sword of Righteousness and Truth Coming Through.") When the CO proposed his initial name for the operation, Operation River Liberty, he said that when the Afghans heard the translation he was greeted by a "big yawn." "But when we talked about Khanjari, that got them going," he said. That was also when he talked about the "Excalibur" moment. It is another exemplar of the power (and importance) of language to unify, move, and motivate in a war.

I attend the Rehearsal of Concept (or ROC) drill. It's in a graduated lecture hall the size of half a football field. There are about 200 people there, and it is standing room only at the back. All the brigade commanders sit down at the front and the drill progresses with all the officers laying out plans for the operations on a giant map of the theater—at least twenty feet square—at the front. The map is also projected onto a cinema screen-sized section of the wall. When they start to get into the detail of operations, an electronic simulation is superimposed. Little black trucks symbolizing a convoy move down the road, following every bend. When they talk about air assets going in, you can see the shadow of a helicopter on the fields and convoys beneath and watch its flight path. Then, wizardry: the whole lighting on the slide changes *as the sun comes up*. The shadows become sharper, more distinct, the greens and yellows of the landscape next to the river become lighter, brighter. But even this wow factor can't last long, as I think of von Moltke's maxim that "no battle plan survives first contact with the enemy." Not even this high-tech one. In fact, it might not even

145

get to the enemy, as the sand and the heat could scupper things long before then.

A month after the ROC drill I go to Garmsir, scene of the solar showers, the Wagbags, the horrible cookhouse, and the heat. It's now in the American AO (Area of Operations) and UK Mil have pulled out, though the PRT maintain a Stabilization Adviser (Stabad) and an office embedded with the MEB battle group that's now based there. There are differences: for one, the solar showers have gone—the MEB have mounted bright blue plastic tanks of water above four wooden shower cubicles with proper shower heads. But that's about the only improvement. The washing facilities remain the same—black basins for clothes, faces, and shaving. The Wagbags are replaced by "portable johns." The packaging is different—a friendlier, hygienic mint green on white, with a softer font bearing an excess of exclamation marks in the instructions. There have been improvements, too, in the FCO accommodation. I have my own pod—though it still has an army issue camp bed—with a TV that has hundreds of Indian satellite stations. I will get very sick of adverts for shampoo that prevents hair fallout over the next few days. I will also start to worry about hair fallout every time I comb my hair. No one anywhere is immune to the power of advertising.

I also have in this pod a shower, a real shower. There's a toilet there too, but it's not plumbed in, so is not usable except through the insertion of a Wagbag or portable john. The Armor Group (AG) guys—our security detail—live in tents in a big room next to what used to be the terrible cookhouse. The Americans haven't yet put in their own cookhouse, so the food is really awful. There are four pathetic plastic trays at the serving counter. For breakfast I shake my head as the cover on each one is drawn back until we run out of options, and I go for the dry biscuits. For lunch you have to pick up your ration pack (Meal Ready to Eat—MRE) between 09:00 and 10:00, and then you can eat lunch whenever you want, wherever you want, on the camp. It's this, the lack of hygiene that shocks me most, I think. There is no requirement to wash your hands before eating, there is no requirement to wipe down afterwards with the (in Lash ubiquitous) blue ethanol wipes. There is a distinct lack of alcohol gel. I'm surprised because in the US itself there is such a premium placed on hygiene and cleanliness. This is a D&V nightmare waiting to happen. Georgie, the AG team leader, asks me if it's OK for the lads to use the shower in my pod in the evening. They usually use it while the evening brief is going on, which I'll be at, so it shouldn't be a problem. And so I say: "No problem."

I'm sitting in my pod writing a report around three in the afternoon when a short burly bloke with a shaved head and elaborate multi-colored tattoos of a geisha on one arm and a dragon on the other comes in with a load of Wagbags.

"Hiya! Ahm Chris. Mind if I use your loo?"

"Knock yourself out," I say, expecting him to go straight in. I turn up the TV a bit more. Those plastic doors are very thin. But he stops to talk.

"Yeah, I think these new American portable johns are better than our Wagbags. They're just easier to operate, aren't they?" he says in a north of England accent—an amalgam of Brummie, Liverpudlian, and Mancunian. I can't tell.

"Haven't tried them yet. I'll let you know."

"Awright!"

He goes in to the bathroom for what I think is an inordinately long time. I turn the TV up another notch. Maybe he really has knocked himself out. He comes out.

"Awright!" He stands holding a sealed silver foil bag. There is no question but that it contains his poo. This could be awkward, but, oddly, it's not. I answer: "Awright."

"The food here's awful, isn't it?" He doesn't stop for me to answer. "Ah survive on protein shakes, me."

He doesn't pause for breath as he moves on to the next topic: "Yeah, ah, me and the lads, like, when we're finished our phys [phonetically: fizz—physical training, working out, exercising] we sometimes go for a swim in the river. D'ya fancy it?"

I love to swim. There is such freedom about it. It's the closest we get to flying, the liquid providing buoyancy such as we haven't known since we all swam in the dark uterine waters.

"Hey, that'd be great. What time?"

He says a time.

"I'll pick you up. Funny though, isn't it, us here chatting over me poo, eh?"

There's just no riposte to that, so I simply smile. He walks out with his foil bag, as casual as if it were a packet of chips.

So at the agreed time he picks me up and we clamber over Hesco walls to get out to the river, which is right adjacent to camp, though when you are in the camp there is absolutely no sense of being next to water. All you see are purple-grey stones and dun sand. The blue tanks for the showers are the most colorful things on base. I'm outside the wire! With no body armor! I am giddy at the thought of it. And the river beckons below, its sweet, salt-free water flowing fast down to the Iranian border.

The Helmand River originates near Kabul, at the foot of the Hindu Kush, which feeds it year round with snow melt. It courses firmly southwest for almost all of its length, just over 715 miles. (That is longer than the UK, from Scotland to the Channel, which is about 645 miles). All along its banks there is a literal "green zone," a sharp and defiant emerald-green ribbon cutting into the sand. Around Lash, and towns above and below it, there is the irrigation system that extends the green reach farther than it goes naturally. Farmers depend on it, irrespective of what they are growing. It is the very lifeblood of the province, the water rushing through the desert like ichor in the very veins of the gods. Even in August things are green. Etiolated maybe—sage as opposed to emerald—but firmly green nonetheless.

As we make our way down the steep sandy bank, stepping carefully over the coils of barbed razor wire, which extends into the river itself, it is like stepping back in time and place, to the sandy dunes of Gyles' Quay and Shelling Hill on the east coast of Ireland, when I was a kid. The white sand and pale and sharp-bladed littoral grasses are the same; as are the roots of shrubs that we used as ropes to lower and raise ourselves over particularly steep parts as children going to the seaside.

But the water is different. It is chalky jade-green. It is so clean and fresh that it tastes almost sweet. The current is very strong, and I am a little bit afraid. I recall that a UK Mil translator was swept away somewhere upstream only a few days previously. UK Mil swept the area with thermal imaging devices, but there was no trace. Looking at the sheer volume of liquid racing to my left, to Iran, I understand that once you lose control in that flow there is no coming back. There will be no swimming parallel to the shore, like in the Irish Sea. And, like many inland lakes and rivers, its treachery, thinly concealed under its beauty and the seductive freedom it offers—especially here, from the heat, from the drudgery of life—comes from its uneven bottom. One step and you are in up to your waist. The next step and you are in over your head. But I am in good hands. I go in wearing my T-shirt and three-quarter length trousers and sandals. I must be the only woman who's been in that particular part of the Helmand River for many years. I immediately attract the attention of about six or seven young boys who've been splashing about in the water. They hover around me like cleaner fish around a whale.

Chris guides me out. We can walk perpendicular to the current, through it, for about twenty feet, and then we are into a more slowly flowing part protected by a sandbank. The absence of salt means the water is much harder to swim in—there's hardly anything holding you up—but I love it. It is cool and refreshing and wonderful. When I put my head down in the water I can still see, even though the speed of the current churns up fine grains of sand making it milky.

We decamp—Chris and Mick and I—to still, deep water in front of a sandbank. We sit, submerged in the water. We have shaken off the troupe of young boys for whom I was obviously a novelty. One of them handed me the carcass of a decapitated carp, likely done where the barbed wire encroached the water. Disappointingly for him I wasn't scared, and lack of reaction meant he gave up and left. Mick says convincingly that carp only breed in water that is really clean. I am easily convinced. Even though there's so much that gets chucked into the river, the quick current cleans it. That's what I'm telling myself anyway.

We talk about what security guys do when they aren't working in Afghanistan or Iraq. There is a story they've both just read wherein two AG guys in Iraq got drunk, got into a gunfight with each other, shots were exchanged, and they ended up killing an Iraqi policeman who tried to break up the fight. "If either of them survives," says Chris, "they'll have to face an Iraqi court. It'll be the death penalty. Wouldn't fancy that."

Mick has worked on cruise ships from Port Canaveral to Nassau. "That must have been a cushy number," I venture.

"Nah, in four months I dealt with attempted murders, attempted suicides, under-age kids getting drunk, rape, gangs from New York trying to rob the casinos," he answers flatly.

For the latter the FBI provided photo-fit images, Mick says, "just like they did in Ireland," and I am reminded yet again that most AG guys are ex-army and that they all served in Northern Ireland. We probably came across each other at checkpoints, on different sides and with different attitudes then.

It feels almost like we're in an outdoor spa, which gives Chris license to soliloquize on his favorite spa treatment—Elemis Lemon and Coconut Body Wrap—"yi've got to relax when you get ourra here, Kate." Apparently Elemis is a really expensive brand. I'm the only girl in the water and I have never heard of it. The two bulky, heavily tattooed personal bodyguards use it all the time. And they extol the virtues of hot stone massages, which I've never had either. The little carp (the ones with heads, smart enough to avoid the razor wire) begin to nip at our ankles and back as we wallow and we head back to the opposite bank. This time you just sit in the current and, like a fairground ride, it propels you along at high speed. The trick is knowing how and when to get off. I don't want to end up in Iran in a wet T-shirt and trousers without hijab. But neither do I particularly want to get out at the place we got in, as it's now occupied by about twenty police officers, come off duty. I am conscious they are all staring, but I have no choice about where I embark on the bank and just hope that Chris and Mike aren't too far away. I put my head down and the three of us walk up, very determinedly, in silence, through the channel of green-gray police uniforms, black floppy hair, and mouths agape.

That evening the shower line starts around seven. Chris knocks. Shack knocks. Mick knocks. Somebody I don't know knocks. They shower, and leave. The next day I'm sitting in my room around three when Chris comes in again, clutching his army green Wagbag.

"God, the Americans have run out of portable johns. We have to go back to using these Brit ones. And can you believe that here we are again sitting here talking about poo, like?"

It's true, it is marginally odd especially as I have just met him the day before. I can only conclude, however, that a diet of protein shakes makes you as regular as clockwork and that here the desert and the circumstances of war are great levelers of social boundaries.

Ospreys hover over Lashkar Gah

# 19. The Helical Screws

MECHANIZED FLIGHT began a long time ago. Icarus didn't do so well, but in the fourth or fifth century AD the Chinese had a toy with a rotating top, arguably the prototype for the aerial screw design that Leonardo da Vinci pioneered in the late fifteenth century. Yes, said Leonardo, if you had a helical screw that was well made of starched linen, then it "should, upon being turned sharply, rise into the air in a spiral." (Note Leonardo's use of the conditional tense.) He also suggested that if anyone ever built his design they really should test it over water. It is a pity that the design needed to wait until the Industrial Revolution and the invention of the engine before his precociously prescient thinking took flight for real. Around 450 years later (in 1907) the first helicopter flight—for around twenty seconds and reaching the heady altitude of twelve inches—took place. A year later a young Russian boy went on a trip to Germany with his father where he learned about the Wright Brothers' aircraft. Originally set to be an engineer, this young Igor Sikorsky decided there and then to dedicate his life to aviation. Emigrating to the US in the wake of the Bolshevik Revolution, he established an aviation company in New York, designing and testing aircraft, applying and amending patents. Twenty years later, in 1940, the aircraft that became the world's first mass-produced helicopter flew in free flight format for the first time.

The big thing about helicopters is that they can do vertical take-off or landing (VTOL) and have rotor (as opposed to fixed) wings or blades. And the reason they need to be able to do this is for rescue or recovery, on land or at sea, in inaccessible places. They are thus perfect for the inaccessibility of Helmand and its conditions—except for the dust, the sand, the heat (the Sea Kings can take five passengers in the summer, twelve in the winter), the number of service hours that they do (VTOL takes it out of them), the number of times that they "go U-S" (unserviceable formally, "tits up" in the military vernacular), and the number of times that they just don't start. (Or the number of times that your helicopter is raring to go, but the other one in the pair is U-S. Or, even worse, the number of times your helicopter is ready to go, the pair is also good, but there is no AH (attack helicopter) to provide top cover.)

Even so, with the advent of the Marines I get to sample the fruits of Mr. Sikorsky's labors. The contract to supply the S (for Sikorsky)-65 heavy lift helicopter was won by Sikorsky in 1962. The military flight controllers (buzzards) post it on their whiteboards as the CH53. We know it as the Sea Stallion, and it seems to us that we often get the very first birds that were produced, way back in the 1960s.

The very first time I got one was in the summer, when Garmsir was in the UK AO (Area of Operations) but transitioning to become a US AO. In those days there might be one flight in and out per week, and Derek and I had already been there for four days—two days longer than we'd expected. Also in those days there were no comms between UK and US flight controllers. The only notice the buzzards would get when a US bird was coming in was the five minutes out warning when the pilot was within range of the ground to air radio. So, when Tank (he is the same size as one), the UK buzzard, yelled at us that there was a US bird coming in (we didn't know where it was going, but we were getting on nonetheless) we ran to the pods, packed, and presented ourselves at the HLS just as the purple plume of the signal flare dropped, a contrast with the dusty gray of the HLS. Then we practically leapt, gazelle-like, over the smooth beach stones of the HLS to enter the metal bird. We didn't think about its age, much in evidence by the fact of its very faded livery on which was painted a big US Marine Corps Star like a postmark on a much traveled postcard. No, we rushed right up to the back end of the bird, like we were the stuffing going into an eviscerated turkey. We just wanted to get out.

We were the only two on board. There's room for 26 or 28 people, but right then there was only the crew and us two. We were so delighted to get out of Garmsir that we indulged in a little helo tourism, taking pictures of us and the crew. Then we looked up. Whereas in the UK airframes there is always some element of mystery about the mechanics of it all, in the Sea Stallion everything is out there, in your face, including in this particular chopper the main rotor hub. It's a small disc of yellow plastic, about the size of a saucer, and it spins and undulates about an inch at the same time: whirring round and round and up and down at great speed, a crazed carousel that holds together the six spinning blades that are over thirty feet long. That's the helical screw Leonardo was referring to when he penned the designs in 1493. That's what will be lifting us up. Instead of well-starched linen we have a body of metal that weighs ten tons when it's empty. That also has to be lifted. And that's what, miraculously, happens: we take off, lifted vertically into the air before swinging around and heading off to Bastion (not where we wanted to end up, but a better place to be for getting into Lash than Garmsir).

We both make the rookie mistake: we sit under the drip. Actually there's not much avoiding the drip, as the whole of the inside of the bird seems to leach lubricant. The plastic piping above us glistens with oil. A nipple of tea-colored liquid is momentarily yet perpetually suspended from the yellow plastic hub of the main rotor before plopping onto the floor. Derek's trousers are ruined. The crew tells us that we should be worried when we don't get hit by the drip—it means that the bird isn't well lubricated, and that's not good.

So I always look out for the drip on the Sea Stallions, hoping it's there but also hoping that I can avoid its direct benison. Yet even when there is a drip, sometimes it feels as if there might be something missing, such as horsepower. When the Sea Stallions lift with a heavy load, it can feel a bit touch-and-go. Consider driving a secondhand car really fast for the first time. You get to a certain speed and the whole thing—the chassis, the engine, the frame itself, the windows—all start to vibrate. You press your pedal to the floor thinking that the metal will have turned to paper and the pedal will touch the tar. But it doesn't—the car keeps going, so smoothly now that you can confidently soar up into fifth gear. (I realize that this will make no sense to anyone who doesn't drive a stick shift, or secondhand cars.)

This kind of thrust and soar doesn't quite work with helicopters. Once, when we had a lot of election materials on board, the old Sea Stallion I was on had a little difficulty. We did the vertical lift off all right, but when we tried to gain altitude gravity was giving us a hard time and it was like trying to drive that car through the invisible barrier. It chugged on, but we weren't really going anywhere. The whole downward thrust and resultant upward lift equation didn't seem to be applicable, even though it was in harmony with the laws of physics. Then it got to be like moving from the car to a bike, cycling uphill at an ever increasing gradient: first you just pull a bit more on the handlebars, then you shift through all 24 gears to get the most length out of the chain. Then you stand up, pressing your whole weight on the pedals, but the gradient gets too much and you lose balance as you cannot pedal fast enough to keep upright. You have to get off and walk: the mountain has defeated you. Except there's no getting out and pushing the bike when you are three hundred feet in mid-air. All you can do, all you can think, all I did think is, "Please let it be quick," if I, like Icarus, am fated to fall to earth.

Of all the things we do, then, the highest risk venture is not the Taliban, or IED strikes, or SIEDs (suicide improvised explosive devices) or even, as has been attempted recently, DIEDs (donkey-borne improvised explosive devices). No, the biggest risk is flight. Actual real, elevated, in the air flight, as opposed to flight from the scene of a crime, or an exploding donkey, say. The biggest risk we face is flying in these wondrous mechanical birds.

As well as Mr. Sikorsky's Sea Stallion there's also the Chinook. I had always associated this with the UK, partly because before the Marines arrived in theater there was no other choice but the RAF Chinooks and partly because Chinooks were something I have associated with the British Armed Forces flying in front of my home as far back as I can remember. So I was mildly surprised to learn that it is originally a US-designed and produced aircraft, and that it is named after the Chinook people of the Pacific Northwest, the Indian people who live by the Columbia River, or the dry hot wind that comes down through the Rocky Mountains. (I haven't been able to establish definitively which—Wikipedia can sometimes only take you so far. There are times when you need real books.)

Whatever its etymology, it is truly a thing of beauty, those two big rotors at either end of its lozenge body delicately and deftly defying contact with each other. I've been there, at Kandahar, where the

British Chinooks go to sleep, just when they are just waking up. The giant metal insects yawn open and shake down their massive double-proboscis, revolving them, first one, then the other, first slowly so that the eye can still see all four separate blades, and then none, like the blur of a hummingbird's wings. Usually they fly in pairs, and when there is only one HLS at a particular location—like at one of the FOBs—only one can land at a time. When that happens, the second craft will hover, stationary in the air, gripping at nothing but magically floating in the emptiness over the great barren desert. The rear gunner, attached to the frame by nothing more than a bit of rope that looks as if it couldn't bear the weight of a small child never mind a fully grown man, sits casually looking out of the ribcage where we are all squashed, his calves and feet dangling over the edge with nothing but a mile of verti-cal air between him and the desert floor. I prefer it when we start to move again—and move we do. It is too easy to lose perspective on the speed of helicopters: Chinooks and Sea Stallions can move with a top speed of around 196 mph. When the pilots plan to have fun at that speed—simultaneous forward and sideways thrust, so we are like a roller coaster that has left the tracks—the rush of the ride is fantastic, and combined with the view (if I get one) exhilarating. You wouldn't think it, but the Chinooks can execute particularly graceful airborne aerobics at high speed, and I still feel safe when they do so.

But if they don't plan the fun, then it's a different story. I've been in a Sea King when the pilot has had to do the equivalent of a hand brake stop and avoidance turn mid-air. We jerked violently to the side, so that instead of being level with those on the seat opposite I was right above them, their new, writhing ceiling. I then (I regret to report) yelped and grabbed Zac's leg. I'm not sure if he was more frightened by the speed and strength at which my hand clawed his leg, or the helo's histrionics. In any event, we recovered quickly and set on our way.

On a trip to Nawa (that I didn't go on), the second chopper of the pair, an old USMC Sea Stallion, started the lift off, but for some reason began to swing out of control. I saw the video footage later. It was as if there was no power at all going to the top rotor—all the thrust was coming from the tail rotor—so the bird was spun slowly round, like a toddler might twirl a toy chopper by its tail, with the nose falling steeply toward the ground. Helos can turn through 360 degrees several times on landing and take off, and some of my colleagues on the bird just thought it was a new maneuver. Others, though, who sat opposite the door, saw the Roshan telecommunications tower—a white and red metal transmitter rising to a hundred feet—come rushing towards them at a speed that was never intended. Only the skill of the pilot got them out of the tail spin, to regain enough control for what is euphemistically termed a "hard landing." This can be anything from a bit of a bump to a full on crash.

At evening brief one night one of the battle group liaison officers (BGLO) reported that a helicopter they were using for a special mission had sustained a hard landing. The brigadier nodded.

"Was it able to get back in the air?" he enquired coolly.

The BGLO shook his head.

"Not yet, sir. We will assess tomorrow at first light and determine what is recoverable."

"Fair enough, carry on."

"Sir, yes, sir." (They really do say that.)

The next evening the BGLO reported on the hard landing again.

"Went to assess damage, sir. All comms and other equipment recovered successfully, sir. The airframe itself was assessed to be too far gone to remove, sir. We then denied the airframe, sir," he said in short staccato sentences.

The brigadier looked at him, his eyes widening perceptibly.

"You mean you blew it up," he said slowly.

"Affirmative, sir."

The brigadier raised his eyebrows and tutted. Everyone else laughed at the linguistic dexterity and energy expended in not calling a spade a spade.

The other thing about helicopters is the price. The Chinook comes in around $15 million each, the Sea Stallion a cool $25 million. They'd just blown up $15 million worth of kit.

These prices pale into insignificance compared to the coolest-looking chopper of all, the Osprey. Ospreys are the new kids on the block, having just recently arrived in theater. They'd been in development for defense production until 2005. The first ones were delivered and saw active operations in 2007. They cost $70 million each, plus approximately $27 billion spent on the development program.

They are true hybrids—the gryphons of the aviation world, with their mid-air metamorphosis between airplane and helicopter, fixed wing and rotor wing. They have a clean sturdy carriage that takes around 24 pax (passengers), narrower than the Chinook or the Sea Stallion, so although there is no oil dripping anywhere it is a little more squashed. They do vertical take off and landing—at amazing speed—with two rotors perpendicular to the ground on landing: either side and at the end of a small fixed wing, squat and black against the clean gray livery of the carriage. Then, when it gets up into the air, the rotors rotate from ninety degrees to one hundred and eighty, continuing to oscillate all the while, so they are parallel to the ground and the helicopter takes on the aspect of a small plane. I've only ever traveled in one once. Inside it is pretty standard, just a lot newer than the other helicopters we fly in, but it is truly impressive watching it then come in to land, like a massive gray swan with wings outstretched and then smoothly folded up, and finishing off with a vertical float to the ground. The downdraft is the heaviest of all the helicopters—roofs need to be battened down, literally, when they come in to land. You need to face the Hesco (preferably holding on to it) and shut your eyes tight, as the draft can easily knock you off your feet. Even the military guys, normally immune to such events, were up on the Hesco taking photos when the Ospreys began to come into Lash. Two of them coming into land will still get some attention—$140 million worth of synchronized swans slicing through the air without ruffling a feather.

But what makes you forget about all the risk and everything that could possibly go wrong is the view. Whether down the river delta to Nawa, up the Sangin Valley across to Bastion, up to Gereshk, over to Nad Ali or down to Garmsir, the view, different on each trip, is stunningly spectacular, in winter or summer. Once, the Merlin crew let me stand up front with the pilots, so I could look out of the windshield. The co-pilot, an Australian woman, was doing the flying (there are more women pilots around than you might think). The cabin is tiny, as cramped as an old Mini, rushing along the scalp of the desert, here and there scraped away to reveal the brown soil irrigated by canals from the Helmand. On the way up to Sangin there are the gray depressed scars of long dead tributaries of the Helmand, and huge sand dunes.

Dotted in between the dunes are Kuchi settlements. The Kuchis are like the Bedouin of Afghanistan; a nomadic or semi-nomadic people, they wander around with their camels and hairy black sheep and live off virtually nothing in the desert. In the time of the Kings they had grazing rights on the great grasslands of the north, and would undertake an annual migration to follow the pastures. Traditionally they were skilled in skinning and slaughtering sheep, and traded these with the settled communities. But there is no grass around the settlements I see from on high. They eke out survival nonetheless—more and more of them are understanding that the wool of their fat-tailed sheep can be combed to create a product, karakul, or astrakhan, that is both expensive and desirable in the rest of the world. They have tents made out of camel skin, and no running water or electricity. It is a brutal existence, and yet relative to the rest of Afghanistan it is more liberal in some ways: I have heard that the Kuchi women rarely wear hijab, for example, but I will never be able to drop out of the helicopter to find out for myself, for helicopters mean another thing: distance, if not alienation.

Coming in to land

160

Whether it is the gravity-defying bulk of the Sea Stallion or Chinook, the sleek lines and prancing dexterity of the Merlin or Blackhawk, or the cartoon audacity of the Ospreys, the helicopters are truly incredible flying machines that connect us to our work and the Afghan government to its people, and in so commuting we get to see astounding panoramas of tough terrain that we simply couldn't traverse without the principle of the helical screw. Thank you, Leonardo. And thank you, Mr. Sikorsky.

Men's polling station, Lashkar Gah

# 20. Election Day (I): Early Morning

IT IS THE NIGHT BEFORE the election. We, everybody, are expecting something to happen. Five days previously there had been an SIED (suicide improvised explosive device) detonated about two miles away. It was a bungled job, rushed, in response to reports that Hamid Karzai was going to be in town. Only the driver himself died, and for him there was only ever going to be one outcome. So he can take the win, but so can we, for there were no other casualties. We were just finishing dinner when we heard him blow himself up. The bang at the center cracked the sky, shifting and separating the air at speed, like cymbals parting and clashing. There is a corona of softer, but strong sound that makes its way to us. It sounds closer than it is—explosions always do—except perhaps if you are at its epicenter. I think it's the Police Headquarters, which is right next to our camp. We finish dinner and go inside. About half an hour later there are two further explosions, their sound smudged by the soft warm breeze that runs along the red ribbon of sunset—mortars. Then gunfire, the sharp bleat of a general purpose machine gun; the single shot spit of pistols or rifles. Even though in our compound we are secure it is the small arms fire that grips my heart most, twisting it in a torque of apprehension. The next day a senior officer tells me that the gunfire was the Afghan National Army simply unloading bullets at the roasted carcass of the SIED's car.

"F**king idiots!" he says, "waste of munitions." He's right, but I can see how they'd want to react like this. It was their compound the SIED was trying to attack, them he wanted to fell. That was last week, but it didn't cause the major disruption and loss of life that the Taliban wanted. And we know that they want to disrupt the elections. They have been intimidating people for weeks. Threatening that people who are found with voter registration cards will be shot, sending night letters (you wake up in the morning to find them nailed to your gate or the wall of your compound) saying the same thing, fining farmers whose cows have inadvertently stepped on a carefully laid IED (even insurgents flush with opium money have limits on resources), threatening that those who are found with indelible ink on their index finger (this is used to mark the individual as having voted) will have that finger cut off. They don't want this election to happen at all, which is why the night before they are pulling out all the stops.

We go to dress state Amber around 20:30. This means body armor to be with us at all times and worn when we are outside hardened accommodation. Helmets are to be carried. Twenty minutes later we go up to dress state Red: body armor and helmets to be worn at all times, inside and out. So I sit and watch *The Wire* with all accoutrements attached. I am quite sure that I must look really stupid, but at least there's no one else around to see, except McNulty and the gang on my computer screen. Half an hour later we are back to dress state Green, which is our normal state—body armor and helmet at accommodation or office, easily accessible. I go to bed early, for tomorrow I am to be an EU Short Term Observer of the elections. This means, security permitting, I will be able to go out and witness the essence of democracy, from which all else is derived: the vote.

I am awakened, however, at one thirty in the morning by the sound of small arms fire. Again that bleating scratching the air. General purpose machine gun, and pops: flares probably. There are small blasts, missiles hitting the dust. This time it's discernibly closer, and I can feel that it's a two-way conversation, a vituperative volley, not just shooting up a dead car in anger or relief. I am not afraid in the sense that I fear for my personal physical safety—I don't—but it signals a potential threat to personal safety that my body does not ignore. My heart thumps loudly in my chest and the moisture retreats from my mouth. I need some water. This happens three or four times in the night, lasts for between ten and twenty minutes each time, the latest at around 04:00. I get up at 06:00, ready to go out and observe the polls opening at 07:00. I am wearing a new outfit which Ahmed, one of our interpreters, brought from Kabul for me on his last leave. It is Empire-line cut, black with a crimson and white embroidery breastplate, cuffs, and a similar frieze around the full skirt and the ankles of the full trousers. Unlike the outfits I get down here, in the deep south, it is cotton, which will be great for the day when I have to wear body armor all the time I am out (normally I take it off once we get inside). But best of all (even better than it being made of natural, breathable fiber) is that there is not one sequin anywhere in sight. It is indeed a special outfit for a special day.

Ballot paper, general election

We set off in four separate convoys of three cars each to different polling centers. As at home, polling centers are mainly in schools but here are strictly gender segregated. As there are boys' and girls' schools co-located (but generally separated by a wall) so there are men's and women's polling stations. We arrive at our first polling station around 07:10. The two ballot boxes in each venue are like giant Tupperware containers, opaque white plastic with gray lids. On the front of each is a label—one in orange, one in green—which correlates with the color of the ballots—one orange, one green—which in turn correlates with the two elections: one for the Provincial Council (orange) and one for the Presidency (green). The ballots are big, but perfectly clear. To reflect literacy levels, all the candidates' photos are on them, as well as their name and a small black and white symbol. The symbols are like those on a slot machine on a seaside pier: three cherries, an apple, three coins. But there are others: a water pump, a canal, three umbrellas. (I have to confess, I had no idea what that was intended to mean. In a country where it rains maybe thirty days a year umbrellas are not going to garner votes. Caroline, my observer buddy on this run, politely points out that they can be used to keep off the sun. Ah.) But the point is that for such large fields (over fifty candidates for one President) and probably seventy odd for fifteen Provincial Council places, the ballots are exceedingly well designed—a simple synthesis of complex information using color, text, and visual images. Literate and illiterate alike can fill them in easily.

Although we arrive after the poll should have started and things are set up, the stations haven't yet opened. This is not uncommon in the Balkans either, nor sometimes in Northern Ireland, and is a very minor irregularity. The most amazing thing is that there are people—women (Caroline and I have come over to the women's side)—lined up to vote. There are about fifteen of them (though it is a little hard to tell, as there are also lots of women staff milling around—about four per polling station, in two adjacent and one contra-corridor classrooms). We have also left our translator behind with the men (we share one per convoy) so we have to get by on my scant Pashto until the woman we are surely perplexing with our fixed smiles shouts: *Arifa, delta rasa!* This I know means "Arifa, come here!", and further that Arifa is likely to be able to converse with us in English. She does so brilliantly. She is about four-teen, wears a neat black hijab over a round face with smooth- skinned, slightly pudgy cheeks and dark eyes. We are so welcome here, she is very pleased to meet us, she is very happy we have come to see their work, this is the polling center manager, if you have any questions we are more than happy to answer them. She loves my Afghan clothes. I explain that I got the outfit in Kabul and that it is having its first outing today. Other women feel the fabric, stroke the broad band of embroidery on the cuffs. I say how much I like their clothes. Burqas cast in a heap in the corner, or carried casually in the crook of the arm, their clothes are as usual bright and cheerful.

Voting at women's polling station, Lashkar Gah

Arifa explains that the set-up is all ready, they are just waiting for the overall station supervisor to say the word. He comes in, right on cue, a tall figure in long white *salwar kameez*, no trousers, just sandals on tanned legs. He has a white beard on his wizened face and wears a white turban. Somehow he appears as an ancient angel bearing commandments from above: "the polling station is now open," he declares, before pirouetting on one foot and heading off to the men's center. I look at the women lined up to vote. It is about 07:25. Then "BOOM!" there is an explosion, we don't know where, but it is quite loud. I fancy I feel the building shudder, but that might have just been the adrenalin streaking through me. Our IBGs (Individual Body Guards) spin across to us immediately: "Helmets on. Stay away from the windows." We're in the corridor and there aren't any windows, but I don't argue. Whatever they say right now, I do, no questions. I don't know what to do with my clipboard (*the* key item for any self-respecting election observer or tally agent) or my notebook. They fall to the floor as my fingers scramble to unclip my helmet and stick it on my head, over my hijab. The women waiting in line giggle at our ineptitude and my ridiculous helmet-on-hijab look. Then they apologize to us for the explosion, as if they are somehow bad hosts because of it. The upside to the blast is that we get to stay longer on that site. Because of security we will only be on each site for half an hour every time, but now we must "stay firm." It gives us time to ask Arifa about whether or not she thinks lots of women will vote today. In Garmsir where I'd been a week before the local Chief of Police told me he expected there to be "zero participation" from women.

Arifa says, "Some women will not come because their husbands won't let them. It is bad. But they should. They should come and vote for their future."

At that we are given the all clear. We must get back to base. We will find out more about the blast there, and see if we will be allowed out again. On the way back we pass walls and electricity poles crammed with election posters. Women buy circles of flat bread. Men squat behind stacks of pale green watermelon. Life goes on.

I get out of the car at the base and meet Greville, the Deputy Commander.

"Are you all right?" he asks.

"Sure," I say, thinking he just meant that we'd been out when the IED went off.

"It wasn't your car, then? We thought it was you."

It turns out that the explosion was a rocket that went off under one of the other three-car convoys. I go to look at the car. The frame is intact, but the back doors are buckled a bit and full of shrapnel. There is no broken glass, though. Ben, another colleague and, like myself and Caroline, an election observer, was in the car. He described it thus: "like a pop under my bottom. Then the AG driver said 'Err, I think that might have been us'—as the dust and smoke began to fill the car. The driver revved up and we sped off. 'Contact! Contact! We are mobile, repeat we are mobile!' You know they have their own language."

The armor plating in the B6 showed it was worth every penny of the £80,000 it cost. It did exactly what it is supposed to do: protect the passengers from mines. The rear brakes were rendered inoperable, but the car was able to be driven back to base. We arrived about ten minutes after them. It wasn't even 08:00 and we were already one car down. But everyone was OK, and there were people lining up to vote.

The Taliban strategy was to attack early, first with the gun fights at night to incite panic and fear, and then with early morning blasts to try and intimidate, to get people not to come out to vote. Our security analysis was that the later in the day it became, the less likely they would be to attack. The information war is just as important—if not more so—as the physical one. The Taliban depend on winning hearts and minds almost (but not quite) as much as we do. They won't want to risk mass slaughter at a polling station where there are no ISAF forces (and there weren't—the security cordon on the ground was provided exclusively by Afghan police and army). But that was the decision that now had to be made: was that it? Would they really back off? Would we be allowed out again, and if so, would we want to go?

The Karzai team, polling station, Lashkar Gah

# 21. Election Day (II): Late Morning, Afternoon

THE DECISION IS MADE. We are allowed to go out, if we want to. I want to. The sight of people lined up to vote in the early morning, without IBGs, armored cars, or Kevlar, is humbling. It's why we're here. We need to support this process, to be able to provide independent evidence that the process was administered by Afghans and it worked. Of course, if it didn't work we'd report on that too, but from the little I'd seen earlier I was fairly sure that the process would work if there were no further external interventions—like IEDs or small arms fire. So even though I am nervous I decide to go out. It is the right thing to do. I walk up the corridor and meet a couple of young Britmil guys. This is what it must be like for them every time they go out—the real possibility of "contact." It's always been there theoretically for me before, but this is the most real it's been.

We approach the second polling station of the day. It's 10:00. The ANP ushers us in. The road is barricaded off with a few pathetic-looking school chairs and some bricks. There's no Hesco here, but it works. There are four women striding purposefully, their burqas quivering with the forward momentum, towards the gate. On top of the gate is an Afghan National Army (ANA) guy with a mounted machine gun, with another ANA guy on top of the school building. It reminds me of my graduation ceremony in Belfast, when police snipers adorned all of the university buildings around us as we ate strawberries and cream in the Quad at Queen's.

Again Caroline and I go to the women's stations first, a different school from our earlier event-filled trip. Again, I am amazed. The place is buzzing with women, voters with Wedgwood Blue burqas thrown back off their faces revealing bright fabrics in all colors in all sorts of floral permutations. I wonder if they have chosen them specially for election day. We are observing so are not supposed to ask them. Anyway, my Pashto doesn't extend to that. Thankfully, we are rescued by another fantastic young woman—aged about twelve or thirteen—who speaks fast and brilliant English in a brittle patter. Razia has learned it here in Lashkar Gah, only started about five years ago and practices by speaking with her father. She wears a black hijab with turquoise flowers that is wrapped around her to her knee, over black trousers. She is like a petite, living mummy. Her confidence is overwhelming. She exhorts her friends at the other stations to come and talk to us. They do so, but more hesitatingly than she does. When we are leaving she even has her photo taken with Brian, our IBG, and she shakes his hand. I've never seen that before. Brian, with his strawberry blond hair and beard, brown baseball cap, and semi-automatic machine gun, says that he's never been approached, never mind spoken to, by any Afghan woman before. But by the end of today three of them will have said hello to him, in English. It is a day of revelation indeed.

The polling staff personnel know their job. The hole-punch doesn't work. It's too stiff to penetrate the laminated plastic of the voter registration card, so the women improvise by cutting off the corner of the card. Voter registration ID numbers are meticulously recorded in neat Arabic font in the ledgers—we can tell exactly how many people have voted at any one time. The booths are three-sided cubicles of corrugated cardboard. I ask if it is OK to take photographs. I need to ask them individually, to give them time if they want to veil their faces. I show them the digital still afterwards so they are not alarmed. The only woman whose face is never visible wears her red and yellow hijab in a mask-like manner, wrapped over her nose and mouth. Even her eyes, peering through a slit in the fabric, are hard to see as she wears a blue FEFA (the official Afghan election observer mission—Free and Fair Election Foundation Afghanistan) pulled low over her forehead. For all that she is slight, she looks a little menacing. The polling station supervisor is no such shrinking violet, however. A solid and stout-hearted woman swathed in a cyan and cinnamon *salwar kameez* with matching hijab, she demands to have her photo taken, and cajoles her shyer friend into standing in with her. When I show it to her she grins, one gold tooth among the white catching the sun.

"Great. Welcome. Thanks," she beams. Caroline tells me later that because she's a polling station official she will have ink all over all of her fingers by the end of the day. Someone asks her if she is worried about the Taliban threat of a more than malicious manicure. She is most dismissive. "But I don't care! Let the Taliban come. I don't care about them, bullies! I'm going to drive from Lashkar Gah to Kabul in two days' time, let's see what they do!"

The sheer spirit of these women is deeply affecting. It is a privilege to be in proximity to it. We walk across to the men's building, through a small door in the wall. This is one day when we actually have more freedom of movement than our male counterparts—we can go to both male and female centers, whereas the men can only go to the men's.

We go up the steps to the men's center. We are greeted again with broad smiles and cries of "welcome," "come in," "come see!" But then our half-hour is up. We are back to base, without incident this time.

We go out again just after 13:00, but at the polling station not much is happening, except lunch. In the women's center the doors are closed and all the staff are eating or drinking tea. I speak with one young man, a clean-shaven authorized agent of Karzai, his accreditation emblazoned across his chest embalmed in a plastic cover. His rather hapless sidekick (with a scraggly beard and a toothy grin with a few gaps) points to the metal badge pinned to his shirt sporting Karzai's picture. He also has a baseball hat with Karzai's portrait on the front, which he rather nervously puts on and takes off as if he is not used to the convenience of headdress that isn't a turban. His more confident friend explains: "There are no people here now to vote. They will be at lunch and prayer. They'll be sleeping now. They will come back at two, or two-thirty. You won't see anything here now." It's not exactly in the Constitution that polling stations are de facto closed at lunch, but it is the culturally accepted thing to do. No one objects. Democracy may be based on consent after all, but in practice where lunch is concerned culture is king here. I ask him what he thinks of the day so far.

"Well, the gunfire last night, that was meant to cause a general panic in the people. To prevent them voting. And people were afraid. And the bombs this morning—security wasn't good then. But it's much better now. People see that others are voting, so they come out too."

He's right. I remember how scared I was on hearing the bullets fly the previous evening. If I wasn't protected by body armor, if I was just flimsy flesh and warm blood and brittle bone, I'm not sure that I would come out to vote. So there is bravery here, but it is not bravado: the atmosphere is genuinely less tense than it was on poll-opening. The process is gaining in confidence as the day draws on.

We go back to the men's center. I walk down the long corridor of the schoolhouse. There are three ANP officers in one of the rooms, one of whom is doing exactly what the young Karzai supporter suggested: sleeping. In the men's center the torpor of lunch has also set in. There are lots of men milling around in the corridor. Across one doorframe is a small bench. We look inside. The polling station staff are sitting on the ground in a circle, eating. We go up to the other end of the school. Our presence attracts many of the younger men. I wonder if it compromises our "observer" status, but in this society we are such a rarity that everyone wants to come and have a look. We look into another room where lunch seems to have finished. We have no translator, but as always we find someone who speaks English and who helps us out. I ask him why he has come to vote today. His answer is simple and succinct: "I must do it for my country." I admire his sentiment, and only hope that it makes some difference. The voters have no choice but to believe that it will make a difference.

Karzai's representatives certainly hold a near monopoly in hats. I take a picture of four of them in a row, all young men, all grinning. I ask the registrar if I can take a photo of him. He puts out his hand: apparently not. But wait—he first wants to put on his Independent Election Commission bib (white nylon, with the IEC logo, a ballot box superimposed on an outline of the state of Afghanistan). He stands up to attention. It wouldn't surprise me if he saluted. I take the photo. Then he sits back down and takes the bib off. It's odd, as usually people don't want to be identified with any organ of the state. Our half hour is up, and we leave.

It is our final outing of the day. Polls close at four. We arrive at the polling station at 16:02. If you are in the line by 16:00, you are meant to be able to vote. There are still people entering the center when we go in. Inside there is something approaching—but not quite reaching—pandemonium. There is confusion and shouting. Men want to vote.

There was indeed a late surge. Kevin and I sit with our orange forms on a low bench in one room that is particularly raucous. The polling station supervisor raises his voice and his hands. I don't need a translator to understand that he is saying "you are too late—you should have been here earlier!" He starts to herd them out of the room like cattle. The men, turbans slipping and sweat dripping—it is still hot, though late afternoon—do not acquiesce quietly, but they acquiesce nonetheless and begin to drift toward the door. All except an old man who hobbles in against this exiting tide of protest. He looks bewildered behind the gold-framed glasses that magnify his blue eyes. He is dressed in white, with a long white beard and white turban, and has a cane because he is old and frail. He doesn't understand why he is being turned away. He fumbles for his voter registration card. You can see the polling superintendent wants to let him vote, but he can't because the other men, sensing an opportunity, slow their roll towards the door. You can see the old man close to tears, his eye glistening, and a lump comes into my throat too. Please let him vote. It's only 16:10, and it's probably taken him ten minutes to walk the hundred yards from the door of the center to the station. But the official, after the moment of near-relenting, cannot allow the man to vote (even though culturally he is an elder and the younger one should always show deference). His face shows the struggle between new-fangled democracy with its rules and regulations and the old ways of respect to the elderly. On this occasion the Constitution trumps culture. The old man is led away without having voted. I think about all the history he must have lived through—the King, the Russian invasion and occupation, the Taliban, the President, and us.

The polling station is now cleared of everyone except the officials and Kevin, me and Brian. We wait quietly for the count to start. Brian speaks with the man guarding the votes, who is unarmed but certainly seems to know about weapons. He is or has been a soldier. He and Brian make different poses and agree on the dangers of various weapon positions. They make small "chah!" sounds and say things like "not good, no, not good." They are obviously bonding. Behind them, outside the window, a crowd of young Afghan men throng at the window, staring at Kevin and me. One of the other polling station staff takes our photo. Then they approach. They've forgotten part of

175

the procedure: to peel a red and white tape across the room in front of the cast ballots. There. Complete. They proudly show it off, the red and white icing on their cake.

Our usual half-hour is up before the count starts. We wait in the corridor and meet up with Ben who has been in the second car in this trip, as he was in the morning convoy that went over the rocket. Down the corridor where the old man has hobbled off, a crowd is gathering at the door. No, they are doing more than gathering. The IBGs go into full alert mode. The crowd outside isn't happy about being denied the right to vote (even with all that cultural constraint people still really want to vote). They huff and puff and they push the door in. But the police and polling station officials are pushing the other side. They clamor back and forth for about thirty seconds, though it seems longer. Voices are raised, some stentorian in tone, some shrill. They aren't happy. We look to see if we can leave by the opposite door. It is locked. One of the police officers raises his gun high above his head. This could turn into a riot, but it's not there yet. Brian says we're going through. We are to line up in single file, behind him, with John, the other IBG, taking up the rear. Will is going first. He flexes his elbows, holding his weapon in both hands, and we walk steadily to the door where the heaving and pushing is still ongoing. These people are not intent on causing harm, they simply want to vote. They part like the waters of the Red Sea (or like the Red Sea would if faced with a general purpose machine gun). They let us pass, and they seem to disperse somewhat in our wake, deflated, as if our leaving has somehow taken some of the passion out of them. We rib Ben about being a bad omen on a trip— things are always eventful when he's around, and he laughs. We pop across to the women's side, which is a paragon of order and calmness. Razia is there, as chatty as before, delighted to see us. The veil of the supervisor with the well-inked hands has slipped, and she looks much younger than I'd thought earlier, less matronly, with lush black hair worn in a center parting and a low braid. She smiles, that gold-toothed smile again. The day has been a success. All of her staff stayed until the end. Women came, they voted. I saw them. The big Tupperware boxes filled with folded papers are silent testimony to that event. Soon it will be time for them to be counted.

Our last half-hour is up: we must leave the count to the Afghans. They will be doing it by themselves, for themselves. And now we all await the result. But just as democracy is about much more than voting, so the day is about much more than the numbers that will eventually emerge. Though there will be many critical voices commenting on election corruption, the day as I observed it—in an admittedly limited locus—seems to me to be a symbolic moment that speaks clearly about desire to move away from the tyranny of the Taliban regime; it reveals articulate, confident people wanting to engage with modernity and the outside world, and it holds within it the inherent courage of asserting choice in the face of those who would grant no freedom of expression, no human freedoms at all.

Swimming Pool Hill, Kabul

# 22. Cityscape (I): Kabul

FINALLY, THE SYSTEM WORKS. I make it to Kabul in less than 24 hours. Rhys and I are the last two people on the Sea Stallion from Lash to Bastion. Then we are the last two people on the C-130 from Bastion to Kabul—the same day! But it doesn't matter: we get there. I have warned Rhys about how traveling with me tends to suck people down into a morass of tardiness and ennui, but he seems to be a good luck charm for me, pulling me up onto a platform of punctuality and—incredibly—precision timing.

This time, only my third, in Kabul it feels like a different planet to Lashkar Gah on every stratum I can think of: geography, topography, culture, dress, fine dining (yes, really), religion. I feel like the country cousin come to gawk and gape at the sophisticated big city folk: there are ten-story buildings here made from concrete, for instance. I haven't brought any Lash-sourced *salwar kameez* with me, which is a bit of a risk—you never know whom you may run into or who wants to meet, but I'm glad. Wearing the red or blue sequined numbers would have meant I'd have stuck out even more than wearing my Western clothes. I have a sense nonetheless of being seen-through, seen to be from the south.

On the level of fine dining, it feels like Europe. Yes, I know—that may seem a little far-fetched, but in Lash, even if we were allowed to go out to restaurants in the evening, there are no restaurants to go out to. But in Kabul I eat out three times, twice in a Lebanese restaurant (wonderful soft and spicy falafel, like I haven't tasted since I bought some fragrantly fresh in a paper cone from a stall on a Beirut street next to the sea in 1993) and once in a French place (the owner, an Afghan woman—yes, you read right, a woman business owner—lived in France for many years and came back to open this restaurant). The steak was cooked to perfection, the caramelized onion jam melded with the meat and melted majestically in my mouth, and the garlic butter (sharp as a knife) saturating the French fries was just such a winning combination of carbs, salt, fat and flavor.

When you are inside this restaurant, you are a million miles from the outside world. Granted, to get in you have to get out of your armored vehicle, go through one doorway opened by armed security guards into a short passageway with more armored guards at the other end. Not until the door closes behind and we are all in the short corridor do they open the next door. The door closes in one country and just six paces away opens on another. For me the vista is hitherto unprecedented: a real restaurant. We enter.

Inside they are serving wine, despite Ramadan. Even in (some respects) very liberal Dubai they don't do this. I feel a little bit guilty, ordering a glass of black-cherry-colored Cabernet. In Lash we try not to drink water in front of local staff when Ramadan is being observed. I find, however, that my guilt dissipates enough during the imbibing of the first glass to enable me to order a second.

But it's not just the wine that makes me forget to wear hijab when I go back out onto the street again once our meal is finished. It's the whole ambience: it's simply not as claustrophobic. It's as if the cultural and religious ceiling has been raised. It's still there, but it's further away —and within the hard, guarded perimeters of the expatiate experience almost out of view. There's just more room to breathe, and to forget the rules. Or maybe it's rather to feel that you don't have to abide by them, that they somehow don't apply to you, that they are too far away to reach you. A few days later in New York (on which more later) I read an article about a conceptual artist who stays in a square box for twenty-four hours or so. It's not awfully original, but this guy's twist is that the ceiling on the cell descends every hour or so. Sometimes it drops a few inches, sometimes a foot at a time, until finally (and unsurprisingly) at the end of the show he is quite squashed but not squeezed. He is restrained, but not by any physical bonds. I'm sure the metaphor has application in New York, built on similarly shaped but differently sized cubes. Conceptual art isn't my favorite aesthetic, but this piece speaks to me of the difference between Lash and Kabul—the ceiling lowered, the ceiling raised; incorporeal repression and restraint. I think it would be interesting to site the show in Kabul for a performance or two.

Still in Kabul on Friday, our day off, I have arranged to go on a city tour. I am quite excited—I've only ever been to and from the Embassy complex and to the NATO bases and usually in darkness, so have no real idea of what Kabul is like, or even what size it is. I'm still in Lash mode and so don't take any hijab with me, my logic being that I'm not going to any meetings, we won't be getting out of the car, so I don't need it. Well, that turns out to be a bit myopic. Nor do I change my shoes—I'm wearing open-toed sandals. In Lash I'd be made to go back and change them to closed-toe boots or shoes. If I have to run, they don't want me doing it in sandals. In Kabul there's no such restraint, even from our own security.

Rush hour, Kabul

I have been warned that the traffic in Kabul is getting worse. Twenty-minute journeys are turning into two-hour odysseys. I don't really believe it, but it's true. We are bumper to bumper for a good part of the drive to the outskirts of the city. The aspirant Manhattan-yellow of the cabs here adds a touch of the absurd, if any were needed. Yellow cabs, forest green police jeeps with mounted machine guns on the back, scrawny brown donkeys pulling carts of pale green watermelons and zucchini, scrawny brown men hauling carts or pushing barrows of the same through the dusty thoroughfares. Man and beast similarly burdened. There are fewer white Toyota Corollas here than in Lash: cars are more diverse in color, brand, and model. It's ramshackle and raucous. But the traffic police don't carry weapons. That just wouldn't happen in Lash. Now, though, it's Friday, the weekend, and it's during Ramadan, so once we get out a bit we start to move.

Kabul is pasted on a huge flat valley around a high hill (TV Hill, I learn later) in the middle, and further out higher mountains at the edges of the valley floor. We set out on a main highway to the King's Palace. Once mighty and magisterial, its damaged sandstone shell still swaggers on a small slope, speaking of the grandeur of the past when it "had it all." It's not hard to believe that it had. It's still beautiful in architectural terms that are much more recognizable to me: European with a strong Greco-Roman influence, tall columns and three-story wings arranged around a massive courtyard that could be Rastrelli's late Baroque in Russia. I am allowed out of the car, so I get out with a camera borrowed from a colleague and start to snap. Then I see the people, men, who congregate around the base of the columns. I immediately feel nervous because I have nothing on my head but my hair. The small boys who come over to beg and ask for "the dollar" don't care, but their older brothers might. They are still quite far away though, so I venture up to a steel gate which lies ajar, underneath massive mute sandstone statues that reach from the first floor to the second, and hold up the third. I wonder if I can go inside. Suddenly a soldier comes out from the shadows and snaps the gate shut. There's my answer: no. I get back into the car and we head off to TV Hill, so called because of the crop of masts planted at its peak.

It takes about an hour to drive the ten miles or so to the top. First we

Grid city, Kabul

skirt the hem of the hill, taking what seems to me the long way round. For a Friday during Ramadan there is certainly a lot of commerce around—locksmiths and bicycle repair shops and car body shops and watermelon street stalls are all open for business, and have customers.

The crumbling hill rises sheer, cliff-like. Houses cling to the slope at impossible gradients. They stick at all angles both to the hill and to each other, like a crazed mud and wattle rookery, and just as vulnerable.

I think that if there's even a slight shudder of the earth, never mind a quake that makes it onto the Richter Scale, everything will split and splinter, fall asunder, tumble, crumble to the ground as if thousands of old birds' nests have crashed from the eaves, raising years of chalky brown dust as they do.

We move to the center of town again and come to a large square. Everyone is out in their Friday finery thronging the streets, crossing the bridge that spans the Kabul River—a pathetic muddy gash of an urban waterway. If there were shopping carts in Kabul, they'd be dumped in its alluvial bed. It is not at all like the Helmand River, though close to and fed by the same snow melt.

183

The people are the same, and different. In among the salmon and blue burqas and the cream and gray *salwar kameez* are many other clothes. Men wear Western suits, some quite spectacular. There's a shiny silver double-breasted number on one man, straight from Duran Duran or Spandau Ballet's New Romantic wardrobe. With his big aviator shades he is the epitome of cool—in his own mind. He's not quite as cool, though, as the man on the poster. He wears a red T-shirt that's been sprayed on, or photoshop pulled: he looks fey, gay, and very muscled. There are too many mixed messages going on there. And then there's the girl.

She is crossing the bridge with her friend. She wears a short cerise and black tartan kilt with a puffball flourish of a finish over black drainpipe jeans and a tight white shirt, with the top button open. Her hijab is in the same pink tartan. It is a Vivienne Westwood interpretation of Islamic dress, closer to how things are done in Bosnia, but somehow a little wilder.

We drive on. On the flat the buildings are an amalgam of some architecture and none at all. There are grand old nineteenth-century villas built by the British colonists, office blocks in what I would call new Islamic style (lots of small arched windows), 1960s communist blocks (self-explanatory), the contemporary European of the oh-so-swish Serena Hotel (deep ochre-yellow plaster arranged in castellated blocks).

Leaving the flat we turn up the roughly hewn track that is the road to the top of TV Hill. There are hairpin bends, but all the way children play and men gather around small kiosks. The view at the top is breathtaking, this wide expanse of a city spread down the slopes and across the flat valley floor. It is like that opening shot of Vegas in *CSI*, but a massive medieval Las Vegas made of mud, and without the gambling.

Our final stop of the day is Swimming Pool Hill. This was the perfect location for an outdoor Olympic-size pool. It is perched on top of a small hill, with fabulous views of the city. On the way up a long-abandoned Russian tank stands mute, an impotent guard. We stop by the pool which is mounted above the road, a huge trapezoid pyre. And indeed sacrifices were made there, for it was where the Taliban used to execute people. The choice was to go to the high dive board (over thirty feet) and jump on to the bone-shattering concrete (the pool was drained of all fluids but blood) or be shot. If you jumped and survived they would shoot you anyway, the Taliban equivalent of the medieval ducking stool or, further back, the choice between Scylla and Charybdis. But today there's enough rainwater and snowmelt still in the pool to allow for swimming, even diving. The water is murky and green, darkly radiant as the sun glints sharply off it. Young boys splash and laugh. They are too young to remember what happened here. I think about the human capacity to absorb awfulness. These people here do it without psychological assistance or support. There is a terrible, quiescent, essential stoicism here. You'd go completely nuts if there wasn't.

The next morning I get on a plane (a new terminal building has been built since I was here last: it's pretty nice) to Dubai. I switch to Abu Dhabi by road and then: New York. But, it turns out, even there I have no way of escaping Afghanistan.

Roof Garden, Metropolitan Museum of Art, New York

# 23. Cityscape (II): New York

I AM ON MY WAY to New York for my two-week leave period. I will be glad to leave Afghanistan behind for a bit. It sounds slightly counter-intuitive but I didn't realize just how hot it was in August, and just how hard it was to work in the heat. Like a lobster being boiled slowly in a pot, my body warmed with the summer. But even the drop of five degrees (from 45 to 40°C) at the end of August was such a relief. I wonder what it does to your body, being in an environment where the external temperature is the same or higher than your internal body temperature. I know it's given me pimples for the first time since I was a teenager. I find myself asking the same rhetorical question now as then: "why do they have to be on my face?"

So a trip out will be good. And there'll be nothing to do with Afghanistan in New York. How wrong I am about that. It is everywhere. It's in my copy of *Gulf Times* that I read at breakfast in the hotel in Abu Dhabi on my way. Then on the plane the complimentary paper has a "down memory lane" piece. This particular piece, from 1988, recalls the tense return to terra firma of a Russian rocket manned in part by the first Afghan in space, Abdul Ahad Mohmand. They had to try three or four times to get back into earth's orbit, returning from the Space Station Mir. The Western media reported at the time that they were nearly out of air. The Russian media robustly refuted it (of course) and played recordings of poor old Abdul and his Russian crew mates laughing. (Actually they did have enough air,[5] but what they didn't have were adequate toilet facilities—whatever the 1988 equivalent of the wagbag was. And just like in a Hollywood script, Abdul wasn't even meant to be there. The other astronaut, the guy who was meant to be the first Afghan in space, pulled out because of a burst appendix. He'd done almost all of the required two years of training, but poor Abdul had just done six months. But they eventually get home, a day or so late.)

5 In case anyone's interested, more on this in *The Story of Space Station Mir* by David Michael Harland.

Part of the mission's purpose was to photograph the topography of Afghanistan because there were so many places so remote that they had never been photographed before. But two-dimensional knowledge of the landscape still didn't do the Russians any good. Yet the very idea of an Afghan in space is a marvelous thing. When I look around at the medieval society in Lash, with its feudal farming staffed by people who are effectively serfs, and try to put that together with the space station Mir, it seems beyond belief. Apparently Abdul the Afghan Astronaut now works in the printing industry in Germany.

I get into JFK on Monday afternoon. On Tuesday I go straight to where I always go first in New York: the Met. I walk from Grand Central Station up Fifth Avenue. It's forty blocks away, but it's a fantastic walk. I pass hundreds of onlookers, cameras ready to shoot as a petite and cream-suited Sarah Jessica Parker sashays down towards Bergdorf Goodman, filming a scene from SATC2. She touches her saucer-sized sunglasses with one hand. A thousand flashes go off from the other side of the street. A woman shouts "cut," closely followed by "that's a wrap." The trees that stake out Central Park are ahead, and I don't stop for an autograph.

Being at the bottom steps of the Metropolitan Museum of Art is always a thrilling moment. You never know what exactly is going to excite you inside, but you know that something surely will. And today, a giant banner is festooned across the façade: *Afghanistan—Hidden Treasures from the National Museum, Kabul.* I'm beginning to think it's following me around. I don't suppose the exhibition can be up to much, but I go anyway. I am captivated and awed by what I see and learn.

First, by the artifacts themselves: a collapsible gold crown decorated with gold leaf, foldable and with its own wooden box; heart-shaped earrings in gold and deep blue; silver and gold appliqués; antelope motif bracelets in gold, turquoise, and carnelian; gold and silver hair ornaments; belt clasps in gold and blue depicting cupids astride dolphins, or warriors (in pure gold filigree); a headdress ornament in the shape of a ram (solid shiny gold); a fragment of a bowl decorated with bulls (gold); a pendant depicting the "dragon master" in gold, turquoise, garnet, lapis lazuli, carnelian, and pearls; a painted beaker. This shows crimson wine being poured from a canary yellow jug in front of a woman wearing blue. The blue cloth is clasped over one shoulder (the other is clearly pinky-brown skin), and she has a yellow wrap thrown across her lap. Green plants are all around and she is wearing some form of headdress. It is all very elaborate, and it is from the first century AD and made of glass. There's also a glass fish, sage-green and midnight-blue. And it's still not broken. But there's more: bronze masks, ivory statuettes, ceremonial plates of silver, a golden belt. It's simply stunning.

These items come from four different sites: graves and a temple at Tillya Tepe, relics from the Indus civilization at Tepe Fullo, two storage rooms from a city at Begram, and a whole city excavated at Ai Khanum. For me the archaeology and history are even more stunning than the treasures themselves (lovely as they are to look at). The book which accompanies the exhibition[6] tells the story of the country long before the Great Game was even considered. First of all, there were three countries, not one. The one country created as a buffer zone between East and West by powers West and East "unintentionally linked the edge of three distinct lands described by the Greeks and Persians two thousand years ago." The three regions were: Bactria (currently Northern Afghanistan), Aria (Western, centered around contemporary Herat), and Arachosia (centered around Kandahar, in the South.) There is also a map detailing the archaeological sites of Afghanistan, and codifying them chronologically. There are five main periods:

(1) Islamic: 7th century AD
(2) Later Silk Road: 3rd–8th century AD
(3) Early Silk Road: 4th century BC–2nd century AD
(4) Bronze and Iron Age: 6000 BC–400 BC
(5) Prehistoric: 15,000–8,000 years ago

There is a site at Lash for each period except Prehistoric. The map, with different colored dots for different eras, also demonstrates just how recent Islam is, and just how much went before. And it holds somehow the notion that it can change again (though I have to say, those digging up Bakelite radios and flat screen TVs eons from now

6 Fredrik Hiebret and Pierre Cambon, *Afghanistan: Hidden Treasures from the National Museum*. Kabul Eds, 2008.

may not find those quite as satisfying as collapsible gold crowns). The other thing I notice about the location of the sites is that while all the periods are represented in close clusters (one Islamic, three Later Silk Road sites, with two Early Silk and maybe one Bronze Age, let's say, in a smallish city like Lash), the only era that really has isolated and self-contained sites is the Islamic. All the others built upon the one before, mixed, fused, amalgamated, assimilated, integrated. But only Islamic sites journeyed out onto the steppes and the craggy rugged mountains where no civilizations had been able to survive long enough to leave artifacts behind before.

The book explains that farmers settled on the plains around the Hindu Kush some 7,000 years ago (it doesn't say where from). They took with them "traditions of building dwellings from unbaked mud brick and making pottery from local clay." Not a lot has changed. Though there are those like the old man with the magpie beard who makes bricks from poured concrete by the roadside in Lash, most of the houses are still made of the same unbaked (or rather sun-baked) mud. So not much has changed in 7,000 years. Anyway, the book goes on to tell how these farmers acquired wealth from the lapis lazuli (recall that the Pharaohs coveted the blue stone) and tin from the river beds. And they put the wealth to good use by installing large-scale irrigation systems, which they first built about 4,000 years ago. Yet they had no writing system, and so they have no name—or rather only the one archaeologists give them: the Bactria-Margiana Archaeological Complex (BMAC) or "Oxus Civilization" (from the Oxus River, today called the Amu Darya).

The Oxus was already involved in international trade when they built the canals. And the canals, like the mud houses, still exist. Farming wouldn't function without them. When you fly from Kabul to Helmand, on a good day you can see that the whole place relies on the irrigation system, green veins that thread across the dark salty clay, giving the country life.

For religion, the Oxus civilization worshipped fire. But wealth creates its own problems. People start to covet their neighbors' goods. So the Persians and the Greeks came in search of bounty. Cyrus the Great, founder of the Persian Empire of the Achaemenids, came through around the fifth century BC and what was to become Afghanistan found itself part of the Empire. Alexander the Great also came through, on his way to India. We all know that didn't end well, but when he departed in 327 BC, he left behind his own FOBs. At one of them in particular he ordered additional men to establish a colony. It was at this base, in Bactria, that around thirty years later Selecucus I founded Ai Khanum. Ai Khanum is named after an Uzbek princess said to occupy its citadel in the Middle Ages. Its original name is lost. And so was it for hundreds of years until one day in 1961. King Zahir Shah happened to be out on a hunt when a villager showed him the fragment of a carved stone. Luckily, the king was an expert on Afghan antiquities and didn't just stick the stone in a storeroom somewhere but reported the find to DAFA.[7] Its director, Daniel Schlumberger, recognized it as a Corinthian capital and concluded that there must be a Greek city somewhere in the vicinity. Excavations began in 1965 and continued until the Soviet invasion in 1979.

What they found was incredible—a really sophisticated Greek royal city, complete with a palace that had a 108-pillar framed outer courtyard and many ceremonial rooms. There was a gymnasium and a two-thousand-odd seat theater in the city. The streets were well ordered by regular blocks of limestone. There were temples and latrines. A short film is part of the exhibition, and still black and white photos of the excavations are shown. Then the site of today is shown: a flat, pockmarked moonscape, with only the barest fragments of those regular blocks of limestone marking the streets. The rubble testifies mutely to what once was, dust settling over the stones in razor-thin layers, getting ready to bury it all again. There is an audible gasp from the audience as the camera pans around the once vibrant, now vacant, site.

A lot of places lay claim to be "where East meets West." Anywhere on the Silk Road(s) seems to stake a claim, but few places are like this one, which truly was a melting pot rather than a mosaic. Apart from the artifacts listed above all being locally crafted, the culture and religion that they articulated, though drawing on the Hellenic, the Achaemenidian, and the Indian, were also local and unique. As the book says of

---

7 Délégation Archéologique Française en Afghanistan

a small gold Aphrodite statue, it is "Grecian" in concept, but has the non-Grecian wings of a Bactrian deity and an Indian forehead mark that indicates marital status. All this, too, could have been lost had it not been for conscientious, caring, and courageous museum staff who hid all of these objects in the vault at the Central Bank and in the Ministry of Interior in 1990. In 2001 the Taliban decided that all "images" must be destroyed, and about 2,500 works of art were annihilated. Some of the material hidden at the Ministry of Interior was discovered and destroyed by the Taliban. But in 2004 the Central Bank vaults were opened up again. Incredibly, the artifacts were relatively intact. It has been a labor of love to curate the exhibition and send it to Europe and America. It still isn't able to be shown in Kabul. The hope is that one day it will go on permanent display there.

Even though I've been to the exhibition, the Afghanistan trail doesn't go cold. As I sit and read the *New York Times* each morning, it's everywhere. Front page, editorial, comment pieces. Is the policy right? Is the policy ready? What should we do? Whither an honorable exit? Rationally I know it's a big news story, but when we are working in our own little bit, out in an FOB in the middle of nowhere, I do lose sight of just how far up the world's agenda these little villages and mighty mountains are.

Rain comes. It's the first rain I've seen in months. And I should be glad, except that I'm due to go to the US Tennis Open the next day. It doesn't pass but just hangs in a leaky cloud over Flushing Meadow. I am impatient and take the 7 Train up anyway because there's just been a break in the cloud and I hope that it will clear up. My brother, more wisely, decides to wait in the apartment. Of course he's right. It starts to rain again as soon as I get off the train. I am determined not to fall prey to merchandizing in the hiatus before play, so look around an auction room full of old tennis artifacts (Althea Gibson's pencil, Martina Navratilova's old kit, Bill Tilden's letters, his classic wool tennis sweater—which Ralph Lauren seems to have successfully "interpreted" for its own product range this year). Nothing that is that interesting to me. Until, incredibly, I'm looking down the auction list and I see the word "Afghanistan." Of course I must read on. I locate the shelf with the articles: two 1968 Afghanistan Tennis Trophies, list price $150–$225.

I read the inscriptions on the two nondescript little chalices. On the first: "International Club Kabul, Handicap Tennis Tournament, 1968." On its reverse: "Runner Up Men's Singles." The second one reads on one side: "International Club Kabul, Open Tennis Tournament 1968." It is the reverse that floors me. It reads: "Runner Up Mixed Doubles."

That little tin cup was awarded to the runner up of a game of tennis played by a man and a woman on the same side of the net. Forty years ago that could happen, and today it can't. Afghan society is now so gender segregated that I can hardly conceive of such a game.

It strikes me, sadly, that the Afghans must look to the past for progress—the astronaut on the space station, the mighty civilizations that tamed the desert, mixed doubles tennis. I know, however, that the Afghans that I speak with want to remember that past, seek inspiration from it, and want to add to the list in the future. But it isn't going to be easy, or quick.

I don't buy the trophies. I don't know if anyone else does either.

Literacy class, Gereshk

# 24. Now She Goes to School

I'VE GONE BACK to Gereshk, the busy hub on the main Kabul–Kandahar road. Lashkar Gah is closer than both, but Gereshk prides itself on its self-sufficiency, enterprise come from the commerce. This is the only community council that has women on it. But all is relative though; we had a tough time once it came to ensuring the women could really participate in the workings of the council. That they could is down to nuanced navigation by Derek.

Now I'm back to see what has happened since we (with the provincial governor's office and the Afghan Independent Directorate of Local Government) established the council and drafted the community plans. The council has three sub-committees: justice, economic and social development, and security. The provision of justice is a key battleground in the conflict—if the government can't provide it, the Taliban will. Which is why we particularly support the justice sub-committees (JSC) as a forum where the local population can go to get lower-level disputes resolved. Of course, this approach is not without risk. These guys use a mixture of Pashtunwali—the traditional philosophical base for the Pashtun people—and Islamic law to figure out disputes and award compensation. They've been doing this for hundreds of years. So women or children don't do well out of the existing system. We know that we're not going to change that through the JSCs, though. That's not their function, that's a long-term development issue. And not something that we, as foreigners, are going to be able to do by ourselves: that will truly need to be Afghan-led, from the highest levels.

No, the work we are engaged in is "hot stabilization," which is (as far as I can see) a pre-development phase of development that draws on Merilee Grindle's concept of "good enough" governance and locates it in a COIN (COunter-INsurgency) context. This means doing the bare essentials so that society does not utterly fragment, so that the center just about holds; so that it knows that there is some government out there, even if it doesn't quite reach all the way down to the districts. Maybe stabilization is best thought of as follows: if journalism is the first, rough draft of history, so stabilization is the first, rough draft of development.

The community councils are a way of representing grassroots concerns while reaching up and linking to provincial and indeed central government from them. It's all about service delivery: security first, then justice, with health, education, and agriculture in the second tier. Afghans like to be on the winning side. Hot stabilization means that we make sure that the governance is visible, and active. Where it can't be, it—and we—are vulnerable to the Taliban delivering services (they have whole parallel administrations, up to shadow governors) in its stead. It's not just a fight over territory.

So that's the theory. Here in Gereshk I'm looking at the practice. I'm a bit nervous because I really have no idea what I'm going to find. There's no judge here, no prosecutor. There's only the JSC—a bunch of farmers mainly who are effectively volunteer councillors (they get a small monthly stipend). They aren't supposed to take on serious crimes like murder or sexual assault, but to deal with the petty session-type cases that involve a greater number of people.

I meet first with the women council members. There are two of them on the JSC. Guliana is the equivalent of a female Elder: a widow, she was a lawyer in pre-Taliban times and is very well respected. Then there's Nagalzi, a younger Baluch woman from a small village close to Gereshk town. I've heard of this village before: Abazhan. Abazhan, we are told, simply refused to succumb to Taliban values or surrender to their force. The village levies its own taxes, its girls go to school, it is the only place for miles around that has managed to keep power generators running, so it has electricity. The secret, it seems, is a strong sense of community identity and confidence. Bullies are usually defeated by confidence and it would seem that Helmand is no different.

We meet in their women's center. It's a simple building, the décor is plain—much plainer (and more palatable) than the many other offices I've been in. There are no gaudy plastic flowers, no loud tassels shimmying from curtain rails—and no photograph of Karzai either.

They love being on the JSC. It's working for them, and for other women that they help. And I learn so much about how the society operates at its most basic level: the family.

Guliana tells me about a domestic violence case: "One woman was beaten by her husband. More and more she wanted a divorce. She didn't want to stay in the family home any longer. She asked for an agreement to be made between her and her husband to divorce."

I ask about her role and that of the JSC: "Oh, I had to go to the guy a few times. The first time he didn't agree. The main cause was that he had two wives. The woman who wanted the divorce was the first wife. She was older. To divorce her would be bad in Pashtun culture. I said to him, 'OK, you might not like her, but there's no need to hurt her. That is not the way of Islam. We are not allowed to torture people. If you don't like her, you can let her go.' After this discussion he came to the JSC and the divorce was agreed."

This was different to the days before the JSC, as she recalls another case with quite a different outcome: "Before the JSC there was one more case. A woman who had been beaten by her husband. We knew that he would kill her if he got the chance. There was no community council then. I raised it where I could, but the woman committed suicide. There was no one to ask at that time. Now we have power, we can do something."

There was another case, a property dispute. It went something like this: "A woman came whose husband had died. She had only one son, a boy of fifteen. There was a lot of property belonging to her husband. Her husband's brother wanted to kill her and her son so as to take the property and sell it. She was very frightened. But the land belongs to the boy. In Islamic law the legacy belongs to the boy, not the uncle. So, we called all the husband's brothers to the JSC. We made a note of all the property, and we got her a lawyer. Now she says I'm not scared any more."

We have been talking for almost two hours, which is something of a record because even though Afghans like to talk they also get tired after an hour or so, so I'm usually careful not to push. I'm also conscious that we are talking on a Friday, their (and my) weekend. I apologize for this—it was the only time I could get flights—but Fatima says, "Pah! Friday is our picnic day, and today we have our picnic with you!"

It's true we've drunk a lot of chai and eaten a lot of brown nuts and yellow-green raisins. Fatima giggles after the two wives and divorce story: "My husband has three wives, I'm the first," she says proudly. For her, and in the culture, for a man to have three wives is a sign of great wealth (at up to $50,000 each, marriage isn't cheap). She is happy and content, she gets to do her own thing. Romantic love as in the Western aesthetic simply doesn't exist here. There's just a whole different way of navigating and negotiating interpersonal relationships.

They take me around the rest of their center. The first room stuns me: it's a gym. Yes, beside these veiled women in a sage-green room are several StairMasters, stationary bikes, a running machine, one of those frame-things to help you do stomach crunches and two of those big air-filled balls in red and purple. They see the look of shock on my face and laugh. "Yes, we work out!" they giggle.

The gym, Gereshk

The next room holds six old Singer sewing machines in black with gold trimmings set on their own tables with black iron treadles beneath. My grandmother had one, and I learned to sew on it. Keeping the tension in the broad pedal taut yet flowing under the table while feeding the cloth through above the table at the same rate is a lot harder than it looks. This is the "arts and crafts" section of their building where women learn tailoring and embroidery. Their wares are on the wall—dresses of deep-colored velvets (plum, forest green, burnt orange) with gold rick-rack or embroidery trims and breastplates, and yellow-tinged tallow of soap and small candles. The room after that one is bare except for a blackboard, well scored with white chalk, propped up against the wall by two wooden chairs painted with the leftover paint from the sage green walls. Four women are sitting cross-legged on the floor, being taught how to read and write. They are all well over school age. A baby rolls in the corner on her belly on the concrete, barely nine months old. I smile at her, and her mother props her up. She looks a bit confused to be taken for the youngest member of the literacy class, but like other children I've come across here she is silent, and smiles back.

I leave the women and go to the men. The district governor has invited me to lunch. The drive into his compound through a gateway is so narrow that it's a real challenge for the Armour Group driver. The governor's staff, tall, dark young men, thin and wiry as whippets, gesticulate wildly and earnestly to assist the entry. They couldn't be more serious if we were docking with a space station.

The house is two-story and made of cement, not mud. But it is nowhere close to some of the new vanilla-icing villas of the narco-barons you can see in Lashkar Gah. This house is dilapidated and shabby, but comfortable. When I go in the men of the community council are there to greet me. The low table is covered in food: round flat bread, boiled lamb, roast chicken, salad, whole fried fish, and massive trays of honeydew melon. There are plates of apples and oranges and black grapes. I learn there are two types of chicken in front of us: Helmandi chicken (rather scrawny and tough, to be honest) and Pakistani (a lot more fatty and fleshy). The cook tells me and the interpreter to dig deep into the Helmandi chicken. We discover a gorgeous stuffing—almonds, hazelnuts, and raisins. The purple grapes are small but sweet. They are from Kandahar. The district governor says they are the best grapes in the world, and I tend to agree.

We talk over lunch. The JSC members tell me about different cases —commercial property disputes—but also cite the difficult cases Guliana spoke about. I start to believe that this thing is really making a difference, is stabilizing the society enough to really get some development work done. As we leave the district governor gives me a gift—a new outfit. It is a red and cream creation with a hearty dose of gold and brass brocade inlay. There are no sleeves. It's quite risqué. But then this is the only Afghan man who has ever kissed me (on the cheek) three times on greeting, as the women do. He takes a risk in so doing, but he doesn't seem to care. He seems rather to care about living his life to the fullest, irrespective of what people say. Somebody always has to move up a gear and get ahead of the pack, to lead the way, to change behavior. He is young and he says at lunch that they are very proud that Gereshk is the only council that has women on it. Clearly he's forgotten that he essentially capitulated in the face of social and political pressure when it came to the initial workshop. That it still rankles is demonstrated by the faces of the others, including the one-eyed Chair. They are clearly not as enthusiastic. He is always in danger of getting too far ahead of the pack, but thus far he has survived. And they, if not exactly following in his wake, have tolerated his moving into other lanes.

On the way back I have a wait in Bastion and I think about the final case Guliana told me about: "There was one very horrible case. A young girl of eighteen years came to me. She said, 'My parents want me to marry an addict. But how can I stay with him? He doesn't care about anyone. I need your help, or I will kill myself.' I went to her house, to speak to her father. At first he didn't allow us in, and told me to go away. But we are Afghan: you must host someone, even if they are your enemy. So we got a cup of tea. The first time we talked, her father took an extreme view. We continued to talk, and he came around. He was worried though, about the marriage contract that he had already entered into. He said, 'I can't do anything about that. His [the addict's] family will take the girl.' So I took her husband and brother and final offer to the JSC. I said to them, 'If you want to give a girl to an addict, why, he is only a half-man. She will kill herself, and this will be on your heads.' The girl repeated in front of them that she would kill herself if they made her marry the addict. That JSC decision was really hard. The session lasted for two or three hours. But eventually they allowed her to go by herself."

I asked what happened to the girl afterwards, what was she doing now?

Guliana smiles. "Why, now she goes to school," she says contentedly, folding her hands in her lap.

You do get some good days on this job.

Discussions on district development

# 25. There Are No Lesbians in Afghanistan

A SORT OF PLAY in which seven persons converse on marriage (again) and sexuality.

**Dramatis personae**

1st COUNCILLOR, *an elderly man with a sternum-long gray beard and crinkled brown leather face crowned by a black and silver turban.*

2nd COUNCILLOR, *slightly younger than the* 1st COUNCILLOR, *wearing a pushed-back turban to reveal a high forehead and large green eyes whose whites widen when he hears strange things. He has a pearl-colored beard.*

JUDGE, *of paler skin, but plumper than the others, he has a squat square face and sharp brown eyes, raisin-like, reminiscent of a cartoon rodent, a hamster perhaps. He is used to being right.*

PROSECUTOR, *a handsome man, he leaves his bald pate uncovered, but wears a thick black leather aviator-style jacket over a cream* salwar kameez. *A smoker, he has yellowed teeth like a jumble of small calcified rocks scattered across his mouth. He was one of only two people in his school to win a scholarship to Tajikistan, where he studied for four years.*

GIRL, *her skin so thin and white it is almost blue. She wears a red hijab which matches her gold-sequinned red* salwar kameez. *Underneath the thin wispy fabric she wears base layer skiwear—black merino wool leggings.*

TRANSLATOR, *a young man with a skull-cap shock of black hair, over a round chubby-cheeked, clean shaven nutmeg brown face.*

FIXER, *an older English man. He takes care of people transiting through Kandahar Air Field, usually known as KAF. His skin is toughened by the suns of Iraq and Afghanistan.*

GIRL Where did you learn to speak English?

PROSECUTOR I had American teachers, here, in Lashkar Gah. My first teacher was Miss Lucas. She was a very kind woman. Very kind. And David Champion. Then there was Miss Jane Bennett. She was the daughter of a teacher and when I was a boy I would do the gardening at their house. So I was their student and their worker. They liked it that I worked so hard at school and in their garden. Miss Jane Bennett, she would come and talk to me in English while I worked in the garden. But I lost touch with her. *[His eyes have a wistful look]*

GIRL What was it like here in those days?

PROSECUTOR Oh, it was wonderful. Lashkar Gah was a great place. And I was able to go and study in Tajikistan. I had two US friends there, Dan and Rachel. She wanted to learn Persian. They were very good friends. At one stage they were going to arrange for me to go to America. But I thought, why would I do that? Things here are great. But it changed, all changed. I did regret not going to America then. The Taliban—do you know about the Taliban, what they were like?

GIRL Er, yes, just what I've read, though.

PROSECUTOR It was an awful time. Awful. They wouldn't allow children to go to school. Now *[he grins widely, displaying the craggy range of yellow teeth]* two of my sons will go to university. And my two daughters are at school.

1st COUNCILLOR *[to PROSECUTOR, in Pashto]* Ask her what age she is!

PROSECUTOR You can't ask her that! *[to GIRL]* He wants to know what age you are.

GIRL It's OK, I always ask you guys lots of questions. I'm forty.

1st COUNCILLOR *[he draws a furry white eyebrow up so far it almost disappears under his turban]* Forty. Four-zero, yes?

GIRL Yes.

1st COUNCILLOR *[to 2nd COUNCILLOR]* She's forty.

2nd COUNCILLOR Yes, I heard. I'm sitting right here.

1st COUNCILLOR And are you married?

GIRL No.

1st COUNCILLOR *[to 2nd COUNCILLOR]* She's not married.

2nd COUNCILLOR Yes, I heard. I'm sitting right here.

1st COUNCILLOR Why not? In Afghanistan you should be married when you are fourteen!

GIRL I'm afraid I'm pretty much the wrong side of fourteen. It seems I'm too late to get married—at least in Afghanistan.

*[PROSECUTOR sniggers]*

1st COUNCILLOR Hmm. *[He eyes the GIRL sternly, as if gauging her worth]* But you are quite pretty. I think you could still get married. You are lucky to be in Afghanistan—somebody will marry you.

2nd COUNCILLOR In Afghanistan, we all support each other in our families. It has to be the family, you see, because the government doesn't. It just can't. So, if someone loses their job, the family takes care of them. If someone gets sick, the family takes care of them. Does that happen in the UK?

GIRL To a degree. But the state also supports, with healthcare, and with some money for people who lose their jobs. That's the theory, at least.

2nd COUNCILLOR Hmm. *[He strokes his pearl-colored beard, widens his eyes]* We are always obedient to our parents. If they say something, we do that. Are people obedient to their parents in the UK?

GIRL When we are children, generally yes, we are. Respect for our parents is a really important value. But when we get older, we make our own decisions—we act independently of our parents.

1st COUNCILLOR Hah! That's not such a bad thing. A good thing. The Qur'an says the same, that people should know their own mind and make their own decisions. Yes, a good thing.

2nd COUNCILLOR And in our religion, we have the mosque—you have the—?

GIRL Church.

2nd COUNCILLOR And you have Allah and Jesus?

GIRL Yes, so the Bible says.

1st COUNCILLOR Hmm. Ah, but we Muslims are very lucky, because we know that once everyone dies they all turn into Muslims anyway. We just have a head start! *[Giggles]*

GIRL So being Muslim is important for you?

2nd COUNCILLOR Very. It's our whole life.

1st COUNCILLOR *[Clearly religion is not a topic that holds him as much as his colleague]* In Afghanistan we have a dowry system for marriage. Do you have such a system in the UK?

GIRL Not exactly, but parents will generally contribute to the wedding costs and all the wedding guests will bring gifts, so the cost is spread around. I have heard that dowries here can be up to $50,000. Is that true?

1st COUNCILLOR Yes, yes.

GIRL How can families pay that much?

PROSECUTOR The Judge would like to ask you a question.

GIRL He wants to know if I'm married?

[*1st and 2nd COUNCILLORS and PROSECUTOR laugh*]

JUDGE Are you married?

GIRL No.

JUDGE Ah, in Afghanistan it is a crime to go past a certain age and not be married!

GIRL I hope you're not going to throw me in jail.

JUDGE No, no! We can have different types of sentence! You see, we are sad because if a man or a woman isn't married, they don't have their full rights.

[*GIRL looks puzzled, so TRANSLATOR explains*]

TRANSLATOR You see, here, it's not like the West. We don't have boyfriends or girlfriends. We aren't allowed to. So if you don't get married you never know how it is to have someone, and that reduces the quality of your life. That's what he means when he says you don't have your rights. And you don't have children. It is a very special love when you are a parent. It is different even from my wife.

GIRL And how did you meet your wife?

TRANSLATOR She is my cousin. We had to do the blood test to be sure that we could marry and our children would be OK. That's how most people meet, through families, and then they stay in the family. But the big family. Can I ask you something?

GIRL Only if it's not "Are you married?"

TRANSLATOR Hah! No, it's not that. Before I come to work in the morning, I play with my daughter and I watch the BBC news. This morning there was a feature on Mexico City. There they now allow two men to get married. Isn't that… [*He hesitates*] wrong?

GIRL Well, we have the same system operating in the UK. [*She believes the nuances of civil partnership and marriage would be lost, so keeps it simple*] Two men, or two women, can get married.

[*GIRL is conscious that 2nd COUNCILLOR, PROSECUTOR, and*

*JUDGE are all listening]*

TRANSLATOR But how do they *do* it?

GIRL Well, they just like male bodies or female bodies. Or, they fall in love with a person and don't care what sex or body the person comes in. For example, I've been to two civil partnerships between two men in the past two years, and this year I will go to one between two women. My gay friends sometimes have more enduring relationships than my straight ones!

TRANSLATOR *[puzzled]* But... don't... they... want... children?

GIRL No, they want puppies. *[TRANSLATOR and PROSECUTOR laugh. 2nd COUNCILLOR looks thoughtful]* But it is a little hypocritical, isn't it, because we know that same sex relations happen here all the time, especially men with young boys. You know that, don't you? That's what we would call child sex abuse. And that is what we would say is wrong, not two people consenting to get married to each other.

TRANSLATOR I know. It happens here. It is wrong. But, this gay rights—is it given in your rights?

GIRL It wasn't always the case, but yes, now we have legal guarantees around gender and sexuality.

TRANSLATOR See, that's what gets me most of all about this country. We don't have any *rights* that are *guaranteed.* They may exist on paper, but we never get them. If I get arrested I may or may not get my rights. It's just too uncertain. What I like most about your country is that your government cares about your rights. *[Pauses]* But also lesbians? How do the women know that it is even possible?

GIRL The same way the men do: they speak with each other, they like each other, and one thing leads to another!

*[TRANSLATOR and PROSECUTOR laugh]*

TRANSLATOR *[confidently]* Well, there are no lesbians in Afghanistan. Our women know nothing about that.

GIRL *[smiling]* Are you sure?

TRANSLATOR *[very confidently]* Yes, because they don't get to see any porn, to learn how to do it. *[Giggles]*

GIRL You watch porn?

TRANSLATOR Yes! We men are always so sneaky. *[Giggles]*

GIRL So you're quite sure they don't watch it while you men are all out, earning a living?

[*TRANSLATOR's jaw drops. PROSECUTOR laughs*]

*The scene is night time at KAF, two days later. GIRL and FIXER have just completed the first check-in for the military flight home after a day of high drama involving the courier (just in time) of GIRL's passport to KAF. Two buses, one white, one red, are parked outside the flightline (a series of concrete block pens, reminiscent of animal husbandry). A pretty young Britmil woman is in charge of the check-in and has been very helpful.*

FIXER She rides the other bus, that young'un, y'know!

GIRL [*puzzled*] The other bus?

FIXER The other bus!

GIRL [*more puzzled*] The red one? Or the white one?

FIXER No, the bloody pink one!

GIRL [*in realization*] Ahh. The other bus. I've not heard it called that before.

FIXER [*laughs*] Ah, but she's a great lass. At first we tried to change her—she's such a good lookin' lass. But she was havin' none of it! Live and let live, I always did say.

GIRL [*thinks*] So there are some lesbians in Afghanistan after all.

The gym, Nawa

# 26. Nawa (I):
# Inside the Wire

THE FLIGHT TO NAWA takes about seven minutes, a straight drop south of Lashkar Gah, but we might as well be landing on a different planet—one with a lot of dust. We fly low and almost directly over the Helmand River, snaking its milky green way around sandbanks and dunes, making small tributaries that branch off and quickly rejoin the main flow, like a solid green staff with crazy filigree the length of its sides.

We land in a field, flat and baked brown, just outside FOB Jaker, formerly occupied by UK military and now home to the US Marines. I can't see anything when I disembark because the chopper raises so much dust. One of our Afghan colleagues hands me what looks like a surgical mask—pale green tissue, elastic straps for the ears. I'm amazed (where, how, did he get it?) but it is just what the doctor ordered. I breathe in much less of the field than if I didn't have it.

There are fifteen of us on the flight, Derek and me and our bodyguard and twelve Afghan colleagues. We're here to roll out the next ASOP community council planning workshop. This is Derek's third trip in three weeks. The previous two times he was putting together an electoral list of around 300 names from all the local elders and all the villages in the district, and then conducting the election, which whittled the number of representatives down to 45. The council is still a roughly hewn piece and in some respects will never lose that edge. And it's precisely that unfinished quality that will continue to claim respect and legitimacy among the community that it represents. We are here to work with them to enable them to really deliver for their constituency by facilitating a draft community plan.

Nawa is a district recently "cleared" by the US. It has a long border with the main Taliban base, Marjeh, surrounded by a deadly minefield that requires a (paid) escort through it by those who laid the mines. There's only one vehicular way through. When the US entered Nawa the Taliban all quickly retreated to Marjeh, their stronghold, so there hasn't been so much as a shot fired around the district center where we will be for the next three months.

For the next six days we will be guests of the Marines. Derek has warned me off, telling me that it will be the most basic FOB I've been to.

"It's just moon dust everywhere," he says. I'm glad Mohammed Noor has given me the surgical mask. Sounds like I'll need to keep it.

As we land outside the wire we get a Marine escort into the base. This in itself is novel—walking next to a real field as little kids clamor around right away, waving, asking for sweets, with dark puppy dog eyes outlined in kohl (as if they needed any highlighting) and impossibly long and thick lashes.

We turn the corner around the Hesco wall (like the desert sand, it gets everywhere) and into camp. Derek says, "Whoa!" (Derek says "whoa!" a lot, like he's pulling up on a horse.)

"Whoa!" he says again. "Where's all the moon dust gone? And there are wooden houses. It used to be just tents. Ten days ago this was a different place! Amazing."

It's true: the Marines have dumped tons of gravel over the sand, a temporary subjugation—it still shows through in places. And they've built three wooden huts to replace the tents. The graveled ground is the color of crushed peppercorns. Nonetheless I quickly conclude that those guys *like* to tough it out, they revel in being able to live in very, very basic conditions.

Derek leads the way to our sleeping quarters—an old mud and straw building with four walls, a hard floor, and a dried palm roof, and no electricity. We dump our bags by the army cots. I get one in a small dark cell the length of the cot, which is about the length of me. If I stretch my arms out I can just about reach both sides, so it is about the width of me at full wingspan. Two sides are the soft mud and wattle walls and I think of Yeats arising now and going to Innisfree. (I'm not sure he'd do any arising if he knew he was going to Nawa.) The other two sides are plywood. There are three wooden/wattle cubicles at one end of the room and one at the other. For the next five nights it's home. We immediately seek out lunch. One has to get one's priorities right. And if eating is one's priority, then Derek is the right person to be with. We go immediately to the food tent. This is the tent full of cardboard boxes of de-oxygenated food pumped full of preservatives.

I've had rather too much experience with the US MREs (Meals Ready to Eat). The previous week, when I was in Garmsir again, I found myself for the first time in my life counting calories in reverse. I had to make sure I had eaten 2,000 of them, or as close to that as I could stomach. US MREs show every single calorie on their food packs. Several days I got to evening dinner only having had 700, meaning I had 1,300 calories to play with—at one meal. And where was the nearest Prêt à Manger Carrot Cake (400-odd calories a slice) when I was actually allowed, indeed required, to have one?

Britmil Ratpacks are different. And because FOB Jaker was once a British base Derek knows that there are still some Ratpacks about. So we leave the food tent with two heavy cardboard boxes, each containing ten 24-hour ration packs.

"So you're sure they are better?" I ask, as the cardboard cuts into my fingers.

"Oh God yes," Derek says. "Just wait." It's true. Though there's slightly more work (popping them into boiling water, and waiting for them to warm up, instead of the as yet unidentified chemical + cold water = heat magic of the US packs) they taste better. For lunch I pop the Chicken Tikka Masala silver foil package into the small water boiler.

"Where do we get bowls?" I ask Derek.

"A bowl?" he says, in the same tone as Beadle said "More?" "The packet—it is the bowl."

Of course that stylish foil is a bowl. I rip it open and the curry is entirely passable. I'm surprised that there are any Ratpacks left because even the Marines see that they are better. Consider our conversation at breakfast with a young (thin) Marine from California called Kevin. Derek and I are munching on our All Day Breakfast and Omelet, Sausage, and Beans respectively. Kevin is eating Imitation Boneless Pork Ribs with Barbeque Sauce, Smoke Flavor Added. Yes, it actually says "Imitation" on the packet.

"Yeah, your Ratpacks are so much better than ours. These MREs, why they've gotta be against the Geneva convention."

"Yeah, an attack on your own troops," I say.

"A blue on blue operation," quips Derek.

"You know, the amount of preservative we eat is having an effect on the rate at which our bodies decompose after death. It takes much longer," says Sarah, who has joined us a day or so after our arrival.

"So we only get the benefit the far side of the line?" I say.

"Yeah, what's that all about?" says Kevin, his surfer's tanned face grinning, his Marine haircut long grown out. He's still too thin though, like a pencil with one of those hairy-troll caps. He should eat more British Ratpacks, even mix and match with the US MREs. But no, that's patriotism for you: stick with the US food.

We have a cup of tea after lunch. The kettle takes ages to boil—it's only fed 110 volts, so that means it takes twice as long as the normal 220 volts. There are no cups in FOB Jaker, only what you bring yourself. I grabbed a couple of paper ones as we left the HLS at Lashkar Gah. It's amazing how many times you can actually re-use them, if you rinse them out and dry them afterwards, and I think of how many we throw away after one use in Lash.

When it comes to toilets, that's not really the case. I never thought I'd be wishing for Wagbags, but here I am, wishing for Wagbags. I never thought I'd be wishing for the wooden cubicles of FOB Delhi. But here I am, wishing for the wooden cubicles. For here there are four, how shall I say it delicately, locations for excreta. But they are all part of the one rough wooden unit. There's a swing door at either end, like a Wild West saloon door, then the row of four platforms with only a panel of wood between each one. For the one place where I don't really want openness and transparency, well, it's quite cozy. The only thing is, it takes your mind off the half-barrels that catch everything that falls from the platforms above. It is as difficult a navigation as walking a plank between two skyscrapers, just don't look down. Sarah asks my advice on using the stalls when she arrives.

"Timing," I say, "it's all about timing. Or else get Derek to stand guard."

The barrels are burned once a day, and the acridity of the smell almost makes me gag. They are right beside the gym area, which consists of a few old and skeletal-looking bits of weights equipment grown more sun-bleached every day, like white bones in the desert. There is no facility for any aerobic workout on camp, the stones are too big to run on, nor is there any running machine in the gym. Maybe it's just as well because the dust that you'd inhale (including the fecal matter) would far outweigh any muscle strengthening benefit.

By 19:30 it's pitch black, and it feels so much later. Your body clock gets much more attuned to daylight and darkness when there is no artificial light to prolong the day. We go to bed about 20:00 most nights. Of course, there is more often than not that middle-of-the-night trip to the toilet, which means getting fully dressed, crunching across the stones for 120 yards and facing the communal stalls in the moonlight. It's a truism of Chicken-Soup-for-the-Soul-speak to say that the darkest time is just before the dawn. But having got up twice one night, it's actually true. Because the blacker the soft inky velvet of sky stretched taut, the brighter the silver of the stars, which shimmer in discernible millions close to earth, while hovering in a bracket above them is the white gossamer veil of the Milky Way, sparkling without a care across the seats of the gods in this heavenly theater viewed from vertiginous earth.

But there is also progress, and an unexpected treat. On the second day a big generator arrives and there is power in our room. Each day thereafter the little Afghan man who is the very competent electrician adds more and more lights to the room, inside and outside. This has its downside, though. Suddenly five laptops appear, with five people working on them. Clearly work expands to fill a vacuum. The five people seem to have endless discussions about filling in timesheets, but the person who's been loudest on the issue I only ever see working on Facebook or Yahoo. Perhaps Facebook has a "work" group that I don't know about. But the real progress comes with the stalls. Three days in, a new set is built, this time with individual doors. Yes, I am easily pleased.

The shower is a delight by comparison, a tiny wood and corrugated tin narthex affair affixed to the outside wall of our building/room, about half the size of an outdoor toilet and with tall beige fronds of palm grass flocked at the corner. If you get there early enough after the workshop you can benefit from the hot water in the solar shower warmed by the sun. You might only be able to use a cupful (which is surprisingly easy to do—again, it is amazing how little you need), but at least it's warm and in daylight. Cold and in the dark is something else. One morning I see a square of toilet paper on the ground beside the shower. On it is written, in careful copperplate: "1935. The US Senate refuses to agree the access of the US to the Permanent Court of International Justice." One of the Marines must be studying legal history while he's here. I'm not sure why he needs to write it on tissue paper though. There is lots to do in their spare time. Some of them do carpentry, some cook (real fries from potatoes and oil that they buy in the bazaar). And some make shapes from Hesco wire. The camp also has the most creative use of Hesco basket wire I've seen. There is a Hesco chaise longue and a Hesco armchair, really well crafted, that would not look out of place in the MoMA.

And there's another treat, a culinary one: real rib-eye steak. About once every two months or so the US will fly out steaks to the troops, and they will simply be barbequed on a barrel sliced in two lengthwise. I have had a run of good luck on this—last week in Garmsir I was there the night they had steak (and grapes). So this steak is the third best steak I've ever had in my life (the other two being on the BBQ at Delhi and at the Capitol Grill in DC). This steak can be cut with the plastic knife from the disposable cutlery set as if it were butter and then it melts in the mouth, virtually fizzing with flavor on the tongue. I don't want to have any of the MREs to accompany it. It is quite glorious all by itself.

Another day we are given a box of pomegranates by Shah Wali (he of the rotund tum). We rapaciously devour the divine pink flesh, the juice running all over our fingers and the sheet of paper we put for a plate. "Whoa!" says Derek, as we are sitting on the pomegranate-stained cot, the bloody aftermath of one of our seed-crunching sessions, "this is just great. We get to do a great job that hardly anyone else in the world—the whole world—does. We get to go camping. And they pay us for it. Whoa! We are bloody privileged."

It's true, even in these rough conditions, we are privileged. Which is why, when we go outside the wire, we need to take care and tread softly, for we tread upon Afghan hopes.

Poetry reading

# 27. Nawa (II):
# Outside the Wire

WE ARE GOING OUTSIDE the wire, on foot. There's me, Derek and Shaq, our IBG (Individual Body Guard), a few contractors, and ten US Marines. We do a drill before we go: "I am one and you are two," says the lead Marine, pointing to the person behind him in the row. "I am two and you are three," says the next guy, getting the Von Trapp children rhythm going.

I get nervous, I'm sure I am going to screw it up and because of my numerical ineptitude will be judged such a liability at the outset that I won't be able to go.

"I am twelve and you are thirteen," I say, pointing at Derek.

"Whoa! What'd you say, Kate? Fourteen, am I fourteen? That means you must be fifteen, mate," he says, pointing to the guy behind him.

I laugh, the floppy top pencil Marine, Kevin, laughs. We finally establish that we are seventeen. The lead Marine explains his mission: to go and speak with a local influential mullah and establish how they might have a relationship. In this war it doesn't really matter how much firepower or how many troops you have—if all they are doing is physically fighting it just isn't enough. They need, at the very least, to engage with local communities as well.

We set off, a numerically challenged rag-tag group, at first along the side of the Hesco wall of the FOB, and then at a T-junction off to the right along the canal. Its banks are barren and black, shaved close to the brown earth from which the scrub has recently been burned off as part of the clean-up effort. Even wearing body armor and with the gunned-up Marines it feels exhilarating, liberating, to be outside.

We walk along the canal, long and straight, crossing it on a narrow bridge—basically a one-brick-wide wall that we reach via a steep descent on loose slippery sand. I'm wearing sneakers with well-worn soles. Derek is wearing loafers with well-worn soles. I'm afraid that either I will slide into the person in front of me or that Derek will fall on me, especially as he's continually taking pictures. And one is not so agile when wearing Kevlar. We cross and now walk down a dusty beaten track through flat fields that I know would be greener or yellower if it were not for the pepper-colored powder of ground sand that shrouds every leaf or ear of corn sheathed in crisp desiccated leaves. There is a small stream and a line of low trees on one side of us, flat fields of grass and corn on the other. Something akin to turf burns in the distance so that a wall of smoke lurks low on the horizon and its smell is sweet and simple and calming and of the brown earth beneath the sun-fired scrub. It smells like being in Donegal in early autumn.

We turn across a small footbridge (wider than one brick) into the mullah's compound. He greets the Marines. We hang back, me especially. I am the only woman of the seventeen, and am only wearing hijab, not full Afghan dress like I usually do when going out. The mullah is said to be very conservative and so I don't want to screw up the mission in a more serious way than not being able to say two consecutive numbers. The mullah is tall, ruddy, and bear-like. He has a great big block of a face, like a wood sculpture with the basic features only roughly chiseled around the natural knots. He looks around the whole group from under his turban and smiles in greeting, slow mechanical nods to everyone except me. I don't take it personally, instead have a chat with the four or five kids who have suddenly appeared.

The oldest child may only be about seven but we do manage to converse, mainly because in response to their questions (Do you have a pencil? Do you have sweets? Do you have pencils? Do you have sweets? What is your name?) all I say is "Pencils I not have," "sweets I not have." They also ask about my family, where I am from, and I ask their names (they laugh when I pronounce these for the first time). There are two boys, with hazelnut brown skin, white teeth, cropped hair in navy *salwar kameez* and little skullcaps. And their sister, without hijab, is beautiful. She is shy and doesn't smile at all except weakly (a twitch at the corner of her mouth) at the very end, just staring with her huge eyes the shade and sheen of freshly unsheathed chestnuts from beneath a fringe of oil-black hair, matted and dusty. I catch the mullah glance over and smile at the interaction with his children, but I don't try to catch his gaze.

The mission is a success, contact has been made and the mullah has put in some requests to help with the reconstruction of his mosque. We move off, but by now a small crowd has gathered, mostly the neighborhood kids.

The Marines and the mullah stand on the bridge and exchange farewells. Other small girls appear on the far bank of the stream, dressed in bright *salwar kameez* and barefooted and bareheaded. I'm slightly stunned, as Derek has told me he hasn't seen one woman, ever, in the bazaar, yet these girl children, though they don't have the cockiness or confidence of their brothers, appear to have the same freedom, certainly in terms of running around and getting mucky among the trees and mud wall compounds, just like we did in our playground of twisted ivy vines and ash and sycamore trees sprouting up around the granite carcasses of old cottages when we were their age. The little boys ask me to take their photographs and crowd round to see the digital image on the back. A man just arrived on a motorbike asks me to take his and insists on seeing it with the same enthusiasm as the kids. The little girls hang back, staring with those big eyes, amazed at the spectacle of padded foreigners at their front door.

We turn back into town, going down a desert track. We are in the green zone, but wherever human hand has not tilled the desert erupts, triumphant. The track is full of moon dust—each step raises a small cloud that billows and seems to take more time to fall than it should, like disturbed sand on the seabed sways gently on the brine before falling slowly back.

We meet a man and a small girl of about eight herding long-haired sheep. They raise quite a dust cloud. There is cultivated land all around us—these people are not lazy or slow. Even though the canals don't function fully, what there is is made use of. A farmer comes up to us and asks for money for fertilizer. A man bathes in the canal, standing up and scrubbing himself down, possibly with soap. A camel is tethered outside a compound, calmly ignoring our party trying again to count to seventeen.

We turn left down to the bazaar. Four months ago it was empty, a ghost town. The canal was choked with rubbish. Now there are around a hundred shops open—covered stalls with people peddling wares:

fruit and vegetables (local pomegranates, Pakistani bananas, onions and peppers), bicycles, car parts (streaked heavily with oil); there are cobblers hammering at shoes, money traders with soiled Pakistani rupee and local afghani notes behind smeared glass shelves. It may not be commerce as we know it, but it is commerce nonetheless.

We turn into the governor's compound, which is flush with the base, and retire for the evening.

The next day it is good to see our team again: Shah Wali, Abul Whakiel, Wahedullah, and Dr. Jawid (finally without a sweater, even though it has started to cool down a bit). There is the usual chaos before the workshop starts, even though we have been through the agenda many times beforehand. These are the most rudimentary conditions we'll have worked in. Even in Garmsir where the FOB is basic the district governor's compound has good rooms to work in, including break-out rooms. We need three rooms. Right now we have two small rooms but no central room for the forty-odd council members.

Shah Wali, a great organizer, is supposed to have organized a tent. It is four in the afternoon and there's no sign of the tent which we need for nine the following morning. It will be dark in two hours. There is a curfew on movement after dark, but really no one needs a curfew, nobody would be foolish enough to travel after dark. Shah Wali says the car with the tent (and here I'm thinking of a marquee-style big top with hard flooring and maybe an air conditioning unit) has left Lash at two-thirty. The journey (for us seven minutes in a helicopter) should only take an hour by car.

"It's four o'clock, Shah Wali," Derek says, "I think I'm beginning to be a little worried." It's not just the arrival of the equipment he's worried about—it's the safety of those transporting it by road.

"I am worried too," says Shah Wali, going out of the room. "I'll call them."

He comes back in, a grin the size of a slice of melon across his face.

"Yes, yes, they are coming. They will be here."

There is a specific worry about this particular community council because over the past three weeks the Taliban's "shadow governor" has sent out night letters—on Taliban headed notepaper—to those

Elders thinking about getting involved in the community council. The message was simple: don't do it, or we will consider you a legitimate target. "Legitimate target": I haven't heard that phrase since the early 1990s—it is exactly the same phrase used by both republican and loyalist paramilitaries at home. And I remember what happened to those who became so labeled.

The next morning the tent is there. It looks nothing like what I expected. It is more like a giant windbreaker that used to be a feature of every Irish beach—coarse canvas pulled around poles to keep you from the icy blast as you changed out of wet swimming gear. Here the cloth is finer and more decorative—giant red flowers on a green background, then another layer of cinnamon specks on a canary yellow base. They are pulled around big bamboo poles. Shaq, our IBG, is originally from Pakistan and says it is exactly like a Pakistani wedding tent. There is a roof of the same material as the walls held up by some mysterious Afghan mechanics connected in some way with the wall of the governor's house. Across the rough cobbles of the stones and the sand underfoot are a series of carpets. On the carpets sit the newly elected community council.

I'm always nervous going into these situations for the first time, before you get to know the Elders. All you see is a sea of turbans and beards and stern eyes, often staring. But you have to earn your stripes with every group, and Derek has assured me they are a good bunch. What I see immediately is that there are more younger Elders than in our other councils. This can happen if an Elder dies suddenly and his son inherits his position in the community, even if he is still in his thirties. There are about four or five in this category. One is like an Afghan Johnny Depp, with a Captain Jack Sparrow facial hair arrangement and cheekbones that could cut steak. His eyes are deep and ponderous and he smiles when our eyes meet. Another has a round chubby face and a stubby beard, sparkling black eyes with lots of laughter lines. He smiles a lot, laughs a lot too. One of the older ones is like a little leprechaun. He has a long beard, and translucent yellow-brown eyes, which change color depending on the light. He is the "waterman," the man who is responsible for seeing that the main canal discharges water into its tributaries at the right time, so that all the villages

villages get enough water in turn for their crops. He's also a major spreader and source of news.

As usual Derek is right. They turn out to be a great bunch. On the third day elections are held for the officers. There are two candidates for Chair. The first is a tall man in a sky blue *salwar kameez* and black waistcoat and turban. He is quite imposing. The second is smaller and looks slightly sheepish, as if he's just been found out in a prank. He is thin, has meek brown eyes, a closed lip smile, and as he stands holding his placard, looks a bit hapless. I think two things: that he doesn't really want the job, and that if he gets it he won't be a good leader. But he, Mr. Mir Wali Khan, wins and becomes the Chair. We go out on another foot patrol with the Marines that afternoon and a car—a white Toyota Corolla, of course—beeps as it drives past us. It is the Chairman, smiling broadly as he drives by, clearly more comfortable in this (his own) milieu than he was earlier. Maybe Mr. Mir Wali Khan will do all right after all.

On the fourth day we split into subject area groups. Mine is security. I am delighted that the waterman is in my group—he has been so welcoming.

Our first session—Dr. Jawid and I are the facilitators—goes well. I am vaguely aware of more staring than usual and of some mobile phone photography but reckon that I am the equivalent of a space alien and if I were them I'd stare too. Plus, we take photos of them all the time, so there's a bit of quid pro quo. I am wearing full Afghan dress and am barefooted because we are inside and no one wears their shoes inside.

When we finish our (three-hour) session I am exhausted. Wahedullah comes up to me and says I need to be careful about how I am acting. He does not elaborate because he doesn't want to offend me, so I ask him to be specific.

"Wahedullah, I can't change my behavior unless I know exactly what the problem is."

"Well, er," he says, his green eyes widening, "your clothes. They are very nice clothes, but…"

"And?" I say, getting a little frustrated.

"Well, how you sit. And your feet. They can see the soles."

I know that showing the soles of your feet is rude, so I have been careful to sit either cross-legged or with soles down, knees bent. But when changing position, it seems, my feet have caused some frisson.

"Well, if they are going to complain about my feet, they can stop staring. And stop taking video footage of me with their phones."

Wahedullah is a paragon of Afghan virtue. I know he wouldn't be saying this to me unless he felt he had to, and I know he probably wouldn't bother with someone he didn't like. I don't mean to be cross with him, but I am. I am petulant and I know it, but just I can't help feeling that they've just moved the goalposts, especially as I had dressed for the occasion. I've never encountered this before.

We have our final session the following day. Before we break into groups one of the worst offenders from the day before in terms of staring is still doing it. There are only two of them—the rest of the men in the group, including the waterman and the big burly red-bearded Chair of the committee are great, they are really keen to engage and we have in-depth conversations about how to deal with the Taliban, especially given the threat level.

But now this man is disturbing. It's crossing the line for me. I speak with Wahedullah again. "Yes, Dr. Jawid told me about it," says Wahedullah. "We are going to get their mobile phones today and we will delete any images."

I'm stunned that Dr. Jawid has noticed any kind of sexual untowardness; he is such an intellectual. It's a lesson to me that the sexual mores are very strict, but observed—in both senses of the word—by everyone, and that they are, though invisible and submerged, at once also ubiquitous and dominant.

The man is spoken to and the images are duly deleted. The staring stops. We finish our work.

The waterman and I talk at the end. He is proud of his two sons going to school, but worried that the teachers are only teaching for two hours a day.

"I am an uneducated man," he says, "I haven't had a notebook in my hand for twenty years because of these wars. I only did two grades in school."

He doesn't say it, but the inference is that he wants more for his children. He is ashamed of his own lack of education but he has been one of the most insightful and engaged speakers in our group; small in stature he may be but he is a giant reserve of wisdom.

On the last morning the Jack Sparrow lookalike comes over. It turns out that he is a poet. He bashfully requests that he be allowed to read his poem to the group. Of course we agree. I immediately assume it's going to a saccharine paean to unrequited pristine love with a highly romanticized syntax to match. I couldn't be further wrong. It is a contemporary exploration of the condition of Helmand over the past thirty years, more like a political Mary Oliver or Philip Larkin than Keats or Spenser. It is hard to get the translation because he reads it straight through in a strong timbre and steady meter, but this (very roughly—I am paraphrasing a non-contemporaneous translation) is how some of it might read if it were written in English:

**Helmand Refugee**
The Russians tried to occupy Afghanistan.
We kicked them out. /…/

The Mujahideen thought that they'd be good.
But they did everything for themselves
Not for us. /…/

Then September 11 happened.
Osama bin Laden thought that he was
A great man for Islam.
But no—he made us fight
Each other for seven years. He was
Behind the Taliban.

The Taliban? What did they do for us?
They made our houses sangars, that's what they did.
And they killed us. And what did you do?
You gave them food and let them use
Your house to shoot from, and then
Complained when the US and the UK bombed
Your house.

Yes, the US came, they are here.
And Britain came again.
They fought and bombed your houses.

Through all the regimes, we the Helmandis
Have been here.
We've been killed, but we have remained.
We have faced tough times, and we
Have been refugees, but we have remained.

You need to come home to Helmand. To make
Your lives here, for we Helmandis will be here
When all the regimes are gone.

This is the truth, I am telling the truth.

I don't know what will happen in this regime.
I am not scared of any regime
The only thing that I am scared of is God.

There is steady applause when he finishes—true appreciation of the arts in this small village in the back end of beyond. Say what you will about Helmand, it always has the ability to surprise. It has been a good week, everyone is happy with the workshop and we are enthused with the plans we have together made for the future. The week has been hard work but today is a good day. The flight even comes early for us. Seven minutes after leaving the dust field we are back in Lashkar Gah in time for our Friday, our precious day off.

But there is a tragic postscript. On Friday Derek receives word that Mir Wali Khan, the Chairman, has been kidnapped. On Saturday his body is recovered by his family. It's the first time the Taliban have so directly carried out the threats in their night letters. It's devastatingly sad, for him, his family, and friends but also for the council—and for us. We know we can't be bound by the thought, but the thought does cross our minds as we have a drink on that Saturday night: were we in some way responsible? Did our intervention contribute in some way to his death? It's not a good day. The next week, the week just past, is not a good week. Derek goes back down twice to commiserate, comfort, and console. It is hard for him, absorbing the grief and fear of others, but he does a good job. Tomorrow he and I will attend a short memorial service for Mir Wali Khan and then we will come back to base and figure out how we are going to move the council forward. If it completely falls apart, then the Taliban have truly triumphed not just physically (with the attendant and immediate sadness) but also conceptually. This may be the time for a short tactical retreat. But it is not the time for withdrawal. We need to remain committed to this for a long time to come.

Community council meeting, Nawa

# 28. Nawa (III): Despair

OTHERS SAID IT WASN'T SO, but Derek and I, we knew.

"It may have been a family squabble," they said, some of those who thought they knew the intel.

"Nothing has been proven," they said, some of those who hadn't been, hadn't seen.

But we knew: we knew the tragedy of last week's footnote could only be due to the Taliban. But that didn't necessarily exclude family members from being the perpetrators. Like houses divided into pro- and anti-Treaty during the Irish civil war—or any civil war for that matter—this conflict sets brother against brother, cousin against cousin, except there's no clear definition of what each other is fighting for because here there is no Treaty, no political agreement or prospect of one to be fighting about. At base there is government and anti-government, yes, but most times the government at least seems so very far away and so fragile and unformed, fearing to step into the sun, to see, to be.

That's what our workshop has been all about—expanding the footprint of government right down to grassroots level communities out in the districts where officialdom fears to tread. We base the title of our report on the workshop from a phrase we heard many times during the week: the delegates all proclaim that they are, or they want to be, a bridge between government and the people.

I write the first draft of our workshop report, and I must comment on the murder of Mir Wali Khan. Death is never something easily ignored, is it? I remember as I write and produce analysis ("It is no comfort to note that the progress made comes at a high cost") the hapless figure he cut as he stood forlornly with the number 1 card perched in his cupped hands at his election. He didn't want the job. ("And for some, the ultimate sacrifice has been made. The message from the Taliban is clear—when they want to, they can still execute a precision strike in the district.") This juxtaposition of analysis about his death and progress and my recollection of his shy self, smiling only as he beeped his car horn as he drove past us, on the dusty road in the low-slung evening sun is just weird. I feel oddly detached, as if I'm having an out-of-body experience, and yet the images of him in my mind are vivid.

Derek goes down to Nawa on Monday. I write the first draft of the report. He adds his part, nearly doubling it in length. He goes back down on Wednesday. I redraft. Thursday is the day that the council is to meet for the first time, and it will be the measure of whether or not the Taliban have scared people off completely.

Derek talks to one of the members that I have worked closely with. He accepts Derek's condolences, sees that we are still there to support, but understands that we can always get into a Sea Stallion and seven minutes later we can be in Lashkar Gah. An hour and ten minutes after that we can be in Kabul, and two and a half hours later we can be in Dubai. But he cannot leave. He is a respected man in the community, with a hefty frame, a florid face, and a big Buddha belly (which I had the misfortune to catch sight of as he rubbed it liberally during our workshop. I still think my feet were less offensive than his belly). He is chatting to Derek through Arif the interpreter when suddenly in the middle of this somber syntax Arif laughs and stops mid-sentence. Abdul smiles and urges him on: "Say! Say! Say what I said!"

Arif looks at Derek, "He says, um." He hesitates again. Most Afghans are very decorous about speech especially in front of foreigners. They simply don't curse.

Derek mirrors Abdul's grin, glad that he can form some facial expression other than the grim grip of sympathy.

"F**k 'em! F**k the Taliban! Tell them they can bring it on! I'm not scared of them!" As he has been in the workshops he is full of bravado, but he has been directly threatened too. He is not out of the woods yet. Nonetheless, Derek laughs with him. It's to be the only light moment that week.

On Saturday both he and I are meant to attend a memorial service for Mir Wali Khan, organized by the provincial governor. The male members of his family will be coming. However, on the Saturday morning they call it off. Not because they have been further threatened, but because there are simply too many people coming to the compound to pay their respects. They come from miles around, in the hundreds we are told, to express sympathy with the family but also disgust at the Taliban for executing him. It's like having the wake after the burial. I grasp at the slightest suggestion that the outpouring of sympathy and support might make some difference to the Taliban, might cause them to recalibrate. All governance requires consent at some level, even tyranny. Regimes can go too far. But it is not to be: the straw is whipped away by the cold and cruel wind that brings the next news.

Our little Lashkar Gah gang is back together again for the first time in months. Fraser, having left Lash in April, has come back to work in Kabul and has wrangled himself (actually: leading a serious delegation) a visit to Helmand. Paul has come back from leave. It's a Monday night, but we are all looking forward to some gin. And, with prescient punctuality, the tonic mailed by my sister arrives that day, so we can have gin *and* tonic. I go round to get Derek, still at his desk at 21:00. He's talking to someone, I can't remember to whom, but the person has imparted the appalling news: two more members of the community council have been murdered. I am stunned.

"Which ones?" I say. My head and my heart are just vacant, a numb vacuum.

"Dunno," Derek says grimly, "I just got the names."

"C'mon," I say, "let's go look at the photos."

Our list of the council members has their names and pictures—in part because they all have similar names (Abdul, Rahim, Arif, Haji, with Mohammed way out in front). I learned during the workshop that the local mullah generally names the children—the male ones at least—so it's not one of the few real choices that any Western parent has.

I am surprised. One of them, Abdul (not "my" Abdul, but another one) is the mullah. He led the recitation of the Qur'an at the beginning of each day, in Arabic. Even as I despair the analyst in me thinks that this killing might backfire on the Taliban. They may not need hearts and minds as much as we do, but they need something of them. Murdering a respected religious leader is not a smart move. But these thoughts are for another forum.

He was quite vocal in the open sessions, and was most animated when talking about education. As a religious scholar he bitterly resented the exodus of Helmandi students to madrasas in Pakistan or Iran. He felt they were taught nothing there but how to put together bombs, and an inverted Islam. He wanted good quality education—secular and religious—at home, in Helmand. He lamented the lack of female doctors in Nawa. The Celtic gene had somehow inveigled its way into his DNA at some stage in the preceding century, for he had pale skin flaked and ruddy now with exposure to the elements, alert green eyes, and a sun- and age-bleached strawberry blond beard. The other man was the deputy Chair. I don't recognize him from his photo, and so cannot think of anything to say about him at all. Derek and I sit for some moments in despair. We did not pull the trigger. We did not order the executions. But as we peer over the precipice into this dark kaleidoscope of contributing factors, the truth is that these three people would not be dead if we had not appeared on their doorstep and encouraged them—literally, we now to our horror find—to put their heads above the parapet.

How to pull back from this? We have a drink, and find ourselves oscillating between the maudlin and the merry in equal measure. We leave the misery and start to have conversations about the best FOB location for food, but then Derek says, "here we are talking about what salads we like, and these guys' families are distraught."

And yet what is to be done? What is the response? Not to give up, but that's easy for us to say. It seems helpless, hopeless. I am reminded now of Hobbes' characterization of society without government, without a social contract: "Lives are solitary, poor, nasty, brutish and short." *Leviathan* could have been written for this situation.

But there is always a response to violent acts, acts that tear lumps out of families and communities. And, though isolated, it is important they know they are not alone. Despair is not omnipotent—it can be defeated. With determination and political will communities can be protected. The government is not without agency here, the regular police are present and the provincial governor both cares about governance and has worked too hard to defeat the Taliban to let this go with impunity. The best CID officials are sent from Lashkar Gah to investigate the triple homicide. The community council is still due to meet on Thursday. Seven out of the forty odd show up. Not that the Taliban read Burke, but if they did, they would do well to consider his view that "The use of force alone is but temporary. It may subdue for a moment; but it does not remove the necessity of subduing again: and a nation is not governed which is perpetually to be conquered."

This all happens around the same time that the five UK soldiers are killed by a person in ANP uniform in Nad Ali, and things back at the PRT—usually an oasis for us when we come back from the districts—are rough too. So all in all it was a pretty grim week.

We go on leave. Not just because we can, but because this time, we really need to, to regroup, renew, rethink.

Out and about, Kabul

# 29. Ticking the Box: Marriage

RASHID IS LIKE a cross between a teddy-bear and a jelly-baby. He's short and squat, with a disproportionably large square head, almost comically brachycephalic. He's a bit wobbly overall and has enormous black eyes, the consistency of poured paint. Rather incongruously, he has a thick stubby moustache over his full lips and this and his girth remind me of the inspector in the animated Pink Panther. He always looks rather anxious, wearing frozen furrows on his big square brow. There's not a bad bone in his body or a bad thought in his head. I doubt there ever will be.

"Did I translate that OK, Miss Kate? I'm sorry, I know I'm not a very good translator. Some words I just don't understand," he says with deep humility. Of course I melt and want to scoop him up, but that really wouldn't be allowed—on a number of levels.

He's not the best translator we have, but neither is he by far the worst. And he is aware that he has more to learn, which is more than I can say for most of his colleagues. So we converse a lot over the few days we are working together. He's from Lashkar Gah, but works in one of the districts. He's the main breadwinner for his family, as all of these young men invariably are. One day we talk about marriage. He's only about twenty-two, so in Afghan terms he's getting on, almost on the shelf.

"So, are you married yet, Rashid?" I ask.

"No, not yet." He hesitates momentarily and then, with a short intake of breath, he says in his Mississippi Delta drawl (he's worked for the US Military before coming to work for us): "There was a girl. Her family wanted her to marry me, so my mawm, she asked me to meet her. Just because it was my mawm, I did. But she wasn't educated, this girl."

"So there was no obligation for you to marry her, if you met her?" I ask. "No. I told my mawm, 'Mom, she's not educated. I would not be happy with her.' And my mawm said that that was OK, she would find a nice educated girl for me."

He lowers his head and is silent for a moment, reflecting.

"The trouble is, there aren't so many educated girls around."

He's absolutely right about that. Especially in the districts there are whole generations of girls growing up without even knowing that there's such a thing as paper. And though girls are much less likely to be educated than boys it is likely that boys in the districts aren't educated either. I remember one of the young journalists I spoke with telling me once that he'd written a short newsletter to distribute to the people of his village (there are no newspapers, no print media, in Helmand; radio or word of mouth is how news is spread). When the villagers saw the printed text they thought it was English (it was in Pashto), foreign and therefore to be mistrusted. The young journalist had the task of explaining that it was in their own language and about things in their province. They'd simply not seen the written word before.

Rashid raises his head and smiles, big white teeth peeking out from under the curtain of a moustache. "But I trust my mawm. She will find a good girl for me, I am sure of it," he says, his eyes sleek and shining like a dark pelt.


Mohammad is a cleaner. He is a long and lean adolescent, with tight curls and delicate Hazara features (the high cheekbones of the Steppes, skin that is more yellow than brown, narrow hazel-green eyes from some genetic fusion on the Silk Road long ago, thin lips). He is not married yet either. He tells me that his father tried to marry him off once before, without him even seeing the girl.

"So I said to him, Miss Kate, I did, that I will respect his choice, but that I will not be marrying anyone without seeing them first!" he says earnestly.

"And how did your father react to you saying that?" I ask, drawn to this minor family soap opera. I am not kept hanging on the cliff for long. Mohammad laughs: "My father says that he doesn't understand young people, that it was different in his day. But he will not make me marry someone that I haven't seen, and even though he will make the selection, I must approve before I will marry her."

He smiles at this small inter-generational triumph. He doesn't realize how universal his theme of the son versus the father is, but he doesn't need to. He will maximize his autonomy, but I still wonder if it's not a somewhat pyrrhic victory.

There is a difference between these boys from the provinces and the boys from the big city. Those who have come down from Kabul mainly work for the military (their anonymity down here means their families are less likely to be targeted than if they were from Lashkar Gah. Plus they've generally been exposed to more English and so have a better grasp of the language than the local interpreters). There is also some rivalry between them. The military terps, out-of-towners, stay on camp while the local guys go home each evening. As far as I can make out, the locals see the Kabulis as interlopers, almost foreigners, with their sophisticated city ways. The irony is that while, yes, the Kabulis may be more sophisticated they are (even though the same age) simultaneously more boyish. The local boys seem to grow up faster perhaps because the Kabul boys are able to postpone the yoke of paternal responsibility for longer. But they all know it is coming.

Sadiq is an incredibly handsome young man from Kabul who wouldn't be out of place in a Benetton or Abercrombie and Fitch ad—a shock of black hair with a perfect meringue of peaks, regular features, thick black lashes fringing dark sparkling eyes. He feels the weight of the marriage path acutely, even though he's only twenty. He wants to travel, to go to the UK or the US to study. His voice is strong when he talks of these things. But when he speaks of marriage it drops to a low susurrus: "I don't want to be married. Not yet. I won't be able to travel if I do."

"It's not possible for you to do both?" I ask, knowing what the answer will be.

"No. Not here. It is not possible here, in Afghanistan," he answers wistfully.

His eyes well up and I think he might cry. But I see him take psychological hold of himself, wipe his eyes, and offer me a wan smile. Then he says something really unexpected: "Can I have a hug?"

It's the Kabul in him coming out. This would never happen with one of the locals. Perhaps I overload this, but it seems to me that he knows that he has dreams and ambitions that are above and beyond most of those he knows. He also knows that they will almost certainly never be realized. He is trapped, every bit as much as the fly in amber. I am overwhelmingly sad for him.

Marjeh is a much more worldly-wise individual. He's also young and from Kabul but a lot more relaxed and confident than Sadiq. Marjeh works as a translator in the districts, currently for us but previously for the US Military. He's one of the best interpreters we have and unusually doesn't take "being Afghan" very seriously. He mentions a girlfriend, an idea at which I am amazed.

"I thought you guys didn't have girlfriends? I thought you just went straight to getting married?" I ask, incredulous.

Marjeh laughs, the brown eyes lighting up.

"Well, I *had* a girlfriend."

"You are messing with my mind here, Marjeh. I didn't think it was possible for you to have a girlfriend, never mind more than one!"

He parries back: "Yeah, we even went on holiday together (I don't probe the detail of this). Up north, close to Tajikistan," he says, grinning. "But then she said, 'You'd better get your father to speak to mine, or else I will move on to someone else!' I said, 'Sorry, I don't want to get married. I want to travel, and I can't do that if I'm married.'"

"To be honest," he continues, talking to me now, not his ex-prospective wife, "and I don't want to sound hard, but for me a wife is like a disease. Look: I'm twenty-two. My family don't care if I'm married or not. They say I can marry who I like, a Russian girl even if I want. I think it's easy to find a girl. I have time."

It's true, he is handsome, educated, and speaks four and a half languages (Pashto, Dari, Urdu, English, and a smattering of Spanish). It's all in the family background, the attitude. And money. At twenty-two he earns more per month than his father ever did. He is respectful of his family, but his earnings give him leverage to negotiate issues like girlfriends and marriage.

"My money all goes to my family. My dad is currently jobless, but he is a tribal Elder so he is negotiating with people all the time, even at [national] parliament."

I'm still reeling from the ex-girlfriend revelation.

"But how do you meet girls in Kabul?"

He grins again.

"It's easy. At school. In the street. But a lot of parents these days don't do arranged marriages anymore. We choose our own lives. We are free."

"Oh yes. Here is very different. I don't know how they do it here. Boys never meet girls and girls never meet boys. But here in Helmand it's different, isn't it?"


Rahim is a Helmand boy through and through. Like his Kabuli counterparts he is multilingual and he's probably smarter than they are. He juggles a job and school. He's about twenty-two. Travel isn't his big thing but making money is. He has a truly entrepreneurial spirit and is always looking round for a new business to start up. He is top of his class in school, but the women in the class are always snapping at his heels. The next five places after him are held by women. Then it goes back to boys again. I find out that the academic positioning is also literal: the girls sit behind the boys in class.

I ask Rahim if he likes any girls at school.

"No, I don't talk to them. I control myself. I have done so for one year and five months now. Anyway, they sit behind us. I don't see them."

I say, "Why do you need to control yourself?"

"Because people will talk. If the girls want to talk, no problem. I will talk to them if we have a science problem."

"Don't you use a mirror?"

He looks at me blankly. Then he gets it. He starts to laugh.

"Ah! That is a very good idea. I will tell my colleagues. We had not thought of that up to now."

"I know, it's my wicked Western mind." He laughs again.

"So how are you going to get a girlfriend if you don't talk to them?" I continue.

"There was one girl's father. He proposed a marriage to my father. But my father said, 'No, my boy needs to see her first.' Then the girl's father, he said 'No, not until the wedding night.'" Rahim smiles widely at this escape, proud that his father has stood up for him. "Anyway, I have time," he continues. "And you are not married, Kate."

"I think it's a little late for me to get married, Rahim."

"But people get married later in your culture."

"That's true. But even so I'm still a little late."

He looks at me rather sadly, possibly overwhelmed with pity, the same way I was with Sadiq—or possibly not.

"But don't you have contract marriages? You just get married for one or two years and then divorce?"

"No!" I say. "Yes, there is lots of divorce, people have very high expectations of marriage. But people don't enter marriage *intending* to get divorced! Unless there's a new social phenomenon that I've missed."

Rahim looks at me slightly askance, as if he simply doesn't believe me.

"Maybe they should not have so high expectations," he says sagely. He continues: "For us, your father will choose the first wife. But you will choose the second. You need to keep the rights of all the wives respected."

"So how do you meet the second wife?"

"Through your family. At social gatherings."

I consider this for a moment and Rahim asks if I don't approve.

"It's not a matter of whether I approve or not, Rahim. It just seems to me to be such a big decision, so much about you personally, but someone else takes the decision."

"But that is the way things are here. And I am happy with that."


It's a Thursday afternoon and John and I are standing outside the office discussing his new job in Brussels, to where he'll travel on Tuesday. Suddenly the rat-a-tat-tat of a prolonged burst of semi-automatic gunfire resonates through the air. We hear it, decide that it's gunfire, but know that we are well behind the Hesco and fear no threat from it. It reminds me of Saturday afternoons in Banja Luka when the fountains of bullets signify a successful wedding party. It turns out that this is exactly what it was: a wedding party.

So on this level, Thursdays in Lashkar Gah seem to be just like Saturdays in Banja Luka. There's a second burst, up into the air, and knowing that's where they are pointed—it simply doesn't feel like the gunfire on the night before the election.

John and I shrug and finish our conversation, but I can't help wondering afterwards about the wedding day. Is it a time for celebration or commiseration? Are there two sets of happy parents satisfied they've made a good tribal and family match? Or two happy young people who are in the (now legal) relationship for all the right reasons? The conversations on marriage—well, on getting married—are (with the exception of Marjeh's story) immeasurably sad for me. They are the opposite of autonomy, which to my mind is what it should all be about. For some of the young men it is good enough. But some want to move beyond the current paradigm. This is love experienced as a prosaic passion infused with the trappings of sentimentalized romance—red plastic flowers, chastity, virginity, semi-automatic gunfire—passing as partnership, friendship, and fidelity. And yet there is also such a belief in the power of love to transcend the brutality of life and offer comfort and affection and companionship. It is as if there are two sets of expectations on the same thing, the romantic relationship and the business transaction, which, like parallel lines, reach to infinity without touching.

It's that Afghan ambiguity again. Yet again I am confounded and moved by it all.

Post-workshop lunch

# 30. Laghmandi Pepsi and the Helmand Star

THE EVENING AIR is the color of licorice and envelops us like velvet—sweet and soft and black and comforting. Unexpectedly, I feel no fear about being outside the wire after sundown, even though it is my first time.

In downtown Lashkar Gah by night I am surprised by how much activity there is. The blackness is ripped in places by single yellow light bulbs, but also by multicolored shop fronts, still open even though it is 19:00, still selling neatly stacked and shiny fruit and vegetables, all things plastic (in all colors), some things metal, some things wooden, and some things sentient: the fat white chickens with the scrawny gut-pink claws and crowns still scratch the dirt in their small wire cages, as they will have done since dawn—unless they unluckily have been selected for a special dining experience.

It is Christmas Eve eve and because there are ten of us invited to dinner at the home of a local official, we are in a six-car move downtown—a convoy that stretches almost half a mile long—all squat steel, fat rubber wheels churning dust and bright headlights tearing through it. There are even two or three other cars, all of them the ubiquitous white Toyota Corolla. There are people walking on the streets—men and young children and even one woman (in a burqa). There are people on bicycles and motorbikes (on average carrying three persons per frame). None of these has lights, so our beams catch them as dark spectral wraiths with their scarves fanning in the downdraft and dust, startled and temporarily blinded by our wattage. But they keep pedaling nonetheless, speeding off (more or less) into the darkness from whence they came.

Even in the darkness I know exactly where I am, which route we've taken. As we pass the final corner before entering the road where our host lives I think I see among the rubble of goods—usually everything from Pakistani chewing gum (with rice paper tattoos in the wrapping)

245

or brushes for the hair and for the floor, to jugs of bleach or diesel—a Christmas tree. It can't be, so I put it down to the distance, the speed, the fading light, and the fact that I'm not wearing my contact lenses. But it did look like a big baby-pine-needle green arrowhead sitting there on the stall front, lit from behind by a weak yellow light.

In fact I am sure that it can't be. This is because on my recent trip to Garmsir the Marines took delivery of their two Christmas trees, and the locals didn't know what they were. As they lay forlornly on the plastic trellis floor one of the community council members came in for a meeting. He had no idea what the trees were, never mind what they were for. I broke off some needles and rubbed them open to release the scent of the sap, at once sweet and astringent. I held it up to Alouja's nose for him to smell. His old eyes lit up as he inhaled for the first time in his advanced life the awesome aroma of pine.

The Danes also brought Christmas trees over land and sea to FOB Price at Gereshk. One morning I was there I had to walk through a small forest of five trees to get to the office. All these trees have a very heavy carbon footprint but given that they are trees, they have probably offset themselves by the time they get to these villages and towns in the desert. As usual the Danes go all out in festive terms: in their evening brief they light four candles on a wreath of pine, the Deputy Commander wears his combat Santa cap (it has white faux fur and a white bobble but instead of red the fabric is Danish battle fatigue).

We arrive at the house and dismount from our heavily armored carriages. The walled garden is a delight—huge and square with a big vase-fountain and round pool in the middle, marble tile paths leading up and away from it, lawn grass cropped close and vine trellises along the far wall. There's a door in the wall, wooden with a cupola-shaped top, and I immediately think of *The Secret Garden*. On the grass are white lattice-work tables and chairs of iron. It could be straight from a (slightly run down) stately home in the UK and bears absolutely no resemblance to the topography outside the walls.

When we turn around the corner we see that the officials have pulled out all the stops for us: a string of blue fairy lights borders the ceiling of the verandah and there are two (plastic) Christmas trees adorned with flashing white and red lights. In the cold and dark it's simply magical and there are "oohs" and "aahs" all round as we come to be greeted by our host (who is delighted by our reaction). As with all magic, though, it doesn't do to really peek behind the curtain. The hot little lamps are very close to the very plastic needles of the tree and it's all held together by a tangle of electric cables of varying quality and four-socket extension leads that have about ten plugs inserted from which a few amber sparks jump from time to time. I decide the enchanting effect is best admired from a distance and so I move away from the power source.

The wide verandah is covered in thick red-themed carpets on which sit the band, a motley crew of musicians. They beat goatskin drums pulled taut and play a squeezebox of some kind—there must be a side pump somewhere—like a horizontal accordion that sits on the ground. The sound it emits (at a fierce pace) is similar to that of the accordion, maybe a bit higher pitched.

I am introduced to a young man, tall for an Afghan, with earnest raisin-colored eyes, smooth clean-shaven skin, and floppy hair. In the Afghan reality show *Afghan Star*[8] (the Afghan *Pop Idol*) he is the representative from Helmand.

"Ah, the Helmand Star," says Caroline.

He beams. "Yes!" he says, grinning widely.

"So how do we vote for you?" I ask.

"Here, you just text to this number."

I try to vote for him but the number doesn't go through. Perhaps that's because the line is jammed with other people wanting to vote for him.

Then he asks: "Do you have any cards?"

I am puzzled and look at him quizzically.

"Top-up cards. Or money? I need to vote for myself but I don't have any money to top up my phone card," he says rather crestfallen.

My heart breaks, but in Afghanistan it's the only place where in one respect I am like royalty. I don't carry cash outside the wire.

"I'm so sorry, I don't have any Afghan money," I say in a voice that I hope conveys that if I did I'd be giving it to him.

He flatlines his mouth, shrugs his shoulders and moves up to the

8 http://www.afghanstardocumentary.com/

stage to sing. And sing he can—he has a great voice. The music had been jogging along in a kind of surreal syncopation like an irregular heart rhythm on an EKG, but songs with lyrics seem to lasso the beat and contain it in a more regular pattern. He sings. And one of the servants, a skinny small man, dances.

And what a dance. It is unlike anything I have ever seen a man do before. It is a bizarre cross between ballet and breakdancing, with a touch of lap-dance thrown in. It seems (to my untrained eye at least) to have absolutely nothing to do with the music, although he manages to start and stop at the same time. He does jerky pirouettes on the dais and then leaves there—clearly moved by the spirit of the music—to dart around us sitting at our fancy tables on the lawn (freezing, I might add. Caroline's turquoise blue and brown ensemble is really only a thin drape; Philippa has put a sports jacket over her blue and silver sparkly number, made possible only by polymer chemistry and not known for its heat retention capacity. I have a wool coat and scarf on but my feet are turning to blocks of ice).

The servant whirls and writhes away, going down on his knees in front of the most important dignitaries at the dinner. One or two of them wave Afghan money over his head when he does so. I don't want to think about what that might signal. It is very different to Western after-dinner entertainment.

I am standing talking to Wahedullah. He has just asked me if I have decided what I am going to do with my life yet. By which I know he means "am I getting married yet?" Given that he last asked me about a week ago and I've been in Gereshk for three out of those seven days and in the camp for the other four, it's not likely. But Wahedullah is eternally optimistic. Or else his ear is much more attuned to the Big Ben of biological clocks than mine.

"You must do this soon, Kate. Or you will get too old."

I laugh and ask him about his latest update. His father has been scouting again but there are no serious deals on the table.

"And what about dancing?" he asks as we watch the dancer take an elaborate, effusive bow, "Do you ever dance? Can you dance?"

"I love to dance!" I say. It's true. "And yes, I can dance." (Possibly this is not so true, but at least in my own head it is true.) "But I know women cannot dance here—it would be culturally inappropriate."

"Yes, you are right," he says, "Even I would not dance tonight, because of my position."

"So when do you dance?"

"At family gatherings, weddings. My brother will get married in Kabul in the spring. Perhaps you can come to the wedding and then you will see how we celebrate by dancing. One of my cousins, she can speak great English, she will translate for you."

"That would be wonderful, thank you Wahedullah," I say, savoring the prospect of an Afghan wedding yet knowing that I will almost certainly not, because of security concerns, be allowed to come.

We have enjoyed fine food—curried lamb, freshly diced salad with cilantro, some form of (incredibly tasty) mashed cheesy and tomato-y cauliflower, skewered lamb pieces fresh from the barbeque, and a turkey (or possibly a large chicken). In Afghanistan it's all about demonstrating hospitality to the guest—the bedizened trees, the bird, the fairy lights—it's all about making the guest (in this case us) happy. And so too with the drink. When we arrived we were served Pepsi. It was not wise to take a big gulp, for it was a special brand of Pepsi. Again, to make us happy, we were served whiskey and cola premixed in 250ml cans—full to the brim. It turns out that this *trompe-l'oeil* of the taste buds is called Laghmandi Pepsi because the people of Laghmandi province are apparently well-known for their duplicity and deceitful ways. This particular legerdemain is honored by the provincial eponym.

Dinner progresses, it gets colder. We applaud the musicians. The song he's just sung is about a small town near Kandahar and basically it says that though the singer has lived in London and Paris he'd give it all up for living in that small town near Kandahar. One of the officials is talking about the song to two of my (male) PRT colleagues.

"Huh! I certainly wouldn't give *that* up for that town!" he sniggers pointedly. My colleagues laugh. I laugh too, and then catch myself—in Afghan society at least I'm a lady and not really supposed to understand the inference. Oops. The official looks at me and apologizes.

"I'm so sorry, I didn't mean to offend you by saying that."

"Oh, that's no problem at all. I didn't mean to offend you by laughing."

We are both skating on the thin ice of the social fabric: who should be most sorry or least offended. We both laugh, the whole table laughs—we are on uncharted territory this evening and I don't know where it will end up.

And that's not all. Next there is dancing. We know as women we are not allowed to dance, so neither Philippa, Caroline, nor I rush to the dais to embrace the funky music, even though it would have warmed us infinitely more than the Laghmandi Pepsi. Instead more of the men jump up, seized with a desire to contort their bodies in time with the jagged beat. It's a traditional dance, very similar to the medieval dances I learned in school: one foot in and one foot out again, clapping with the hands on the one foot in. A troupe of men soon circle around the square of lawn grass, some getting the esoteric rhythm, some not. Some of them are in *salwar kameez*, some in Western civilian clothing, some are in UK military uniform, and one is in US Marine Corps uniform. They lurch from side to side like a drunken caterpillar in a conga. Of course we applaud wildly. It's a literally fantastic sight.

But that's not all either. Next thing the same man who told the semi-smutty joke offers me his hand looking toward the dance floor. I will admit that being demure does not come easy to me but I try really hard (I only have eyes for my icy feet) and think I pulled it off. But no: failure. He insists and before I know it I am up on the dais, with him holding my hand above his head and my own.

I have no idea what to do. Do I move to the music (if I could), or would that cause offense? I decide to keep my hips as stock still as I can as I follow his feet on the red carpet. He is still holding my hand. The audience is applauding loudly. Then some of the senior officials who have been danced to (or at, I'm not really sure which) earlier rush up on to the stage and wave money around my head. I am still not sure what that means. Is there commerce going on here? I have rarely moved so little on a dance floor but feel that in the circumstances less is most definitely more. Yet again new ground has been broken, new boundaries established, a subterranean social order shoved a little closer to the surface.

I sit down, relieved, and thank my partner. He immediately extends his hand to Philippa (he is on a roll) who after (I must report) only the merest millisecond of hesitation is up there. How she manages to disengage from The Hand of Dance I'm not sure. She struts her stuff for a few minutes (again adopting the same minimalist approach as me) and then it is Caroline's turn. She makes quite the splash with her turquoise full-length scarf although there is a (happily averted) near disaster when she almost steps on it. Who knows what might have ensued had she fallen over? When we are all sitting again the man with The Hand of Dance leans over to me and says:

"Thank you for the dance. It was really great. I apologize if I offended you by touching any of your private parts."

We all, including him, collapse with laughter. I still have no idea if he was laughing with, at, or in spite of us but he seemed to be at every party I was at for the next few days and was very friendly.

On departure the host gives us all very fine gifts—fabric for the men and made-up dresses for us three women. He makes a speech in which the word "love" features a lot, and expresses deep appreciation for the fact that we are away from our families at Christmas time, that we have chosen to work for Afghanistan instead. I think he ascribes more altruistic motive to us than perhaps we warrant but his position is reflective of the deep Afghan commitment to the family: no Afghan would be away from their family at Eid, for example.

We step back into the cars and drive up through town, at around 23:00. This time the streets are truly deserted. Every so often there is a yellow bulb over a shop front but I only see one private house with any discernible electric light. The stalls are closed, the chicken coop is empty. The only faces we see are those of young police officers as they stand guard at mud and Hesco checkpoints, and only then because we pick up the whites of their eyes and the cold glint of their guns in our headlights. Night duty on the flimsy checkpoints in Lashkar Gah: that has got to be scary work.

Guard duty, dancing, drinking, Christmas trees, mixed gender company. It all happens under the vast vault of the blackcurrant-colored sky spotted with stars. I think about the degree of energy it must take to control it all, the tension between the constraining architecture of the social surface with that which riots perpetually beneath. Afghanistan is as fragile as the skin of a wave.

Embroidery classroom, Gereshk

# 31. Hey Mr. DJ, Put a Record On...

I AM BACK in Garmsir, doing some work with the justice sub-committee and the security sub-committee of the community council. We are lucky to have been able to come into the District Center to meet them, even though our base camp is only about 500 yards away, because there have been high winds overnight and the threat of a sandstorm is only a whisper away. No helicopters are able to fly, even though the visibility looks, to us landlubbers, quite good. Technically we are on "Air Red" which means that no air assets can be used either for regular transport or even for emergency medical evacuation (medevac). If there is no medevac that normally means that we can't move anywhere, by land or air. In short, we are grounded. Yet there is a little local flexibility. If the local commanding officer gives the green light to limited movement his vehicles can go out, even without aerial cover. Today we are to travel in the US Marines' MRAPs, huge hulking custard-colored Hummers on steroids (their wheels come up to my shoulder and they are almost as broad as my arm is long). And the local commander, John, a thoughtful and charismatic leader of men, says "yes."

I've never been in the back of any military vehicle before but I have seen into the back of the UK military Land Rover: those have simple board benches in the back. I am surprised therefore to find that the foam-padded black seats in the MRAP are really comfortable. It's not illogical though—for long trips through the desert the last thing a commanding officer needs is for his men to have bruised posteriors or stiff backs. They need to be alert and ready to fight. I remember Paul saying how important it is to always wear a seatbelt in military vehicles. They may have sturdy metal exoskeletons like a prehistoric beast and if they go over a mine the metal monster may leap awkwardly in the air, but they will likely absorb the blast. The danger, though, is what happens on the inside. Inside what can happen is that the flimsy bodies of humans get flung around, and if they make contact with the shell, that's when it can get messy. So I put on my seatbelt. I look up and see that the ceiling is also padded, but only thinly. If my skull hits that at high velocity, that will be messy too. I decide to put on my helmet though no one has told me I need to. The only discomfort comes from the fact that the gunner, standing now (though with a detachable padded knee rest if he needs it) in his swiveling mechanized circle, is smoking, and the smoke blows down into the cabin. As I dismount I think about how our fat column of three of these tanks must look as they thread through the narrow streets of the bazaar and how easily they could flatten a child or a sheep. The driver probably wouldn't even feel it, nor would I on my padded seat. I walk away from the hypertrophic tires and into the district governor's compound. There three workers are repainting over the big Afghan flag on the lintel of the small concrete atrium: solid blocks of red, green, and black. Many of the fabric versions have gold fringe and corner tassels, but they don't go for this degree of sophistication out here in the sticks.

The MRAPs aren't the only thing we borrow from the USMC that day. We also have Andy the DJ, who is here to record some of the messages from the trainers so that they can be broadcast on the local radio, Radio Garmsir, and Mohammed the interpreter.

Mohammed is a bit hapless from the outset. His default position seems to be bewilderment at the world in general. He's a big Hazara kid from Kabul, clean-shaven, pale-skinned, and wearing tinted glasses. Generally the Hazara have a great attitude and are good translators, but Mohammed just wants to go out and have a smoke as well as to eat (more than one of) the purple foil-wrapped, strawberry-flavored Iranian cream cakes we are served with our tea.

Working with translators is always a delicate business—you generally have to work together for a while before you find your level. My aim is not to get too stressed if the conversation moves on before I get a full translation (knowing that I am never going to get absolutely all the detail). For them the challenge is to give me a good flavor of what I need before I burst blood vessels and to keep the conversation moving. So I know I need to be patient, but after ten minutes of Mohammed the meeting is making absolutely no sense to me at all. So I ask him what it actually says on the presenters' flipchart paper: "I'm sorry, I don't get it. I can't read."

"You can't *what?*" I exclaim internally. "Oh, is the writing too small?" is the out-loud thing I say. He is wearing glasses after all. He looks miserable.

"No. It's not that. I can't read Pashto."

"How come?"

"It's not my first language. Dari is. I can't really speak Pashto either."

I do wonder about the hiring process that resulted in this gentle and rather feeble person being appointed. And also: what happens if he has to translate something really sensitive on the front line, in a live kinetic environment when a commanding officer has to explain something important like why there are civilian casualties in the area, or what compensation deal he will strike for persons whose compounds are appropriated for military use?

"OK, Mohammed. I think it's best if you went and got Andy. Does he speak Pashto?"

"Yes," he says sheepishly, shifting his well-padded backside from the chair and shuffling off to fetch Andy.

Derek looks up from the paper he's been writing.

"Where's he off to?"

"I had to fire him."

"Whoa. Why?"

"I speak better Pashto than he does, that's why."

Andy arrives. My first question is "do you speak Pashto?"

"Yes," he says, "it's my first language. My family is from down south, from Kandahar; though we moved to Kabul about twenty years ago we still all speak Pashto. And Dari. And English." He grins, straight white teeth flashing against his swarthy skin. He has a short black beard and close cropped hair and wears US Marine Corps desert uniform. Though he's only here to record the session he readily agrees to translate.

During the tea break, we talk. He is the DJ on Radio Garmsir, broadcasting about four hours daily—two in the morning and two in the afternoon. He receives about twenty letters a day from local residents. He is a celebrity to the small boys who pepper the bazaar and around the school.

"I can't believe it," he says, "here they are, these kids from the back end of beyond, and they know exactly which are the best Afghan songs to play. They are really with it. Cool." He speaks in a cross between Kabul and Hollywood patois. "Yeah, they are giving me high fives every time I see them!"

"I hear people send you poems as well," I venture.

"Yeah, and I hate to say this," he says nonetheless (though to be fair it is in a bashful tone), "I even have some girls who are in love with me."

"Really?"

"Yes, but it's very sad too. They are stuck here."

"But how do they contact you?"

"There's a girl, she sewed a message onto a piece of cloth, then she sewed up the cloth. She used silver thread to do that stitching thing, how do you say it?"

"Embroidery," I say.

"Yes. Yes."

"But how did she deliver it to you?"

"She got her kid brothers to drop it off at the gate of the camp. There is a box there for collecting the requests. She sewed it up so that they couldn't see it."

"And what did she say?"

"Well, she had sewn—embroidered—a note to say she really likes me, liked my voice. She drew a flower and put my name on one side and hers on the other. She's done this a few times. She's even given herself and her sister a code name. So those are the names I read out. Only I know her real name."

He smiles wanly, in clear sympathy and respect for the girl.

"Yeah, she is smart too. She wrote to me once that her mother was sick and wanted to know if she could come to the camp for medical treatment. I was able to give her the right time to come over the radio —using her code name—and sort out with the doctors in here to treat her. That's the real good part of the job. That and being able to put on great records, knowing those kids are listening."

It's easy to think of DJ Andy (that's his USMC name. I asked for and use his real one with him—he's not the only one with a code name) as cool and liberal. But his accent and his easy charm belie his roots somewhat. At lunch I ask him about his family. There are signs of liberalism—he mentions his sisters when I ask him about siblings. (It's relatively common that when you ask some of the Elders about their children they'll say something like "two." If you express surprise—Afghans have big families—and ask "is that all?" they'll say "oh, I have seven daughters as well." It's not universal, but to a large degree the boy child is all.) Andy's sisters go to school. I ask if they'll go to university. He doesn't know but thinks that maybe there's no need. He's happy to be in a position to provide for his whole family. His father was in the Afghan police for thirty years. Now he's retired and working as a driver. As a translator (and DJ) Andy makes $800 a month, a colossal wage for Afghanistan and enough to provide for education, food, and housing for everyone in the household.

But even though he is young and liberal compared to some of the men in the room (and was embarrassed to translate for me some lines about sex that came up in the workshop until Derek chided him into it. "Oh my god," he said, giggling, "I would never normally talk about this stuff in front of these guys! I didn't know these guys even knew about this stuff!"), he is still Pashto.

His sister used to wear full Afghan clothes—"like you, Kate"—but then she started to wear *salwar* and jeans. Then the jeans got very tight. Then she started to wear Western tops as well. So Andy had the "big brother talk" with her: "If you want to dress like that, dress like that. But you need to think about what kind of statement that makes about our family, what it says about our honor."

She went back to wearing the long *salwar* and the wide, wide pantaloons when out on the street in Kabul. It's not just the old men that young women are constrained by, it can also be their peer group.

And yet he still plays the requests of the young seamstress, flirts with her in a very abstract, yet Afghan way, a way that could be seen as unseemly.

I think of the young girl in the mud hut sewing elaborate Pashto letters in silver thread. It's relatively easy to coax straight-backed Latinic font into letters with thread, but the filigree curls and curves of Pashto would need hours of patience and determination, not to mention much creativity. It's the Western equivalent of having a poster of a pop star on her bedroom wall, or Tweeting a celebrity.

Except that it's so much more poignant, harder, and the stakes are so much higher for her. And all this risk for a boy whom she will never ever meet, but who holds something in his voice, his words, the music that he plays, that lifts her out of the mud compound of her reality and into a fantasy world where she is free to love whomever she wishes.

Security planning, Nawa

# 32. Nawa (IV):
# Return to Tralfamadore

IN EARLY FEBRUARY I had tried to get to Nawa, thinking I could add it on to the most recent Garmsir trip, but there was a storm, a great desert storm, almost a year to the day since the last one when the transit camp tent at Bastion was ripped asunder and fell on my head. The wind had howled for hours, whipping up dust so that the air became a pale yellow opaque sheet like solidified sugar that dimmed the desert sun to a low wattage. So the storm stopped play that day, and I had to wait and go back to Lashkar Gah with Derek the following day.

I knew that if I didn't go during this rotation it would be the end of March before I'd be able to go. When I got back after the Garmsir trip, on a Tuesday, then, there was a decision. The following week I was due to fly to the UK to take part in the Command Post Exercise (CPX) —effectively the final training exercise for the next Brigade Headquarters coming out to Helmand. It took the form of a five-day 24-7 simulation that the Brigade Headquarters had to lead, and respond to some curve balls. Some of the curve balls were incidents that I recognized from the past year (a woman turning up at the PRT seeking protection from domestic violence; eight police officers poisoned then shot at their checkpoint; organize a shura on short notice because someone was going on leave). But perhaps more of that later— the point is that I was the only one going from the PRT and it was pretty much imperative that I get there on time. I was due to leave Lashkar Gah the following Tuesday. Since you need 96 hours to book a flight, the earliest I could book it for was Saturday. The problem with Saturday was that it was one day after Friday, which was when the big Op (Operation Moshtarak) was due to start. (We'd been planning and re-planning this since the previous September, and had been exhausted by the institutional inertia brought about by too many Powerpoint presentations and multicolored sync matrices—events on a timeline, a campaign plan, I used to call those, but we're all in the army now and so they are, in their singular form, a sync matrix.) The language hasn't got any easier for me, especially since I'm fairly sure the Taliban don't have PPPs. Indeed, as one of my Danish colleagues noted when we went over the plan for the umpteenth time to the umpteenth general who came to visit, "What I want to know is, how the f**k did we win the Second World War without a sync matrix?"

And the point of all this? Well, that air assets would be at a premium for the Op, and not for ongoing work. Once the fight started all bets were off, even if you did have an officially approved Air Support Request (ASR) on Marine Air or Air Movement Request (AMR) on Royal Air Force. At any time helicopters could be diverted to deal with the fight—to medevac casualties (civilian and military) or to offer hardware support (i.e. to attack from the air or take aerial photos of the enemy), and so those with ASRs or AMRs would be (rightly) de-prioritized, left with nothing but that three-letter acronym which only applies to one time, one date, one place. Once you are 24 hours outside your ASR it no longer exists: there are no rollovers.

So I proposed to Derek that I would travel on the Saturday, do the two meetings with the security sub-committee and the justice sub-committee and come back on the Sunday, a mere two days before my wheels up on the Tuesday. It would be cutting it very fine. Predictably Derek's first reaction was "Whoa!" accompanied by a deeper frown than normal, "are you sure?"

"Yes. I really need to go. You said yourself they need some direction and a bit of a nudge. If I don't go now, it will be the end of March. That's too long to leave it."

"Whoa. Yes, I suppose. When do you go to the CPX?"

"Leave here Tuesday. I have to be in London Wednesday night."

"Whoa. And you do know that the Op's going to be starting on Friday."

"Yeah, I read that in the *New York Times*, Mr. Derek. The whole world knows that."

"Whoa. Well, if I was you, I wouldn't go. It's too risky—you'll definitely get stuck."

"Which is why I'm taking my passport with me. If I get stuck there, I'll just go straight to Bastion and on to Kandahar."

"Just as long as you know..." Derek concluded wistfully, shaking his head regretfully at my youthful folly. It's not for nothing that we refer to him as "the PRT Elder."

There are additional dramas on Thursday and Friday as the flight is on, then off, then on again. Joe, the US Marine Colonel who acts pretty much as the official ASOP fixer, does a sterling job, from an original flight time of leaving Lash at 03:00 and departing Nawa at 08:00 (where in the world does business between 03:00 and 08:00?), I get to travel down on Saturday afternoon and back on Sunday afternoon. The Osprey comes and the trip takes only five minutes.

I'm nervous about seeing the council members again. I haven't seen them since the murders, four months previously. But before I see them, there are new things to see in Nawa. Ian, the stabad (stabilization advisor) for Nawa, shows me around the new governor's compound. It's based on a standard Afghan model for government buildings and—apart from the lack of stair rail at the very top—is basically sound. The stairs don't even lurch off to the left, as they do in the same building in Gereshk, and the AC wiring doesn't go through holes in the window glass, as it does in other places. Ian and I go up onto the roof, flat and smooth except for a few thin chimneys. Immediately below us are piles and piles of big white and peach-colored straw bags. These contain wheat seed that is being distributed to local farmers—an alternative to planting poppy. To the left of the wheat heaps is another mound—this one of rust-colored wheelbarrows. They are stacked so precariously that they seem to seethe like a column of blind beetles trying to find a safe place to dock with the land. Even though it's late afternoon, there are people abuzz below.

But the most astonishing sight is not the mass and its energy at our feet, but the view beyond that. It is positively bucolic, an agrarian tableau right out of the nineteenth-century European landscape painting schools. The sun, a timid circle of coral, bleeds pink into the blue-white sky over a flat brown field, its earth exposed in straight furrows. Three tall trees at the edge of the field cast long shadows over it and over the next-door field—of bright green grass on which a few goats feast. A small fire burns at the base of one of the trees, sending wisps of white smoke up through the lattice of its branches and into the cloudless sky. It is an effortlessly serene scene, Arcadia in Afghanistan. We turn and go back down the straight marble-clad stairs and across to the camp as the sun makes its final descent below the horizon.

The next morning we make the short walk across to the governor's compound. The well they had been working on in November has been completed and there's even a proper door in the wall (previously we'd clambered over it, weighed down by our Kevlar and helmets). We meet the governor in the yard. Arif the translator begins to shout at him in Pashto and I am momentarily alarmed. I look at Ian who mouths to me that the governor has taken his hearing aid out to answer his phone (which rings a lot through our conversation) which is why Arif has raised his voice. The governor is ebullient, beaming: on his own initiative he has brought down a few Lashkar Gah journalists to do a "day in the life" of his good self. It's really good initiative, made all the better because it's purely Afghan and nothing at all to do with us.

The community council members quietly accumulate around him. They are so thin and timid that they seem to materialize like ghostly wraiths out of thin air. They hover around the governor for a while and then we retire to the same small silver-green room with the red velvet cushions where we'd had the original workshop. I have taken note of the dress code violations I made the last time I was there and keep my socks on this time (just as well, because it's freezing in the room). I also make sure to wear a dress that's at the longer and baggier end of the sequin spectrum.

I apologize for the length of my absence and offer sorrow and sympathy for the loss of the three council members. That this is appreciated there is no doubt, but it is simultaneously held with an almost extreme stoic fatalism, verging on that of the Tralfamadorians of *Slaughterhouse Five*. And they mean it. When we speak about the possibility of talking to the Taliban they do not shirk from it, even as they bring evidence to the meeting of further and recent (the previous evening, around the time that Ian and I were seduced by the bucolic scene from the roof) threats.

"We have to do it," one man says simply. His wizened skin is the color of an iodine stain and he wears a grubby white turban and robes. And they have plans for how to. It's tremendously brave. We have security on our camps but these men will go back to their unfortified compounds and live as best they can.

They are also working on representing their communities. I ask if they are able to keep records of their decisions. They show me a hardcover notebook. "No, we hadn't," says the wiry and wizened Chair of the justice sub-committee, "but now that we have this (he opens the notebook), we will be able to."

This tells me two things. Firstly, they don't always tell us what they think we want to hear, and secondly, it's taken them four months to get a notebook.

The rest of our conversation tells me something further about the idea of death among them. It's not that death is a non-event (the number of people attending the houses of those murdered testifies to that) but that it is—even without the overlay of the war—an omnipresent event. It is banal but not trivial. There's so much of it around and it's up close and personal (not for them embalming parlors, funeral homes, morgues, or polished hardwood coffins with trimmings of brass). Their stoicism means that death is absorbed and accepted as very much a part of life. They will fight—to the death sometimes—for life, for land, for honor and the tribe, but they will not struggle against the dying of the light in the way that culturally we do.

I ask them if the poet has written anything further since the poem he last read for us in November. They smile and say no, but that they will tell him I have enquired so he might be prompted to write something new. They tell me that there has been better security since I was last there, and they have been able to persuade the authorities to construct several more police checkpoints at key junctions. This is progress: they are developing their own agency. It is all the more remarkable given the continuing spate of threats to their lives.

"Run-bathing" on the HLS, Lashkar Gah

# 33. Recreation

MY FRIEND JOHN asks me, "How do you live without *things?*"

We are in his house, which is full of things. Several generations of things, in fact, things from his generation, things from his father's generation, and things from the generation that came from Scotland to here. There are things here also that were bought when we were in different places in Europe: the small painting of the French Drawing Room that he spotted first in the window of an antique shop in Budapest, several carpets that were bought in Sarajevo, some from Shiraz (imported directly by Mohammed whom we got to know well through our frequent negotiations. He wrote poetry in his spare time) and some antique Balkan kilims of ochre and olive, the color produced purely from vegetable dyes.

They are very beautiful things and they make for living in this old Canadian farmhouse, plumb in the middle of the vast Ontario wheat plains, very wonderful indeed.

I too have many beautiful things but they—the paintings, the carpets —are under wraps in my brother-in-law's shipping container. I haven't seen them in a long time.

"You get used to it," I say to John, "very quickly."

And it's true, you do. But one doesn't do without everything: small things can make a big difference to quality of life inside the wire, inside my room. A colored duvet cover, paper copies of de Chirico's *La Grande Torre,* Breughel's *Tower of Babel,* Hopper's *New York Movie,* Wyeth's *Christina's World,* a tiny El Greco, a map of Helmand, and a plant that extends its territorial reach daily. It has bright yellow-green leaves that both reflect and bind the sun so that it shimmers on the sill. I don't mind that at all.

Our rooms are where we spend a great deal of time inside the wire so it's important that we make the space as habitable as possible. Women are more likely than men to make an effort with interior

267

décor. Men are more likely to personalize by moving furniture around. What you do with the minute physical space is linked to how you deal with the vast psychological space. For the other question is: what do you do when you aren't working? You can't go anywhere, not to a restaurant or a cinema or even for a walk in the city.

We all come shrink-wrapped to Helmand. A psychological assessment is done before we come out, which is valid in theory for about a year. Then you have to do another one. If you are a permanent staff member of the Foreign and Commonwealth Office, mental health professionals are available for you to talk to roughly every six weeks. The rest of us, a rag-tag bunch of subject area experts, contractors, and consultants, could talk to them if we really wanted or needed to I'm sure, but mostly when we need to talk we talk to friends.

You make friends quickly here; the environment is so small, so intense, we are all working (almost literally) on top of each other. If you move away from your desk for a day the chances are someone else will be at it when you return, we are so short on computers. Friends are important here for all the reasons they are universally important—people to laugh with, people to vent with, people to be with, people who have an understanding of what you are about, people with whom you can really be yourself. People whose very presence is comforting, especially if they are proffering gin and tonic (sometimes with sliced limes, or pure lime juice ice cubes). In this situation friends are doubly important. We hang out in each others' rooms a lot, and in a way it's like being in student dormitories except that we are (theoretically) more mature now. That means we have better posters on our walls. And we can afford nicer gin.

Yet there is also a need to make space for yourself. People do this in different ways. Every lunchtime Philippa plays her clarinet, and the notes, slow and melodious, come wafting down the corridor, calming and comforting. Kevin and Dave play guitar. Another Kevin plays air guitar in the Clubhouse and Wii Tennis in the Brown Lounge (so called because the sofas are brown and the walls beige. Our other lounge has brown sofas and pink walls. Guess what it's called). For a time Wii Kevin and I ran World Cinema Saturday—our attempt to bring in celluloid magic and broaden the movie minds of our colleagues. We try

German, Brazilian, Korean, Japanese and, of course, French. Not every one is everyone's cup of tea, but we are satisfied that we've done our bit for culture in the boondocks.

The other vital ingredient for survival in the Lashkar Gah Main Operating Base (MOB) is exercise. There is the volleyball court—builders' sand brought in to fill it and lined with military sandbags—which sometimes doubles as training ground for the demining team. You see them there in full uniform in the midday sun snaked on the ground, inching forward—literally one square inch at a time—practicing with props. The real thing could kill them.

Close to the volleyball court is the military gym, two rooms of a crumbling concrete building with twenty bikes, six cross trainers, about eight running machines, two rowers, and a selection of weights. The dirty lemon yellow walls host the painted logos of brigades past—a white parachute with blue wings, a big ochre sword, two crossed canary yellow swords overseen by a red crown, the number 12 set in an army green ace of spades—and muscle charts of the body. There's an outside part as well: floor mats, bars for doing pull-ups, bars for doing push-ups, and benches of the type I'd last seen in primary school. In the summer the equipment is moved outside (there's no AC to speak of inside). That's fine in the short term but it only means the sand gets in and corrodes the machinery. The gym maintenance people come every six months or so, but they haven't come in a while now. They say it's too dangerous.

Then there's running around the camp (about a two-thirds of a mile circuit) or around the HLS (350 yards). There's a part of the camp run which is long and narrow, overhung by some razor wire. It's strictly just one person at a time. Recently I encountered a guy coming the other way (clearly one of us was following the wrong one-way system). I decided, to be polite, to move to the side and run under the razor wire. It would still give a couple of inches grace between me and the sharp edges. The problem was I was too polite, too early. There were still about ten yards between me and the other runner. What I didn't realize was that the ground under my thudding feet (loose stones on sand) was rising—by a couple of inches. We continued to run towards each other when suddenly—aieee!—an involuntary screaming noise thrust itself out of my throat as the razor wire embedded itself in my skull. I was like a kitten caught by the neck—my arms and legs are in motion but there was no movement. I was caught on this single point. It wasn't quite as bad as the time I got a fishhook stuck through my hand (because you just have to push it on through as it won't move backwards) but it ran a close second. I had to reverse off the blade. I put my hand to my head and a clump of wet hair slid off. I asked the guy (whose face is contorted as if he'd eaten a lemon or raw sewage) if it looks deep.

"Oh, it's all right," he pronounces, "you'll be fine."

So I ran on. I applied some TCP when I got in, and tried not to think about the new fringe sprouting at the crown of my head. It's true what they say: most accidents happen in and around the home.

Nothing quite so messy for Derek and Paul, who have perfected the art of multitasking as they are able to run and sunbathe simultaneously (run-bathing is the technical term) and as a bonus manage not to shave their heads on the razor wire in the process. They accomplish these tasks merely by the device of not wearing shirts. In the summertime their dedication often knows no bounds. Today, though, Derek fell in almost the same place I got caught on the wire. My bottle of TCP is being well used. I hope it lasts until the end of my tour.

Halfway through the year our clubhouse opens. The clubhouse is really one room with cream walls and a cream ceramic tile floor, very small windows framed in burgundy wood, bad lighting (too bright), three leather sofas, some wicker bar stools, two beer/soda fridges, a bar, and a big TV mounted on one wall. This means there is (sometimes) beer to buy but mostly we drink spirits because beer simply takes up too much space to transport. We must source it in Kabul and then find a way to bring it down. That it is a logistical problem is bad enough, but there's an additional obstacle as it is forbidden to take alcohol on a military flight. But we are nothing if not creative and so generally there is beer to buy on a Thursday night. Usually there's just one pack of 24 cans, which means that it can be sold out by nine o clock. The profits from the beer buy equipment for the club: an ice-making machine, the air guitar, a karaoke machine (which we've used once, on New Year's Eve), a good iPod speaker. On occasions we dance, clearing a space in front of the TV like in a student house party. The music and the move-ment transport us far away, over place and over time. Sometimes we'll have a coffee morning on Fridays. Rory and Marlin will take out the Nespresso machine and we'll have real lattes and cappuccinos and sit on the deck in the sun around the green faux wrought-iron café tables. We could be anywhere in the world that serves good coffee.

On special occasions Judy sings. No one can say her second name (it's African and is a collection of consonants—"k's" and "p's" pushed right up against each other—with a token vowel at the end), but eve-ryone knows she can sing. Before she opens her mouth she attracts attention from the Afghans. She has a gorgeous voice. It vibrates like struck silver with a range that reaches down to the underworld, up to the heavens, and across the earth in between. I don't particularly like the songs she sings (*Hero,* some stuff by Whitney Houston) but there is magic in the air when she engages her vocal cords with her soul and we are all both transfixed to the deck and transported far away by its singularity and beauty.

We have theme evenings. When (yet another) Kevin leaves to take up a post in Miami we have a Miami Vice party. Everybody makes what they can of what's in their wardrobe. Derek gets the prize for sleaziest Don Johnson lookalike—those turned-up cuffs and the shirt opened several buttons too many work for all. Speeches given at these going-away evenings are heartfelt and funny. Hugh has a spectacular capacity for meshing the two. He has us all in fits of laughter when recalling some of Kevin's moments in the PRT, then tugs at our heartstrings as he breaks all the rules by revealing something from Kevin's "360° feedback." This is a process by which anybody can offer a confidential view of what their experience of working with the person has been. The idea is that the person's line manager will take into account these views when doing their staff appraisal.

"You don't expect that stuff to be confidential, do you? More foolish than I thought, you lot," says Hugh, before going on: "Kevin has been a great Deputy Head of Mission, a fantastic deputy to me, he is more than competent, but, as many of you noted in your comments on him, he could do so much more if only he had more confidence in himself."

Not a dry eye in the house. And we all know that we are all but transient, itinerants, at best guests here, in this country of dust and desert and green crops close to mighty rivers and high, high mountains. Our time to leave will come as mine comes now, hurtling toward me to arrive in a mere three weeks' time.

Springfield in the Balkans: Obilić power station

# 34. Another Place

EVEN KABUL AIRPORT has an airbridge these days, so that (depending on the plane you are on) you no longer have to get the rickety bus and walk the final fifty yards into the airport building. The pilots no longer pray before flying either. (I wonder if that's progress.) But the small airport I descend into now has no such sophistication. It's essentially a big hangar. As usual I get into the wrong immigration line. There is an interminably long discussion between the immigration official and the man at the head of the line. When he eventually gets in (the other two lines fill with entirely new people in the meantime) another official invites another man in front of me to come through without even showing his passport. That wouldn't happen in Kabul either. Checks there are fastidious.

The driver is there to pick me up when I eventually get through (on the plus side there is no waiting for my luggage, it's sitting by the carousel). He has gray hair, watery gray eyes and no beard. He has broken English and, attuned though my ear is to this type of patois, it's difficult to converse. I know it's a risk but his age is such that I am pretty sure that he will speak at least two other languages, one of which is the language of the oppressor, but it is one I know. So we switch and then it works. We can communicate.

It turns out that he's a driving instructor, as is his wife, but now he works for this international organization in his country because, as usual, the money is better. His name is Feta.

"Like the cheese," he giggles.

The houses of this country—and the airport is in the countryside, no sign of a city anywhere on the flat dull-green plain—are fairly uniform in architecture. They comprise bricks of red clay framing two or three-story boxes, a family apartment on each floor, each with full-length wood-picket balconies slung across their fronts so that the balmy summer evenings may be enjoyed to the full. A tiled gable roof with several smoky chimneys tucks it all in. The red boxes are set in muddy-green fields with brown gashes where early ploughing has begun. There are tractors and horses, some cows but no pigs.

The first sign that we are anywhere near a city is from the big factory on the crest of the low hill to our left. From one cavernous concrete chimney it belches charcoal-colored (and -loaded) smoke. From another the gaseous excreta is off-white, but no less polluted. If Homer Simpson were to work in a factory in Europe, this would be it, Springfield Nuclear Power Plant's twin.

And like Springfield it's a small town. The driver knows exactly what I'm doing there. He's seen the bosses' schedule. He wishes me good luck as he drops me at the hotel, a four-story building as narrow as a Dutch townhouse but with much less character and not fronting onto a canal. Instead it fronts onto a small parking lot framed by plastic bins on four castors. They are brimful and smell. The exterior, once white, sports sooty beads under the window sills and in the corners. The interior, of royal blue and post-box red, simply overwhelms the small wall space. That the receptionist is smoking is bad enough, but she looks at me coolly and says, "Do you mind if we move you to another hotel? We have a delegation in today, and you are double booked."

"*I'm* double booked," I think, "I don't think so." But of course I say nothing, just feebly nod and go to the identical building next door. At least the receptionist there isn't smoking. There are no lifts and I am on the fourth floor.

I have an appointment with the most prestigious hairdresser in town at four o'clock. I have never been but I know it will be the most prestigious because my friend Lynn, who lives in this town and who is the party responsible for me being here, has booked it.

I call her and she gives me directions; we arrange to meet for dinner later on.

I find the hairdresser's very easily—just down the road from the UN Building and just opposite the main police station. As expected, it's very stylish, a swirl of gleaming toothpaste white in the midst of a row of soot-sodden peaches and grays. Inside they are all young and trendy, too young and trendy for me, but no one will know me so what does it matter? But they do know me.

"I have an appointment at four," I venture timidly, in English.

"Ah, you are Lynn's friend! Please, come in! Lynn is wonderful."

I am happy to bask in the reflection of Lynn's reputation. Everything is great except: they are smoking—inside. I'm back in the smoking section of Europe.

There is a short conversation to establish what I want done today. One woman translates for the woman who will be in charge of the scissors. When the translation has finished she goes off to make me a cup of tea.

I smile at the woman with the scissors. She is small and young and thin, with long fine hair drawn back in a single braid that settles down her back. Her name is also Feta. She has wet doe-like eyes, brown against make-up struggling not to be tangerine. We smile at each other again. This is going to be a long haircut so I ask in the same language I spoke to Feta the driver earlier if she speaks that language.

There is an emphatic "No" in response. And she immediately begins to speak in very passable English. So now I am beginning to understand that age is a determinant of linguistic range. Perhaps the younger generation, the ones who have no memory of cultural, religious, and linguistic dualism, are the ones who reject Serbian. But I can't conclude that just yet—I've only been in the contested country three hours by this stage. After my faux pas I go back to smiling and we continue with the haircut.

"Shall we have a fringe?"

Perhaps communication has been a mistake. For some crazy reason—perhaps I am overcome by the smoke—I say, "Sure, why not?"

She cuts away.

"Maybe a little more," she pouts.

"Maybe not," I say, probably not as firmly as I should have.

"OK," she says, in acquiescence. Or so I think: she cuts a little more anyway.

I leave with a glossy mane nonetheless and head off to dinner to meet Lynn. It is spitting rain, rain which absorbs the factory smoke and a host of other pollutants on the way to reaching my new hair. It is cold and dark and there are potholes in the pavement. Cars pay no attention to red lights and selfishly I make sure to cross the road with at least two people between me and oncoming traffic.

I get to the restaurant first and sitting down run my fingers through my lovely new hair. They are stopped in their smooth, cuticle-flattened tracks by a foreign substance, a repulsively soft clay-like substance. Yes: a bird has shat on my lovely new hair. That's never happened to me before. I'm not liking this place.

Lynn arrives. I tell her about the foreign substance in my heat-trained tresses. Surprisingly, she is not surprised.

"Yes, I know. That happens all the time here. It's just full of crows and blackbirds. And they are always cawing. Sure it's where the name of the country comes from: Kosovo. It means place of the blackbirds."

"And you want me to come and live here?"

"You will love it!"

Then the singing waiter comes. I'm not good with waiters being anything other than waiters when they are on active service as it were. And having been a waiter for a long time myself, I have a sense of entitlement about adopting this attitude. Not only does he sing (and also jiggles his not inconsiderable girth in what he surely believes to be a rhythmic motion akin to dancing) he "has fun" pretending to give us our meals. He holds out my plate, I reach for it, and he withdraws it. It's not fun at all.

Lynn sees that there is a divergence of opinion about the function of waiters in front of her.

"He reads the weather on local TV every night," she giggles, hoping to lead me away from the situation by the addition of even more absurdity.

"Well, I think if that's where his talents lie he should really pursue that, and just give me my food."

Eventually he withdraws. It really shouldn't be such a struggle to purchase pre-cooked food at a restaurant.

I sum up the evening: "Lynn, a bird shat on my new hair. People smoke in public. Everybody is named after cheese. The waiter sings. I don't like this place."

"Nonsense, you'll love it once you're here! We'll have fun, you'll see, you'll love it."

Next day I have my meeting, and leave. A week after I say "yes" to the offer of a job in Mitrovica, Kosovo. So I will be going back to the Balkans: Lynn had better be right.


On my way back into Helmand for the last time then, I am sitting beside Steve, one of our close protection team. It's two in the morning and we are sitting in the pale green phosphorescence of the military plane that will take us to Camp Bastion. I tell him I'm leaving and he asks where I'm going next. Kosovo, I say.

"They're as bad as each other down there," he says. Like a lot of the close protection team he is former UK military. His Balkan tour included Kosovo.

"I know the Serbs did bad things. But I remember one village where I was. There was this old Serb couple who'd been shot, caught in cross-fire. The old woman, she died almost right away. By the time we got there it was too late for her. But her husband, he was wounded, but still alive. He needed to go to the hospital. But the Albanians, they refused to take him. So he died, right there. An eighty-year-old man. There was no reason for him to die. And what harm was he going to do them?"

It may not be quite that raw today, over a decade later, but the twenty hours I spent there demonstrated amply the fissures and pitfalls that remain.

Yes, it's going to be another interesting posting.

The desert near Gereshk

# 35. Progression, Regression: Hello, Goodbye

THERE ARE THREE THINGS this week.

The first thing is a good thing. I am going to a meeting in an administrative department, to meet among others one of the first people I encountered when I first arrived: Karima, who works there. That she is still alive after the year is a minor miracle—threats were made against her in the run-up to voter registration, and this morning she tells me about further threats. After so many it is not the danger anticipated by the threats that is the most difficult thing, it is that she is weary. Threats wear you down. But she manages to keep going and to keep her office going.

Karima comes out to the front door to greet us. There's me, a US Marine Corps officer who's just arrived, and a Britmil officer. On the way in Karima speaks to us in English. When I arrived she spoke two or three words but over the course of the last year she has been attending the English classes organized in her center and now speaks well, and a lot. It puts me to shame, my Pashto is so weak. The other women who are teaching and learning come out of the classrooms and flock around us, the two women in their combat fatigues, one gray-green, one beige-brown, and me, in purple crepe cloth that swirls under my navy body armor.

We speak to one of the young women. She's shy at first but shines a smile at us, her cheeks and eyes emitting a small sheen.

"Hello. My name is Zarima. I've been learning English just for six months here at the center. I never get a chance to speak to foreigners to practice," she patters out at a rapid pace, "can you understand me?"

She has very little accent, the words are vertical, only slightly round-ed and evenly sized.

"Of course we understand you, you speak very well," I say.

She casts her eyes down again towards the patchy carpet, then looks up.

"Thank you. When we speak with ourselves we never know if we are speaking correctly or not. We never get to speak with foreigners," she repeats.

"Well, why don't you come and translate our meeting?" I ask her.

She looks a little doubtful. She's never done it before.

"I'm not sure I can," she says.

"Of course you can," I say. "If you get stuck on any word, my terp is here, he can help you out."

I look over at him, who is about the same age as Zarima, maybe a year or two older.

He responds immediately with a broad grin and says, "Yes, that's no problem, I will help, but you should do it." He looks encouragingly at her.

And so she did. She sat on the sofa beside Karima and interpreted thoroughly and with precision, in both direction, English to Pashto and Pashto to English. After each utterance she giggled and tugged her veil over her mouth, at once exhilarated, exalted, and embarrassed at her own daring. Once or twice she got stuck and directed a rapid fire question to my terp, who mainly answered, "yes, yes, you're right. That's it." He was tremendously and enthusiastically supportive.

It's a first for any meeting I've done in Afghanistan: a female interpreter. Yet they are there (and more capable than some of the young men that we've got), submerged beneath the sand like an oil-field waiting to be discovered. She will just get better and better, but then there are two avenues available. She will either get more frustrated as the social framework suffocates her ability to move as an equal in a world of men, like an iron corset around her essence, snuffing out any ambition she may have had to do so. Or she will study the design of the corset, scope out its weak points, scoop out some room for herself within it, maybe even sculpt something of note, like some of the older women in the province.

The second thing is a bad thing. It concerns one of those older women who have worked the system through several regimes. It's not something I have seen but it is something I have heard. It is about Guliana, one of the women on Gereshk Community Council and one of the women who have successfully navigated the shifting social mores of Afghanistan over the past three decades. Like Karima there are threats and intimidation against her precisely because she's active in her community, because she's been able to mold herself a small space of her own—saving the young woman from marriage to a drug addict, enabling her to go to school is but one example. Now she's prominent in the Women's Center, in the community council, and a host of other things. It's too much for the Taliban and so they lay IEDs near her house. The days when women could drive have long gone. Guliana read the runes well and so she no longer drives herself. But nonetheless she is in a car being driven, when it catches the edge of an explosive ordnance. It blows up, throwing the car and throwing Guliana. It does not do as much damage as it should or could. She is not badly injured. And this happens only a week after a local school was burned down and the teachers—among them another community council member—threatened and intimidated.

And so it goes on: we make progress, we regress. We go forward, we go backward. It is as inexorable as the way that waves come and go at the ocean's edge.

The third thing is a mixed thing: the goodbyes and some hellos. We are switching over brigades again, on both the US and UK sides. From the UK side this will the fourth brigade I'll have seen, and from the US side the third. It means for us every six months a new set of relationships to be forged, for them a new set of information to be absorbed (no matter how much pre-deployment learning, they always have the same questions for us) and plans to be made and executed. All in six months.

Some military, though, do longer. A few US colleagues have been with us for a year (with only one two-week break). Michelle, Jerry, and Joe have all left us in the past weeks; a few Stabilization Advisors—Ian, Jim, Peter with whom I've worked a lot—are leaving after almost 18 months' service. Erika, who always cheerfully fixed my computer when I did something inexplicable to it, left the other day. We develop a small ritual of seeing people off—a trip down to the Helicopter Landing Site (HLS). It's right beside the concrete casing of the sewage pit whose stench is getting more raw, more ripe as the temperature rises (we are in the mid-30°s C now), so goodbyes are generally gently scented as well as emotional. The final photos are taken under the "LASHKAR GAH HLS" sign, black lettering on white wood hung above the buzzard's desk by two small chains.

Then the buzzard gets the bundle of people into order: "Sirs, ma'ams, ladies, gentlemen. Your Merlin pair are inbound, five minutes out. Can you put on body armor, helmets and can I have the following pax line-up along the Hesco and wait for our call to bring you out?" She rolls off the names, apologizing for her mispronunciation of some of the Afghan ones.

At that there is a hefting of heavy things, armor, backpacks, hearts. There is a shifting of canvas straps onto backs, into hands, a shuffling toward the Hesco, a signal once the dust has settled, and they are off.

They leave us, they leave Zarima, they leave Guliana. And off the Merlin pair come new boots on the ground: ingress, egress; progress, regress—as inexorable as waves on the shore. For now.

Qala-e-Bost Arch

# 36. Qala-e-Bost

DEREK AND I are going for a Sunday afternoon drive. We're not really supposed to use resources (for only two of us it's a four-car move) for tourism, but since there are few sites of interest around, since we've been around for a while and not done anything touristy, and since it is my end of tour trip we don't feel so guilty. We are heading south of Lashkar Gah, and it will be the furthest that either of us have ever been in a car in Lash. We go through the town as normal (our base is right at the northern edge), down past the governor's office, past the power station, and onto the cobbled road that leads to the airport. The airport is usually the furthest I've been and it is quite thrilling to drive past it, into the great unknown.

The road undulates in all directions—up, down, right, left—its smooth surface solid in the surrounding sand and dirt, as out of sync with its environs as if it were a cobbled version of the Yellow Brick Road. We find ourselves very quickly in rural Lash. Houses grow sparse and give way to wheat fields filled with waxy green wands luscious against the dull sand. There is no poppy here so close to town, yet even three years ago there would have been. Brightly colored doors—turquoise, crimson, yellow, orange—mark the entrances to dun-colored compounds, and then we go through a set of ancient mud watchtowers at one of the erstwhile gates to the city. Once through those we are very quickly but very completely in the countryside. There are roadside wells (though I wouldn't fancy drinking from the one that actually sits in one of the graves in a small cemetery), roaming goats and, as we round a corner on the crest of a small hill, an open compound that contains a haystack, two camels, and a donkey. A curlicue of charcoal smoke reaches up to the sky, sun-bleached blue and crystalline above us. There are still electricity poles this far down the road, though—thin wires stretched precariously across bamboo poles, probably because the power station is just on the far side of the airport on the southern edge of town and so these houses are not so far away from the local grid, which now offers a much more reliable electricity supply than when I arrived.

By the time we pass a small village, about five minutes later, there are no more bamboo poles, no electricity, no connection to modernity. We've only been driving for twenty minutes in total but already we are in a completely different landscape. The smattering of stunted mud houses then make way for an even more alien—and ancient—architecture. We come upon buildings two or three stories high but stretched at the corners and hollowed in the middle as if they were giant, broad egg-timers made from chewing gum. Windows are holes in the malleable walls, black spots dotted all over, so the structures come across as bizarre multi-eyed but placid monsters, mulling by the side of the road. Those windows have witnessed a few things in their time, and they will continue to look out at all the travelers on this road in time to come.

Then we reach trees, a small wood—a completely new and magical topography for me in Helmand. They are old and tall and their trunks, of soft red wood, are wide, perhaps three feet in diameter. The leaves are a muted green, veiled by the dust, but they are manifold, fed by a small stream, an offshoot of the Helmand River that now meanders momentarily by the road. Then the road bends through the trees and rises up imperceptibly almost as if it was stretching to kiss the walls that surround our destination: the ancient fort at Qala-e-Bost, or Kalibist as it is said in Pashtun.

We enter through tall wrought-iron gates as if we were entering a mud Manderlay, and then we see the famous arch. It's nothing short of spectacular, but there's something not quite right with it, something different from the famous National Geographic photo. It takes a second but then I grasp what it is: underneath the arch are columns of rough wrought bricks interspersed with thick wooden beams that look almost like an artificial climbing wall. Clearly it was thought that the arch was in danger of collapse and the wall underneath is there to support it. Sitting in the shade afforded by the coarse brick are two intrepid tourism entrepreneurs, old men with long beards and a disproportionate sense of optimism. One carries a small sign printed in English, which proclaims him as the watch keeper of the fort and can we give him some money to enable him to maintain his employ. Of course we have no cash and can only smile and apologize.

"Who'd have thought you'd see an old codger like that out here!" exclaims Derek as we walk away round to the other side of the arch, "actually expecting tourists! I wonder how many he sees. But it can't be worth his while," he muses.

"Well, what else is he going to be doing?" I say. "He's hardly going to be going to the office."

"True," says Derek, pursing his lips, still surprised.

The arch is flanked by rectangular citadels, the alternate turquoise and white tiles on their upper halves preserved better on one end than the other but both still carrying in them the care and craftsmanship of their creators a thousand years ago. It is a thing of beauty but the thing that excites me more is the fort, which we see properly as we round the end of the arch.

It is set on a small steep hill in the middle of the vast, flat alluvial plains from both the Helmand and Arghandab rivers. There is very little left on top except a relatively recently abandoned Afghan police checkpoint (the ramparts crumble as we clamber over them) and the view. It is simply stunning. We are overlooking the peninsula that pokes into the confluence of the two great Afghan rivers in a rich patchwork of fields. To the right, across the Helmand, is the Bolan desert, where the Taliban reside; to the left the Arghandab snakes through the land, making it verdant, giving it life. The late afternoon sun hits the rivers' waters and the confluence—islands of silver-sage green liquid—shimmers beneath us, cleaving the land in three or four places. It's so beautiful, and silent.

Derek takes some video footage, turning full circle. To the north is a big square area, the size of several football fields, of hard, packed mud surrounded on three sides by vast walls that look like cliffs, but are man-made—the original walls of the fort. To the south is the meeting of the waters, to the east is the small forest, to the west the Bolan desert.

"You'd never think there was a war going on," says Derek, overlaying his footage with a wry commentary as he wheels slowly around, having the lens take in the full three-sixty.

But there is a war going on, as there has been for pretty much the whole of Qala-e-Bost's history. There's very little historical fact available about the arch and even less about the fort except that it was the winter palace of the great Ghaznid Emperor Mahmud, so the view we have now is the one that Mahmud had. Most agree on the date of the arch to be around 1100 but Wahedullah tells me later that the fort, the site of the palace, is much older than that, around two thousand years old. The claim that the city of Bost (Lashkar Gah didn't arise until much later) has been mentioned in Zoroastrian hymns and in the writings of historians in the first century AD support Wahedullah's assertion.

We come down a little way from the top. I want to see the well-like store chambers. I've read about them, there is meant to be a stairwell that descends almost 200 feet into the earth, and I want to see if I can see it too, even go down. About a third of the way down the hillside I see the first of the well-like structures—a big rough circle of crumbling brick at the top, about twelve feet in diameter. Below the surface, though, the engineering is near perfect. The brick is tight and smooth and there are perfectly arched doorframes stacked the whole way down, as if a medieval cloister has been furled around an invisible column, an enormous circular lift-shaft. I imagine cowled monks on every level, pacing, meditating. I ask Derek to borrow his camera.

"Hold my feet!" I say as I flatten myself on the small part of the wall that rises above ground, positioning the camera over the edge to get a better picture.

"Whatever you do, don't drop that camera!" he says as I shuffle my face and hands and the camera over the edge. I am reminded of the time I peered over the Cliffs of Moher in a similar position, only there is no wind and no Atlantic below me now. I get the shots, hoist myself back and immediately want to descend. Wahedullah says that at the bottom there are tunnels that lead to the river, which is how they got water into the palace. To get there, there's a tunnel with some rough steps about thirty feet from the edge of the giant lift shaft. Cat, one of the CP team, advises against going down.

"Come on, Cat, there aren't going to be any Taliban down there," I say, half-joking.

"No," he says, "but there's a shitload of bats."

"Oh," I say, "best not to interrupt their sleep, then."

"I thought you'd say that."

We take a final look around the vast lunar playground we find ourselves in. Being outside, walking around—even carrying the extra twenty-odd pounds of body armor—is exhilarating. You really could be forgiven for forgetting that there's a war going on: Helmand gets a very bad press, even among other Afghans. I am reminded of something that the Helmand Star, whom I first met at the Christmas party a few months ago, said at an event I was at recently. While he was taking part in a heat of the Afghan Star contest in Kabul he reported that all the other contestants were scared of him because he was from Helmand. "They think we are all terrorists in Helmand," he told us glumly, "just because we are from the south." That in turn brought me back to the days when Northern Irish people didn't like going to England because they felt that everyone there thought them terrorists too, and were wary of their accent. Media headlines defined a whole people. Even people from the South of Ireland thought it: a (mostly) unspoken assumption that we harbored violent intentions against those we were visiting, that we were nothing but trouble. They were afraid, at that time, to take the time to find out that we were warm and generous and lived in a beautiful place. This is how people from Kabul view Helmand—only through headlines. Granted, Helmand is a dangerous place, much more dangerous than Northern Ireland ever was, but dangerous is not the whole story; media headlines may be accurate but they are not absolute.

Back down at the arch our tourist information manager calls Derek over. When he gets into the car he hands me a small dark wooden carving, a crude representation of the arch. It's been given to me by the old codger even though we had no money to give him. No matter, we are guests in his arena, he is the now the king of this crumbling palatial place and he is a good host. Derek has been given a coin, disfigured with a salty crust of verdigris. It has either been dropped by the Emperor Mahmud or planted there by the old man. I suspect it may well be the former. I think that archaeologists would simply adore this place—there must be much more down in the column of cloisters than the bats. Just as there is so much more to Helmand than the headlines.

Kids at play

# 37. Leaving Lash

I AM GOING for my final drive through Lashkar Gah. I know in this environment that you should not think of things in these terms but I can't help it. In part because there are so many movies based on the flimsy premise that things go wrong "on the last job" and in part because at the last memorial service we attended—now permanently moved to the front gate, since the camp is expanding too much to allow us the luxury of an emergency HLS—one of the young men whose life we commemorated for twenty minutes in the late afternoon haze had been killed on his last patrol. Not only was it his last patrol but he was the last man on the patrol, and he was the one who stepped on the mine. Not only that, it was the last of his three tours in Afghanistan. To compound the tragedy, he left a pregnant fiancé.

I'm clearly not going to be exposed to the same threat level as the military but I am uncharacteristically nervous nonetheless—if anything is going to happen it will be the very last time you do it. I had managed to do my last helicopter ride without thinking it was the last one, and I thought that I'd done the last drive through Lash—two days previously—without naming it so, but Wahedullah, Shah Wali, Abdul Nazir, and the rest of the ASOP gang have invited Derek and me to a farewell lunch in the WADAN office. So we are surprised that as soon as we arrive Abdul Nazir and Hafizullah are heading out but not so surprised that there's no sign of Wahedullah. Though he's improving he's pretty much always late. We chat with Shah Wali for forty minutes before the others arrive, in Afghan time. Of course this is preceded by several phone calls where Wahedullah says progressively: "Don't worry, I will be there in five minutes" and "Don't worry, I am here."

There is an exchange of gifts (ornaments of mottled Helmandi marble, Chinese glass and Irish linen), words and tears, and then we eat. We have Derek's favorite: meatballs, which are spicy and float in a (only slightly oily) lentil suspension. There's also roast chicken, rice,

293

apples, scallions, tomatoes, cucumber, huge sheets of bread, Miranda orangeade and Pepsi all set out on the floor of the little room where we've worked and eaten so many times before. Both Derek and I are wearing Afghan dress today—me in a cream cotton affair with brown hand-stitched embroidery around the cuffs and collar, made by the women in Karima's office, and Derek in a pale blue *salwar kameez* with white stitching on the breastplate and sleeves.

We take lots of photos at the end of the meal and on the way out, weighed down with marble (all I can think about is that my baggage allowance is now well and truly shot), we pass the montage of photos that Shah Wali has pasted on the atrium wall. We all feature in many of them: from the first workshop with the community council in Nad Ali to those in Gereshk, Garmsir, and Nawa. Five of those people that we worked with, people who are in the photographs, were killed because they were brave enough to stand up and be, as the waterman from Nawa put it last week in Marjeh, presidents of their own land. So there is sadness on the wall but there is no regret. And there is no fear. There is also hope and happiness for herein lies the future of Afghanistan: confident communities taking responsibility for their own governance, linkage to the central government, and guidance on so doing coming from talented, courageous, and committed young Afghans like the young men we have just eaten with. We only half jest with Wahedullah that when he is a provincial governor or even a national minister, Derek and I will come back as his advisors.

The wall also serves as a lens through which to view our work over the past sixteen months. When you are in the middle of it, doing the rounds of workshops and the grind of follow-up meetings—building capacity is hard work—coaching and supporting, working on the same concepts over and over again, waiting for helicopters that don't come, sprinting for those that come early, sitting in the back of a B6 or an MRAP in the blast of mid-summer heat, it can sometimes be hard to see where you are heading or what has been achieved. If you are building roads or bridges or police stations or government offices it's easy: you can see and touch and feel these things. Bricks and mortar are tangible. But they are no good if they are not populated. The building of democratic and administrative infrastructure is less tangible but it's what it's all about: creating a social contract. And, when you see it working, when you see a person who's been elected to represent others actually doing that, making life better for someone who isn't able to make life better for themselves, resolving a problem, providing public agency for an individual who has no personal agency, it's worth it all. Everything we see on the WADAN wall shows our efforts in making that happen, and I am proud to have been associated with those. We've also had more than our fair share of laughs while doing it, which is an extra bonus. Sometimes I am amazed that I get paid for this. We say goodbye and I am tearful as we drive away. I know I'll see Wahedullah the next morning as he and Derek will be off to Nad Ali to conduct new elections for the community council there, due to new boundary changes because of Operation Moshtarak—the operation to liberate Marjeh.

As we go back up through town we note changes over the past year. There are more cars and not all of them are white: there are reds, grays, and silvers around too. They are still all Japanese but not all of them are Toyota Corollas. We drive on black-top roads all the way from the governor's office to the base. These streets are now smooth and tarred. And there are street signs—white text in Pashto and English on an orange background. Now I know that a certain street is called Paktia Street or Lashkar Gah Street, or that there's a Kandahar Junction. On the newly asphalted streets there is less rubbish lying around. It all lends a greater sense of order and normality to the city. Six months ago we would have been driving on hard-packed dirt and my only idea of where we were would have been visual. Produce remains seasonal though, except for the white chickens; unfortunately for them, they are never out of season. Watermelon season has arrived and mangoes will be here in another month.

The next morning I go down to the HLS to wave goodbye to Derek, Wahedullah, and the gang. I bring the maps with the new boundary changes. In the Portakabin that is the HLS waiting room we unfurl them and we discuss them with the governor. Suddenly Derek exclaims, "These are the wrong maps! These have the old boundary markings. Shit!"

"What time are the birds coming?" I ask.

"Ten, fifteen minutes," says Derek, exasperated before the six-day trip even—literally—gets off the ground.

"Why don't I go back up to Geo (the military map makers) and get the right ones. If I run, I should make it?"

"OK, they should have them printed out. The young corporal, he did it last night for me," said Derek.

It would be tight, but I should make it. Especially if the birds do their usual thing and are a little late. At the back of my mind as I set off on the third-of-a-mile trip to Geo is the little cloud of knowledge that any bird booked for the governor is likely to come on time.

I reach Geo after a slow jog because I have done another "last" thing earlier that morning—a six-mile run around camp—so my muscles are more jelly-like than anything else. The young corporal that Derek said had done the map is nowhere to be seen. His colleagues look at me blankly and say that they have just given the maps out.

"Can I see the map on-screen?" I ask.

One guy duly opens up and I see where the changes should have been.

"Yes, you printed out the old maps. This line here between Nad Ali and Marjeh should be straight along this road. And up here, we want to get these desert people included in the Nad Ali district. How long to print out this version?"

"About ten minutes."

"OK, let me see if there's time."

I call Derek to see if there's any delay. About five minutes. The margin of possibility that this will work falls to wafer thin.

"Will I give it a go?" I ask.

"Whoa! OK, let's try it," he says.

"We need to print it," I say to the printer.

The map room is really very cool. There are two enormous printers each over three feet across, and the ink needle runs smoothly back and forth, forth and back. It seems an interminable time before the paper even starts to come out of the other side—a perfect representation of Nad Ali district in lines of blue, red, pink, and black.

Wahedullah calls. They've been given their five-minute warning, to put on body armor and helmets, line up at the Hesco wall.

In an ironic role reversal he asks, "Are you coming?"

"Yes, don't worry, I will be there."

There's about five minutes left in the printer. There's no chance that two copies will be ready in that time, but this one copy just might. It's the ultimate in watching a pot boil. My stomach churns as I irrationally will the machine to go faster. At last the machine crisply cuts off the paper. I snatch it out and start to run fast, though it is a case of the spirit being willing but the flesh being weak and quickly flagging, so the speed doesn't last too long. I steady my stride and pace myself better but then I see the green of the second Merlin taking off, popping out the white phosphorous ribbons of its flares as it rises into the air. I'm fifty yards from the HLS, holding a now damp but still accurate map of Nad Ali. They have gone.

Three hours later so am I. It seems that today is the day for aircraft being on time. I'm lunching with Philippa thinking that the flight will be late as usual, but it's not. It's right on time. We wolf down some food and go to get my gear. There are hugs and then I have to go. Soon I'm back on the black cobbled road to the airport. As we draw close I have to look twice at a sign. I've never seen it before, even though I'd been down that road only five days previously. It is made of metal and has a green background—the exact same color green as road signs for primary roads in the US. The white graphics depict the road we're on, the turn-off to the airport to the left just ahead and beside the straight arrow pointing towards Qala-e-Bost is lettering in Pashto and English that says "Garmsir District." It couldn't be more wonderful than if it were showing the way to the Emerald City. For the sign is not just a sign but a symbol. Yes, it illustrates where the airport is, where Garmsir is, but it also indicates more than direction. It says that you can travel this way—that the province is linked by road, that there is a normality that is possible, that there is modernity. Life goes on, in some places it is lived, in Helmand endured: people survive. But the sign says it is possible to do more than just survive. It says there is a government that is here to stay. It says: expect more; have ambition, for yourself, for Helmand, for Afghanistan.

# Afterword:
# A Little Bit of Politics

So, there are signs that things are pointed in the right direction. While there will always be setbacks and steps forward at the micro-level, the level at which I worked, the key question, as troop draw-downs continue to be announced and implemented, is: will the underlying trajectory continue to be upward and onward, or will it slip, irrevocably, backward? And, even if it is upward and onward, is it sustainably so without our continuing intervention?

One man put it to me this way:

> It is like a giant set of scales. Each side is heavy. But right now the government is very active and so people see this and say "let's work with them right now. The governor is coming and there is the wheat seed distribution program." But if the Taliban is in control, the people—who are not [members of the] Taliban—will follow them.

Thus in Afghanistan, government is about presence, physical presence. And the absence of government means a vacuum that the Taliban will fill with their presence. It's akin to a pendulum of perpetual motion. As I have noted in another place,[9] for Afghans in Helmand the essential survival tool is that of being on the winning side. The bottom line is that whoever is the provider of security is of less relevance than the fact that security is provided, so that people enjoy protection and relative safety. Security is the overriding concern; it trumps rights, ideology, tribal identity, religion or custom, particularly for the poor and vulnerable.

So we shouldn't deceive ourselves—if we can't provide security, if the Afghan government can't provide security, then the Taliban will exploit that absence and return. And they will be knocking at a door

9 "Proximity, Pragmatism and Pashtunwali: Informal Justice at District Level in Helmand," at www.stabilisationunit.gov.uk/.../64-proximity-pragmatism-and-pashtunwali-informal-justice-at-district-level-in-helmand-province.html

ajar, for the Taliban smartly appropriate the ancient customs and traditions of local tribal Elders. They simply apply more extreme versions of them.

As responsibility—rightly in the long term—is transferred to Afghan security forces (army and police) we need to consider the fact that this is an asymmetric shift. For our effort is not exclusively military—it is a joint civilian-military effort. We may not have always gotten the balance right between the two, but it was always more than just boots on the ground. As the military draws down, it has, at least in form if not in substance, institutions to hand over to: the Afghan National Army; the Afghan National Police. But the development and governance side of things (much smaller in number than the military side) will need to remain since as yet there are no Afghan institutions to hand over to. The community councils that we continue to establish are a start, but they need much nurturing. Further, civilians can't work safely when they are not protected by the military, or operate in areas that have not been "cleared."

The counter-insurgency theory that underpins our strategy is based on the "ink-spot" theory largely credited to the British in the Malaya campaign of the 1950s. It goes something like this: Phase 1, where the military use force if necessary to "clear" an area of the local insurgency. Phase 2, where they establish a perimeter and "hold" the area in order for civilians to come in to this secure Petri dish and—in Phase 3, "build"—grow governance, construct roads, schools, wells, and generally generate economic and social development. The idea is that credit for successful "ink-spots" would be taken by the Afghan government and, further, that the spots would gradually spread and link up, creating a critical mass of confidence, democracy, and development so much so that the insurgency could not compete, even in terms of security.

At home we have a saying: "If you're part of the problem, then you're part of the solution." This is not absolute, but it is a general rule of thumb that a solution—however limited—requires all parties (who want to be there) to get around the table. To effect transition from a conflict there needs to be a negotiated political settlement, in which nobody gets all of what they want, but everyone gets something of what they want. This was true in Northern Ireland, it was true in Bosnia and Herzegovina, and it is one of the reasons why Kosovo is so difficult, where even though there's a framework, not everyone has signed up to it. An agreed overarching blueprint providing tramlines for the future to which everyone has subscribed, or at least accepted, is essential for navigating the complex path from war to peace. This is particularly the case when the international intervention is as multi-lateral as the Afghan one is: NATO leads the military effort (it too is asymmetric—there's no equivalent organization on the civilian side). Different countries do diplomacy, development, deterrence, and defense in different ways, but at least if the ultimate goals are agreed in-dividual nations' efforts should cumulatively contribute toward those. Right now we don't have any shared vision of the end-state among internationals, yet alone a political agreement between Afghans.

To compound matters further, in Afghanistan a negotiated political agreement is all the more difficult due to the diffuse and fragmented nature of the tribal structures. Tip O'Neill may have coined the phrase "all politics is local" but nowhere it seems more so than in Afghanistan, where a family compound can be an independent republic. Further, the Taliban are similarly fragmented. Local leaders will declare for the Taliban one day, and against the next. Think back to the giant set of scales. So any political settlement will have to involve the Taliban, but deciding who is truly representative of the Taliban—and how much influence they actually have over those they claim as constituents— will be difficult. And representatives to talks have to be broader than the Taliban; it needs to be an inclusive process, inclusive of the tribes, inclusive of the provinces, inclusive of the young and the old, inclusive of women.

However, amid all this fragmentation, there is one thing about which I discovered consensus among the population (including local Afghan Taliban), and that is that it does want its voice to be heard, both individually and collectively. And that individuals—women and men both—are capable of articulating what they want: to live free from fear; to have real choices in their education, public and private lives. There is no doubt but that our interventions raised expectations in these areas. There is no doubt but that our interventions raised the risk for those taking part, and their extended families. But neither is there any doubt but that those who were involved wanted to be involved, welcomed the chance to participate, the chance for change. The moral question arises, however, if, having raised risks and expectations, we then withdraw support before the fledgling institutions are ready to fly by themselves.

The road to hell is paved with good intentions. While there was much folly and fault with the Helmand Valley Authority project that temporarily transformed Lashkar Gah and the surrounding area, at least there was commitment over the long term—some thirty years. And so too this incarnation of invasion and occupation of Afghanistan: this is about taking the long view, considering and agreeing what we want the political end-state to be some twenty-five or even fifty years from now, and working collectively and inclusively, as internationals and nationals, toward delivering that. Some long-term vision and leadership from both civilian and military components would go a long way toward realizing that.

In the meantime, since I left, people continue to pay the ultimate price: many NATO soldiers from many nations have been killed; the handsome husband of feisty Tutija the teacher was murdered because of her involvement in the community council in Gereshk. Her colleague Guliana now no longer travels, as her car was bombed several times. More members of the Nawa community council have been killed. But the rest keep going. Derek had 2,000 people put themselves forward to the meeting that elected the new Marjeh community council. As long as that desire for change is present, should we not be too?

# Index

304